Freedom, Repression, and Private Property in Russia

This study demonstrates how the emergence of private property and a market economy after the Soviet Union's collapse enabled a degree of freedom and simultaneously supported authoritarianism. On the basis of case studies, Vladimir Shlapentokh and Anna Arutunyan analyze how private property and free markets spawn feudal elements in society. These elements are so strong in post-Communist Russia that they prevent the formation of a true democratic society, while making it impossible to return to totalitarianism. The authors describe the resulting Russian society as having three types of social organization: authoritarian, feudal, and liberal. The authors examine the adaptation of Soviet-era institutions like security forces, police, and the army to free market conditions and how they generated corruption; the belief that the KGB was relatively free from corruption; how large property holdings merge with power and necessitate repression; and how property relations affect government management and suppression.

Vladimir Shlapentokh was born, raised, and educated in the Soviet Union. Before immigrating to the United States in 1979, he worked as a Senior Fellow in the Sociological Institute in Moscow, where he conducted the first nationwide public opinion surveys in the USSR. He is currently Professor of Sociology at Michigan State University and is the author of eighteen books.

Anna Arutunyan is a Russian-American journalist currently based in Moscow, where she is a senior correspondent for *The Moscow News*. She has reported on Russian politics for ten years and is the author of *The Media in Russia* (2009) and *The Putin Mystique* (2012).

Freedom, Repression, and Private Property in Russia

VLADIMIR SHLAPENTOKH
Michigan State University

ANNA ARUTUNYAN
Independent Journalist

CAMBRIDGE
UNIVERSITY PRESS

CAMBRIDGE
UNIVERSITY PRESS

32 Avenue of the Americas, New York NY 10013-2473, USA

Cambridge University Press is part of the University of Cambridge.

It furthers the University's mission by disseminating knowledge in the pursuit of education, learning and research at the highest international levels of excellence.

www.cambridge.org
Information on this title: www.cambridge.org/9781107042148

First published 2013

A catalogue record for this publication is available from the British Library

Library of Congress Cataloguing in Publication data
Shlapentokh, Vladimir, author.
Freedom, repression, and private property in Russia / Vladimir Shlapentokh (Michigan State University), Anna Arutunyan (independent journalist).
pages ; cm
Includes bibliographical references and index.
ISBN 978-1-107-04214-8 (hardback)
1. Russia (Federation) – Politics and government – 1991– 2. Democracy – Russia (Federation) 3. Civil rights – Russia (Federation) 4. Property – Political aspects – Russia (Federation) 5. Free enterprise – Political aspects – Russia (Federation) I. Arutunyan, Anna, author. II. Title.
DK510.763.S498 2013
947.086–dc23 2013007198

ISBN 978-1-107-04214-8 Hardback

Contents

Preface

In the preparation of this book several people took important roles. First of all we would like to mention those who edited it – Judy Spanogle, Eric Beasley, and Jeff Oliver. We highly appreciate their efforts and their willingness to enhance the quality of the text. Our special gratitude goes to Jeff, who prepared the text for the publisher. We also want to say thanks to Vera Bondartsova, who with her research work helped us a lot in the writing of the book.

We also want to convey our gratitude to those whom we addressed for advice and information – Vladimir Kontorovich, Dmitry Shlapentokh, and Lubov Shlapentokh.

Of course, we want to express special thanks to Robert Dreesen, who was the first "outsider" to appreciate the value of our attempt to make the comparison of various regimes that ruled the Russian people in the nineteenth and twentieth centuries as objective and detached as possible.

Introduction

Private Property as a Source of Both Freedom and Repression – The Russian Case

Introduction

In the first years after the collapse of the Soviet Union in 1991 it appeared that the new Russia would be so different in all possible aspects from the old regime that the comparison between it and the Soviet past would be monotonously uniform, as happens in the case of the comparison of the life of a slave before and after liberation. It even seemed to some observers and analysts of a new Russia that their knowledge of Soviet society had become almost superfluous for understanding a new free society and could be used at best for understanding the residuals of the Soviet mentality in the mind of the citizens. Indeed, the experts on Polish or Estonian societies that brusquely broke with the totalitarian system hardly needed to know a lot about the role of the Communist Party or the Verkhovnyi Soviet (the Soviet parliament) in the Soviet political structures to analyze the current political system, in the same way that the researchers of economic life of East Germany hardly needed deep knowledge of the planning economy of the German Democratic Republic to monitor economic processes in that part of the Federal Republic of Germany after 1989. In 1990–1992 the same feeling was typical for those who watched the formation of a new democratic Russia. The absolutely free election of the first Russian president; the almost, as it seemed then, total elimination of the KGB from life in the country and the disappearance of the fear of political police; the debates on any issue without any restraint – all these and other similar events suggested to Russians as well as to foreigners that the Soviet political system belonged to the past along with other unpleasant times in Russian history, like that of Ivan the Terrible or Alexander III.

However, already after President Boris Yeltsin's shelling of the Russian parliament in October 1993 it became evident even to some of his admirers that the new Russia would have to be analyzed not from the viewpoint of "emergent theory" – which places the focus on the birth "of novel and coherent structures, patterns and properties during the process of self-organization in complex systems," in the words of Jeffrey Goldstein,[1] but from the viewpoint of a historical approach with its focus on continuity of social structures. After 1993 the similarities of the new regime with the Soviet past became more and more striking. With the ascent of Vladimir Putin to power in 1999 the problem for analysts who tried to be "objective" was not how to argue against the comparison of Putin's and the Soviet regimes but how to escape the equation of Putin's political order with the Soviet. Now the major goal of the researcher became to find out the proper weight of the commonalities and differences between the 2000s and the 1960s–1970s. In other words, in comparing Putin's regime with the Soviet past the researcher has to avoid both mistakes – overestimating the similarities and underestimating the differences.

The necessity to look at Putin's regime from a comparative perspective rejuvenated interest in the comparison of the different Soviet regimes. As a matter of fact, in Soviet studies before 1991 as well as after, it is easy to discern two approaches – one that has focused on the unity of Soviet history and another that has tried to find out differences between the different stages of this history.

In many cases, the first approach was developed by the totalitarian school, whose members tended to emphasize features typical of a totalitarian society and in order to grasp the essence of the Soviet system preferred the use of constants in its description, paying minimal attention to the changes of Soviet society in their analysis.[2] The major arguments of the first school can be described in this way.

Whatever the extent of these differences, the major institutions and ideological postulates of Soviet society as it emerged almost immediately after 1917 remained the same until the end of the Soviet Union.[3] From the beginning, the totalitarian state and socialist ideas were consistently used for the

[1] Jeffrey Goldstein, "Emergence as a construct: History and issues," *Emergence: Complexity and Organization* 1.1 (1999), 49–72.

[2] Merle Fainsod, *How Russia Is Ruled* (Cambridge, MA: Harvard University Press, 1963), p. 87; R. Conquest, *Russia after Khruschev* (London: Pall Mall Press, 1965); see Hannah Arendt, *The Origins of Totalitarianism* (s.l.: Harcourt Brace, 1951); Carl Friedrich and Zbigniew Brzezinski, *Totalitarian Dictatorship and Autocracy* (Cambridge, MA: Harvard University Press, 1956); Robert Tucker, *Philosophy and Myth in Karl Marx* (New York: Cambridge University Press, 1961); Robert Tucker, *Swollen State, Spent Society: Stalin's Legacy to Brezhnev's Russia* (s.l.: s.n., 1980); Robert Tucker, *Stalin in Power: The Revolution from Above* (New York: W. W. Norton, 1990); Robert Daniels, "Russian political culture and the post-revolutionary impasse," *Russian Review* 46.2 (April, 1987), 165–75; Alex Inkeles, *Social Change in Soviet Russia, vol. 57* (Cambridge, MA: Harvard University Press, 1968); Richard Pipes, *Russia under the Old Regime* (s.l.: Collier Books, 1992), pp. 3–4, 1993, pp. 497, 500; Martin Malia, *The Soviet Tragedy: A History of Socialism in Russia, 1917–1991* (New York: Free Press, 1994).

[3] Ulam was correct when he pointed out that Lenin, in the aftermath of the revolution, "enunciated what would become the pervasive characteristic of Soviet society and communism." See Adam Ulam, *The Kirov Affair* (New York: Harcourt, 1988), p. vii.

modernization of the country in order to catch up with the West, maintain the empire, and expand Russian influence throughout the world. The major institutions of society also remained essentially the same after their creation by the leadership: the political monopoly of one party; the absolute dominance of the supreme leader in the decision making process; the political police as the most powerful instrument of the regime; the militarization of society; aggressive imperial policy; the totalitarian ideological indoctrination of the population; the ban on religion; the complete monopoly on media, education, science, and culture; the dominance of the central administration over the provinces; the complete absence of democracy; the official emphasis on class and class warfare; the centralized control of the economy; public property as the means of production; and the rejection of private economic activity.

Alexis de Tocqueville's assessment of the American experiment stands out as an exemplary social analysis that focuses on the essential elements of a given society. Tocqueville focused on the essential elements of American society instead of drawing attention to the changes. The authors of this book follow the same approach. Tocqueville's vision of America was not fixed on forecasting change, and yet he did not ignore the potential for transition. During his brief travels in 1831 he came to understand the fundamental elements of American society, elements that persisted for more than one hundred and fifty years. His discernment of American federalism, a virtually unknown phenomenon in Europe, was brilliant. Tocqueville also recognized American individualism and the role that associations play in American society.

The second approach made the evolution of Soviet society and the differences between "good" and "bad" periods in Soviet history the center of its attention. This approach was mostly popular among the revisionists, who, denying the totalitarian character of Soviet society, looked for the dynamics of "political pluralism," of "conflicts between political elites," in the educational level of party apparatchiks. For members of this school, the differences between Lenin and Stalin, or between Stalin and Khrushchev, or Khrushchev and Brezhnev were more important than the description of Soviet history as a whole.

Revisionists attacked the views of totalitarianists who believed that society under Lenin, Stalin, Khrushchev, and Brezhnev stayed essentially the same. Moshe Lewin wrote about the genuine proletarian character of the October Revolution and the radical differences between Lenin and Stalin. From Lewin's perspective, Stalin destroyed Lenin's heritage (1968). Stephen Cohen refused to see the society after 1953 as "totalitarian" (despite the radical conservative turn during the Brezhnev regime). Cohen wrote that after the death of Stalin, "Stalinism no longer defined Soviet reality" (1980).

Those revisionists who recognized the totalitarian character of Stalin's regime were inclined to label it "exceptional," like the period of "primary accumulation of capital" in Western society during the seventeenth and eighteenth centuries, rather than an "abnormal" or "accidental" stage in Soviet history. After 1991, many Russian liberals and their sympathizers in the West described the harsh life of Russians in the same way, as "a period of primary accumulation."

Revisionists typically maintained high regard for Stalin's opponents such as Nikolai Bukharin. Bukharin and others, by their estimations, would have brought about "socialism with a human face" if they had taken control of the regime. Revisionists expressed obvious sympathy for socialism. They resolutely rejected the thesis "Stalin is Lenin today." In this way they followed the line of Soviet propaganda after 1953, which tried to separate "socialism" from Stalin's horrors.

Revisionists based their thesis on the fundamental differences between the Stalin and post-Stalin societies, with the argument that these societies were institutionally different. This point of view was publicly rejected by most Russian intellectuals after 1985.

This school even included Hannah Arendt, whose interests in totalitarianism made her more eligible for the first school. Among other members of this school were Stephen Cohen, Severyn Bialer, Jerry Hough, Sheila Fitzpatrick, and those who exaggerated the differences between Soviet society before and after 1953.[4]

The authors of this book gravitate more to the totalitarian school and share with it the belief that the Soviet system essentially did not change until 1989–91. However, they are far from underestimating the differences between various periods in Soviet history, even if these differences are much less strong than the differences between Putin's regime and the Soviet regime as a whole.

It is important to explain, even if briefly, the nature of the differences between the Soviet regimes. It is possible to separate this history into six different regimes: those that functioned under the guidance of Lenin during the Russian Civil War and War Communism (1918–20) and during the NEP (The New Economic Policy) (1921–8); Stalin's regime (1928–53); Khrushchev's regime (1954–64); Brezhnev's regime, which was continued by his two heirs, Yury Andropov and Konstantin Chernenko (1964–84); and Gorbachev's regime (1985–91). For our analysis we decided to operate mostly with three regimes – Stalin's, Khrushchev's, and Brezhnev's – bearing in mind that only with Stalin was the Soviet system ultimately formed while under Gorbachev it changed radically.

The changing role of the state is definitely a major factor behind the differences between Putin's regime and the Soviet past. But it is also behind the differences between the various Soviet regimes. Certainly, throughout the whole Soviet history, until the breakdown of the Soviet system in 1989–91, the Soviet state remained a totalitarian institution, with the characteristic described previously.

[4] For the difference in views between Ulam and Arendt, see Adam Ulam, *The Communists: The Story of Power and Lost Illusions, 1948–1991* (New York: Scribner, 1992).

However, having said this, there is much evidence that the degree of state intervention in social life changed a lot. Essentially, we mean the activity of the repressive apparatus that determines when the totalitarian regime is hard and when it is soft. The ebb and flow in repressive activity of the Soviet state set up the role of the political police in society, the level of fear in society, and the probability that the Soviet citizen would be persecuted, fired from a job, arrested, or even killed for political reasons. The level of repressive activity determined the character of human relations, the degree of trust people have in each other even inside the family. The same level in the most conspicuous way affected the selection of cadres; the creative activity in science, education, and culture; the professional level of scholars and all other intellectuals; and, of course, the degree of openness of the country to the external world. One of the authors who lived during the three Soviet regimes – Stalin's, Khrushchev's, and Brezhnev's – can attest that for him as a human being and not as a researcher, the differences were enormous. He was full of fear before 1953, then could breathe and enjoyed some modicum of freedom in his creative activity as a founder of Soviet sociology, and then became despondent and harassed with the restoration of some elements of Stalinism under Brezhnev.

The Soviet regime at the times of the NEP (1921–8) was much milder in comparison with the cruelty of "War Communism" (1918–20). Hardly anybody will argue that Stalin's regime was hard, while Khrushchev's regime that replaced it was soft. At the same time, Brezhnev's regime was harder than Khrushchev's. It is more than obvious how much Gorbachev's regime, even in its beginning, 1985–8, was softer than what preceded it.

It will be quite reasonable, as some authors do, to use the same criteria – the extent of repression and fear – in a comparison of Putin's regime with the Soviet past. There are authors who suggest that the difference between Putin's regime and the Soviet past is also the level of repression and fear, which in contemporary Russia is lower than in any other times in Soviet history. Indeed, after 1991 and even since Putin's rise to power in 1999 the degree of fear in society is much lower than even in the first years of Perestroika, to say nothing of the Brezhnev years. And yet, as we will show in a special chapter, in fact fear among people who challenge or want to challenge Putin's regime is quite high. In other words, Putin's regime has demonstrated itself to be authoritarian, and yet it has still presented one of the mildest forms of authoritarianism that Russia has ever known. To show this, we will concentrate on the differences between Putin's and the Soviet regimes.

In this book, we will focus on one of the key elements that have accounted for these differences between Putin's regime and the Soviet past – the emergence and role of private property. Taking a new theoretical perspective, which we call the "segmented" or "hybrid" approach, we suggest that private property and free markets spawn feudal elements within society. On one hand, these elements are so strong in post-Communist Russia that they prevent the formation of a true democratic society. On the other hand, they also make it impossible to return to totalitarianism. As a result, Russian society can be described as having three different types of social organization: authoritarian, feudal, and liberal, albeit with a clear preponderance of authoritarianism.

We will try to prove that the main causes of the differences can be found in the emergence of big private business accompanied by big money, which in the specific context of the 1990s opened the gates to feudal tendencies and to the essential weakening of the central administration and an outburst of corruption unprecedented even in Russian history. As we will show, big money and corruption influenced all sides of Russian society including those elements that it shared with the Soviet past as well as those that were introduced by liberalism, including the role of the state, ideology, the morals of society, the behavior of political leaders, the parliament, the political police, relations between the center and regions, foreign policy, ethnic conflicts, activity of the opposition, science, the army, the professionalism of cadres, emigration and immigration, and the motivation of the younger generations.

In terms of specific cases from Vladimir Putin's Russia that illuminate how private property and a free market economy function within a clearly authoritarian model, this work goes beyond the idea of private property as a benevolent driver of freedom. Instead, we argue that private property – a dogmatic concept that has spread throughout Western social science since the time of John Locke and has been used with special fervor by the contemporary scholar Richard Pipes in his analysis of Russian history – can also foster the harshest forms of government repression. Furthermore, Russia under the reign of Vladimir Putin presents us with an invaluable insight into how this happens.

This book focuses on specific examples of how property relations have fostered authoritarian control in the last ten years and how they foster feudal tendencies in the country. Moreover, the authors examine such historical occurrences as (1) how the adaptation of Soviet-era security forces to free market conditions spawned rampant corruption in all levels of society; (2) the reality that the KGB was relatively free of corruption; (3) how large property holdings merge with power and necessitate repression, as in the Yukos affair, when Soviet leaders were free of the impact of private property on their behavior; and (4) how property relations affect government management and suppression of the masses and how little this affected the behavior of the apparatchiks in the Soviet Slav and Baltic republics (the republics of Central Asia and the Caucasus region are another story).

In addition, the book shows how property relations determine Russia's standing in the world and its foreign policy, even as the property factor had zero impact on Soviet foreign policy. Finally, with a strong focus on sociological analysis and original reporting, the book reflects how these factors are affecting the people in contemporary Russia who are involved in these processes and how these developments were absent during Soviet times. Two examples of affected groups are former security officers trying to make sense of their new role and average workers caught in the power struggle between factory owners.

Although the authors firmly believe that private property has led to feudal elements within society, they do not underestimate the importance of liberal elements within Russian society. Thanks to the existence of private property, Russians can now choose business-related professions, albeit within the context of many bureaucratic impediments that are reminiscent of the Middle Ages. They are also able to accumulate money and transfer it to foreign banks, freely move inside and outside the country, as well as benefit from freedom of the press.[5]

In a world recovering from the effects of the economic crisis and the fervent quest for the explanation of why it happened, a subject that became a crucial theme during the U.S. presidential election campaign in 2012, the analysis of the role of big property and big money in Russian society through the lens of our new segmented theoretical perspective will shed new light on the role of property relations in impacting different types of societies

Breaking with past traditions that either criticized or defended free market reforms from an ideological perspective, this book examines the problem on its own terms rather than through a political prism. What emerges is a candid picture of market capitalism acting in synergy with an autocratic state structure. The analysis relies on several publications that deal with Russia in the last two decades, which were either written or cowritten by Vladimir Shlapentokh.[6]

This book strongly differs from recent publications on Russia in the West as well as inside Russia. Certainly, a number of these books deal with corruption in Russia as the government and corporations blend together. They include Yury Felshtinsky and Vladimir Pribylovsky's *The Corporation: Russia and the KGB in the Age of President Putin* (2009), Andrei Soldatov and Irina Borogan's *The New Nobility: The Restoration of Russia's Security State and the Enduring Legacy of the KGB* (2010), as well as Lilia Shevtsova and Antonina W. Bouis's *Lonely Power: Why Russia Has Failed to Become the West and the West Is Weary of Russia* (2010). However, none of them can claim to explain

[5] Analysis of the impact of private property and free markets is not only relevant to all post-Communist countries but also to the West. In some ways, this book continues the line of analysis developed by Vladimir Shlapentokh in the books *Contemporary Russia as a Feudal Society: A New Perspective on the Post-Soviet Era* (Palgrave Macmillan, 2007) and *Feudal America: Elements of the Middle Ages in Contemporary Society* (coauthor) (Pennsylvania State University Press, 2011).

[6] In addition to the books already mentioned, these books include Vladimir Shlapentokh, *A Normal Totalitarian Society* (Armonk, N.Y.: M. E. Sharpe, 2001); Vladimir Shlapentokh and Eric Shiraev, *Fears in Post-communist Society* (New York, Basingstoke: Palgrave, 2002); Vladimir Shlapentokh, *The Last Years of the Soviet Empire: Snapshots from 1985–1991* (New York: Praeger, 1993); Vladimir Shlapentokh, *Soviet Intellectuals and Political Power* (Princeton: Princeton University Press, 1990); Vladimir Shlapentokh, *The Public and Private Life of the Soviet People* (New York: Oxford University Press, 1989); Vladimir Shlapentokh, *The Media in Russia* (New York: McGraw-Hill, 2009).

the differences and commonalities between the Soviet and post-Soviet regimes. These books, which are the closest to ours, discuss the Russian development in a descriptive way but do not analyze it from new theoretical perspectives.

The case is even truer for books such as Edwin Bacon's *Contemporary Russia* (2010), which describes the differences between Putin's regime and past Soviet ruling power. Our book is not meant to be an indictment of Putin's regime or the institution of private property. Rather, it draws on academic research and recent reporting in order to weigh both the positive and negative effects of the emergence of this institution on Russian authoritarianism.

1

Private Property and Big Money in Political Regimes in Soviet and Post-Soviet Russia

A Theoretical Overview

Debates on Post-Soviet Russia: The Consensus on Authoritarianism

The people of any country, and historians thereafter, sharply debate how the country should be portrayed or labeled. In contemporary America, we see arduous debates centered on how to characterize the country politically, economically, and culturally. The range of labels placed on U.S. society is so long and diverse that it seems as though the critics and observers of the United States are talking about several different countries.

The United States is not, of course, the only country where people debate its defining characteristics. The Soviet Union, for instance, was given a wide range of labels. Until its collapse in 1991, many observers – both inside and outside the country – treated the USSR as a true socialist society, while others regarded it as a brutal totalitarian regime.[1] However, post-1991 Russian society is even more complex than it was during Soviet times, and this complexity serves to make the interpretation and labeling of its essence even more varied and debated.

Post-Soviet society, as we knew it in 2012 (as this book was being written), was shaped in the first few years immediately following the collapse of the Soviet Union. The major elements of this society have not changed power in any essential way after Boris Yeltsin shelled his parliament in 1993. Remarkably, it took the Bolsheviks about the same short amount of time to build the Soviet system. Most of the features of the Soviet system (the lack of individual freedoms; the absence of a division of power; the mere imitation of democracy in lieu of real democracy; the economic and political dominance of public property and the central planning economy; the incredible power of the political police and the omnipresent fear in the people as a result of it; the state's absolute monopoly

[1] Vladimir Shlapentokh, Eric Shiraev, and Eero Carroll, *The Soviet Union: Internal and External Perspectives on Soviet Society* (New York: Palgrave Macmillan, 2008).

on the media, the educational system, and the scientific community; and the pervasive xenophobic ideology) did not change until 1991.

Post-Soviet Russian society had its core identity shaped by the middle of the 1990s and, like its predecessor, has not changed over many years. This new society comprised many elements of the Soviet system. However, several elements in the political system that emerged in post-Soviet society had not existed previously: the openness of society to the external world, freedom of speech, the freedom to leave the country, and the existence, even if very weak, of a civil society with independent organizations.

The main features of the post-Soviet economic system born in the mid-1990s were a combination of new and old elements. On one side, private property became a normal phenomenon in a society where, only a few years previously, it was widely considered an inimical notion. Economic competition, free prices, and the consumer's right to have a choice in purchases became common aspects of life. Concurrently, on another hand, the state continued to play a crucial role in the economy. For instance, private and state property tended to overlap with each other; government officials became stockholders of major companies, and the government was able to use the courts to confiscate any property – and could even send the owners of said property to prison. With the help of the government, big companies, which were the object of the political elite's material interests, procured a monopoly on the market and were able easily to fend off domestic and international rivals.

Yeltsin's Regime: The Dominance of the Liberal Belief in Private Property as an Automatic Producer of Democracy

Many liberal politicians and intellectuals focused on the liberal changes that occurred in the country after 1991. They viewed Boris Yeltsin, the first Russian president – and not Mikhail Gorbachev – as the founder of both Russian democracy and free market reform. Despite the evident lack of democratic developments, many Yeltsin enthusiasts took the liquidation of the Soviet-command-planning economy and the emergence of private property in each sector of Russian life as irrefutable proof of Yeltsin's democratic credentials.[2]

The liberal admirers of Yeltsin's regime disregarded his authoritarian streak because of two factors. One was primarily emotional – having suffered repressions under the Soviet system, many of Yeltsin's supporters, consciously or not, sought revenge against the Communist Party. A second, equally important factor was a confusion of economics and politics that was common to both the Russians and their Western advisers. Yeltsin's admirers believed that the dismantlement of the planned economy and the introduction of free markets and

[2] See, for instance, Marina Shakhina, "El'tsin. Chelovek, kotoryi umeet delat' vybor," *Novoie Vremia* (1994).

private property would automatically result in democratic institutions, thereby precluding any return to authoritarianism. For many Russian liberals, the idea of private property as an automatic generator of democracy was as obvious as the law of gravity. It was this conviction that lay behind Prime Minister Yegor Gaidar's policy of shock therapy and rapid privatization. Indeed, Gaidar would go on to develop his ideas on the dependence of a country's political order on the level of privatization and the size of income per head in a series of books in the 2000s.[3]

Gaidar and other supporters of market reform disregarded the criminal consequences of privatization. In particular, they ignored the rampant corruption that proliferated as private enterprise sprang up in a society lacking the rule of law, which made democratic development very difficult.[4] Many Western scholars shared this belief in the simplistic positive correlation between wealth and democracy. They also fell for "the economic trap," believing that an increase in wealth would inevitably lead to democracy. This notion played into the central dogma of the American mind. The legitimization and veneration of this correlation have dominated the sociological and political literature since Seymour Lipset's article (1959).[5] The prominent political scientist Rudolph Barro, an expert on the Communist states in east Europe, vehemently defended Lipset's thesis in his famous article, "Determinants of Democracy." forty years later.

Among those Western authors describing Russian society who believed in the high correlation between market economy and democracy was Andrei Shleifer, a former adviser to Gaidar's government, who offered (with his coauthor Donald Treisman) a vision of the world where a free economy made political institutions truly democratic. He viewed post-Soviet society as a "normal democratic society" on the basis of its income per capita.[6] Later, in 2011, Shleifer recanted his previous label, no longer considering Russia to be a society with normal democratic institutions. Shleifer abandoned the "economic" approach and recognized that "although nearly all transition countries have eventually converged to some form of capitalism, there has been a broader range of political experiences, from full democracies, to primitive dictatorships, to just about everything in between."[7]

3 Yegor Gaidar, *Dolgoie vremia. Rossia v mire. Ocherki ekonomicheskoi istorii* [Long time. Russia in the world. Essays in economic history] (Moscow: Delo, 2005); Yegor Gaidar, *Anomalii eknomicheskogo rosta* [Anomalies of economic growth] (Moscow: Evraziia, 1997).

4 One of the authors of this book already demonstrated it in an article in the 1990s. See Vladimir Shlapentokh, *Russia: Privatization and Illegalization of Social and Political Life* (Cambridge: Conflict Studies Research Center, Royal Military Academy, Sandhurst, 1995).

5 Seymour Martin Lipset, "Some social requisites of democracy: Economic development and political legitimacy," *American Political Science Review* 53 (1959), 69–105.

6 Andrei Shleifer and Daniel Treisman, "A normal country," *Foreign Affairs* (March–April 2004).

7 Andrei Shleifer, "Seven things I learned about transition from communism," February 5, 2012, http://www.voxeu.org/index.php?q=node/7593, accessed March 1, 2012.

Several other prominent Western scholars were also mostly blind to the authoritarian elements of Yeltsin's and even Putin's regimes.[8] Timothy Colton primarily described Yeltsin as a champion of democracy.[9] This view ignores Yeltsin's role in sponsoring enormous corruption, his systematic fight against democratic institutions, and his violation of virtually all of the electoral rules. Colton, following Gaidar and other Yeltsin admirers, showed his strong belief in the impact of privatization on democratic progress.[10] Leon Aron, another prominent American expert on Russia, shared the same view as Colton in the early 2000s.[11] Michael McFaul also characterized Yeltsin as a revolutionary in his presumed attempt to build a democratic society in Russia. He even spoke rather positively about Yeltsin's use of "military force" in October 1993 (which included the shelling of parliament), stating that the acts were reasonable in the pursuit of "his objectives."[12]

By 2000, with Vladimir Putin continuing to steer the country away from democracy, it became clear that Russia was essentially not a democratic society. But the mainstream literature ignored the pivotal role Yeltsin played in shaping the post-Soviet regime; several books published in Russia and the West in the twenty-first century glorify Yeltsin as a true Russian democrat. Only a few liberal authors in the late 1990s managed to overcome the economic myopia and saw Yeltsin and his regime as being essentially authoritarian in nature.

Putin's Regime (2000–2012): The Near-Consensus on Its Authoritarian Character

The debates about whether Russia was a functioning democracy or a moderate autocracy changed markedly with the ascent of Vladimir Putin. Even

[8] In the last two decades, this theory has been the object of severe critiques by a number of prominent scholars: Lawrence E. Harrison and Samuel P. Huntington, *Culture Matters: How Values Shape Human Progress* (New York: Basic Books, 2000); Ronald Inglehart, *Modernization and Postmodernization: Cultural, Economic, and Political Change in 43 Societies* (Princeton, NJ: Princeton University Press, 1997). The Russian experience supports the exact opposite of Lipset's postulate. What is more, this experience is another piece of evidence in favor of the concept advanced in the early 2000s by a group of authors headed by Daron Acemoglu. These authors "argue that this evidence is consistent with another well-established approach in political science, which emphasizes how events during critical historical junctures can lead to divergent political-economic development paths, some leading to prosperity and democracy, others to relative poverty and non-democracy" (Daron Acemoglu, James Robinson, and Pierre Yared, "Reevaluating the modernization hypothesis," *CEPR Discussion Papers 6430*, August 2007).

[9] "As a democratizer," Colton writes, "he is in the company of Nelson Mandela, Lech Walesa, Mikhail Gorbachev and Vaclav Havel. It is his due even when allowance is made for his blind spots and mistakes." See Timothy J. Colton, *Yeltsin: A Life* (New York: Basic Books, 2008).

[10] Colton, *Yeltsin: A Life.*

[11] Leon Aron, *Yeltsin: A Revolutionary Life* (New York: St. Martin's Press, 2000); Leon Aron, *Russia's Revolution: Essays 1989–2006* (Washington, DC: AEI Press, 2007).

[12] Michael McFaul, *Russia's Unfinished Revolution: Political Change from Gorbachev to Putin* (Ithaca, NY: Cornell University Press, 2001) p. 265; see also other American authors inclined to look more or less benignly at Yeltsin's and Putin's regimes, such as Marshall I. Goldman, *Petrostate: Putin, Power, and the New Russia* (New York: Oxford University Press, 2008).

while the regime continued to view itself as democratic, its autocratic character burgeoned.

Officially, President Vladimir Putin has insisted – as did Yeltsin – that his regime is a democracy; he has persisted with this assertion in all his public statements, domestically and internationally. Putin consistently appeared to take sincere offense over direct or implied criticism from Western leaders who questioned Russia's democratic credentials. Most notably, in his Munich speech in 2007, he contended that the West, instead of "teaching us ... has to learn itself what genuine democracy is."[13]

Putin's successor, Dmitry Medvedev, was touted by both domestic and foreign observers as a more liberal politician when he became president in 2008. Yet, it soon became clear that, despite a few rhetorical criticisms he made about the lack of political competition in Russia, Medvedev largely continued along Putin's path. Although Medvedev, at one point, came close to mocking the idea of "sovereign democracy" – a model advanced by the Kremlin ideologist Vladislav Surkov in 2005 – he nevertheless continued to insist that Russians live in a democratic society. During his fall 2010 speech in Yaroslavl, he contended that "Russia, without any doubt, is a democracy."[14] Several Russian intellectuals rushed to support Medvedev's view, relying on convoluted arguments about the complexity of democracy and the impossibility of comparing Russia with the West.[15]

Putin's regime was able to recruit a number of known social scientists to argue that his regime was democratic. Roy Medvedev, a famous historian, declared his confidence that Putin's Russia was gradually becoming a democratic country with new political, socioeconomic, and value systems.[16] He was joined by the prominent sociologist Olga Kryshtanovskaya, who suggested that the Russian political regime thoroughly satisfied the requirements of a democracy.[17] A few Western authors, like Marshall Goldman and Douglas Blum, rejected the labeling of Putin's regime as authoritarian and tried to refute the arguments of those who did.[18]

[13] Vladimir Putin, "Vystuplenie i diskussiia na Miunkhenskoi konferentsii po voprosam politiki bezopastnosti," *Prezident Rossii*, February 10, 2007, http://archive.kremlin.ru/appears/2007/02/10/1737_type63374type63376type63377type63381type82634_118097.shtml, accessed October 30, 2010.

[14] Dmitry Medvedev, "Vystuplenie na plenarnom zasedanii mirovogo politicheskogo foruma 'Sovremennoe gosudarstvo: Standarty demokratii i kriterii effektivnosti'," *Prezident Rossii*, September 10, 2010, http://president.kremlin.ru/transcripts/8887, accessed October 30, 2010.

[15] See texts of presented papers at the Yaroslavl World Political Forum in September 7–8, 2011, http://www.gpf-yaroslavl.ru/about/doklady-i-vystupleniya, accessed March 1, 2012.

[16] Roi Medvedev, *Vladimir Putin: Tret'ego sroka ne budet* (Moscow: Vremia, 2007).

[17] Olga Kryshtanovskaya, "Demokratiia ochen' sil'no izmenilas," *Yaroslavl', Mirovoi Politicheskii Forum*, September 17, 2010, http://www.gpf-yaroslavl.ru/presscenter/publications/Demokratiya-ochen-sil-no-izmenilas, accessed October 30, 2010.

[18] Goldman, *Petrostate*; Douglas W. Blum, *Russia and Globalization: Identity, Security, and Society in an Era of Change* (Baltimore: John Hopkins University Press, 2008).

However, despite Putin's efforts, the absolute majority of Russian intellectuals, media people, and politicians – whatever their political and ideological orientations – accepted the idea that they lived under Putin in an authoritarian society. Among them, even the universalists, who believe in a democratic society as the best choice for any country, have acknowledged Russia's inability to join the club of democratic countries (Lilia Shevtsova,[19] Anna Politkovskaya,[20] Andrei Piontkovsky,[21] Mikhail Delyagin,[22] Andrei Illarionov,[23] and Masha Gessen[24]). Still, some universalists have remained optimistic about a democratic future for Russia, such as the editors of a book that summarized the results of Putin's regime.[25]

Most Western authors writing in the last few years – Richard Rose,[26] Richard Sakwa,[27] Stefan Hedlund and Steven Rosefield,[28] Stephen Kotkin,[29] Andrew Wilson,[30] and Stephen White[31] – have also defined Putin's Russia as an authoritarian society.[32]

Is Putin's Regime Similar to the Soviet Regime?

Naturally, many who describe post-Soviet Russian society as authoritarian choose their own reference point. Some of them prefer to see Putin's regime in

[19] Lilya Shevtsova, *Putin's Russia* (Washington, DC: Carnegie Endowment for International Peace, 2005).

[20] Anna Politkovskaya, *Putin's Russia: Life in a Failing Democracy* (New York: Holt Paperbacks, 2007).

[21] Andrei Piontkovsky, *Tretii put' k rabstvu* [The third way is to slavery] (Moscow: Moskva, 2011).

[22] Mikhail Deliagin, *Rossiia posle Putina. Neizbezhna li v Rossii "oranzhevo-zelenaia revoliutsiia"?* [Russia after Putin. Is the orange-green revolution unavoidable?] (Moscow: Veche, 2005).

[23] A. Illarionov, "Dekabr'skie tezisy dlia grazhdan Rossii," *Grani.ru*, December 27, 2011.

[24] Masha Gessen, *The Man without a Face: The Unlikely Rise of Vladimir Putin* (New York: Riverhead Books, 2012).

[25] Gabriele Gorzka and Reinhard Krumm (eds.), *Rossiia: Itogi poslednego desiatiletiia (1998–2008) i perspektivy razvitiia* (Moscow: ROSSPEN, 2010).

[26] Richard Rose, William Mishler, and Neil Munro, *Popular Support for an Undemocratic Regime: The Changing Views of Russians* (Cambridge: Cambridge University Press, 2011).

[27] Richard Sakwa, *Putin: Russia's Choice*, 2nd ed. (London and New York: Routledge, 2008).

[28] Steven Rosefielde and Stefan Hedlund, *Russia since 1980: Wrestling with Westernization* (Cambridge: Cambridge University Press, 2009).

[29] Stephen Kotkin, "Sticking power," *Times Literary Supplement*, March 2, 2012.

[30] Andrew Wilson, *Virtual politics: Faking Democracy in the Post-Soviet World* (New Haven, CT: Yale University Press, 2005).

[31] Rosefielde and Hedlund, *Russia since 1980*; Stephen White(ed.), *Politics and the Ruling Group in Putin's Russia* (New York: Palgrave Macmillan, 2008).

[32] See Michael Stuermer, *Putin and the Rise of Russia* (London: Weidenfeld & Nicolson, 2008); Henry E. Hale, *Why Not Parties in Russia? Democracy, Federalism, and the State* (Cambridge and New York: Cambridge University Press, 2007); William A. Pridemore (ed.), *Ruling Russia: Law, Crime, and Justice in a Changing Society* (New York: Rowman & Littlefield, 2005).

the context of the whole of Russian history, portraying it as a typical Russian authoritarian society (e.g., the historians Yury Pivovarov[33] and Victor Danilov[34] and the philosopher Vadim Mezhuev[35]).

The majority of those who have seen Putin's Russia as an authoritarian society have preferred to make the Soviet system the major point of reference.[36] Especially popular was the identification of both Putin's and Brezhnev's regimes as times of stagnation.[37]

While making several statements that were seemingly intended to characterize it as being deeply democratic. Putin still expended a great deal of effort in making his regime symbolically similar to the Soviet one by restoring the Soviet hymn and the Russian banner for the army, ordering a rewrite of the official Russian history in order to present the Soviet past as a stage in that history that is worthy of respect, and, particularly important, rehabilitating Stalin's reputation by presenting him as a "great manager."

What Differs between the Authoritarian Regimes?

Authors of various political affiliations recognize the similarities between the Soviet and Putin regimes. Yet, from communists to liberals, only a few deny the existence of serious differences between the two regimes. As mentioned, there are a lot of political and economic elements of post-Soviet society that would never have existed under either Stalin's rule or the post-Stalin regimes. However, even those analysts – in Russia and abroad – who focused on the differences between the Soviet society of yesteryear and the modern post-Soviet society did not offer a theoretical explanation for them. Some of them typologized both of these as authoritarian regimes but still did not propose the latent variable that would explain the differences. These authors based their typology mostly on the role of elections and political parties and proposed labeling countries as exhibiting semidemocracy, semiauthoritarianism, soft authoritarianism, electoral authoritarianism, competitive authoritarianism, or façade democracy.[38]

33 Yury Pivovarov, *Russkaia politika v ee istoricheskom i kul'turnom otnosheniiakh* (Moscow: ROSSPEN, 2006).

34 V. Danilov, "Rossiiskaia vlast' v 20 veke," in T. Zaslavskaya (ed.), *Kuda idet Rossia. Vlast'. Obshchestvo. Lichnost'* (Moscow: Vysshaia Shkola sotsial'nykh i ekonomicheskikh nauk, 2000), p. 6.

35 V. Mezhuev, "Traditsiia samovlastiia v sovremennoi Rossii," in T. Zaslavskaya (ed.), *Kuda idet Rossia. Vlast'. Obshchestvo. Lichnost'* (Moscow: Vysshaia Shkola sotsial'nykh i ekonomicheskikh nauk, 2000), pp. 81, 86.

36 Andrei Piontkovsky, *Neliubimaia strana* (Moscow: RDP "Yabloko," 2006).

37 Piontkovsky, *Neliubimaia strana*.

38 See, for instance, Larry Diamond, "Thinking about hybrid regimes," *Journal of Democracy* 13.2 (2002); Steven Levitsky and Way, Lucan, "The Rise of Competitive Authoritarianism," *Journal of Democracy*, 13.2 (2002), 51–65.

While the approach focusing on the quality of elections has some merit, it is not reasonable to look at the character of the elections in both regimes as the main factor that explains the major differences. Indeed, the elections in Putin's Russia, with all their well-known flaws,[39] are still much more politically important than Soviet elections were. The Soviet ruling elites used tremendous resources to get the necessary electoral outcomes, using the results as a major criterion to evaluate the performance of governors and all other administrators in the country. But at the same time, elections in Soviet Russia, from the late 1920s on, were actually a minor item in the agenda of the party apparatus.[40] Few issues drew its attention during the election campaigns of national and local rubber stamp legislatures. Those that did were not related to the outcome of the elections but to the level of the participation in them. Many citizens – particularly in post-Stalin times – avoided election stations to show their negative attitudes to the local authorities, and even to the supreme leadership; many people also wrote negative statements about the bureaucracy on their ballots.[41]

This stated, we still cannot use the character of elections, or even the level of political freedoms, as the major variables for illustrating the differences between the Soviet and post-Soviet regimes, nor with various other authoritarian regimes of the past and present. In fact, the character of the electoral procedure and process cannot be the major explanatory variable because an election, in and of itself, is a function of some deep-rooted factor inside a society.

In our opinion – and this is the main idea of this book – the cause of all of the major differences between the Soviet and post-Soviet regimes, as well as the cause of the differences among authoritarian regimes in general, lies in the radical differences in property relations: the dominance of public property in one case and of private property in another. While the emergence of private property in post-Soviet Russia could not exterminate authoritarianism, as Russian

[39] It is possible to note several facts among them: the opposition has no access to TV during the election campaign; oppositional parties are not registered; the authorities of the ruling regime use their administrative resources for persuading and forcing people to vote for the ruling parties and candidates; and rigging election results is a common practice. Belief in widespread dishonesty in the electoral process was the major trigger of mass protest actions in Moscow in December 2011 and the first months of 2012. Still, even though the existing practices drove so many people to the streets in protest, the election process in post-Soviet Russia was markedly different from the election process during Soviet times.

[40] In the early 1920s, the elections of local authorities were relatively free, and the party was concerned about the results. See Vladimir Brovkin, *Russia after Lenin: Politics, Culture and Society, 1921–1929* (New York: Psychology Press, 1998).

[41] Alla Vekhovskaya, *Pis'ma v redaktsiiu i chitateli* (Moscow: Izdatel'stvo Moskovskogo Universiteta, 1972); Dmitry Shlapentokh and Vladimir Shlapentokh, "Letters to the editor on the ideologies in the USSR during the 1980s," in Anthony Jones (ed.), *Research on the Soviet Union and Eastern Europe* (Greenwich, CT: JAI Press, 1990); Vasily Davydchenkov, "Organizatsiia sotsiologicheskogo obsledovaniia i vnedrenie poluchennykh rezul'tatov v tsentral'noi gazete," in Vladimir Shlapentokh (ed.), *Sotsiologiia pechati* (Novosibirsk: Nauka, 1970), pp. 147–77.

liberals thought, it was able, nonetheless, to transform many dimensions of political life in the society.

Most authors who write about societies that are considered authoritarian tend to underestimate or ignore the huge influence of private property on the functioning of those societies. Some examples of this nonemphasis of private property are evident in the typologies of authoritarian regimes created by such authors as Steven Levitsky and Lucan Way,[42] and Taras Kuzio.[43]

Following this tendency to underestimate the role of big private business, capital, and property in an authoritarian society, several authors who equate the Soviet and post-Soviet regimes also ignore property relations as the major factor differentiating the two regimes. Brian Taylor's book *State Building in Putin's Russia: Policing and Coercion after Communism* (2011) is typical in this respect. He talks, for instance, about the similarities of the KGB and FSB without focusing on the fact that many of the leading generals of the FSB accrued great fortunes. (We will speak of this in detail later.) Instead of focusing on ownership and the control of private property, Taylor, in elucidating the differences between Putin's Russia and the Soviet system, concentrates on the fact that "Putin didn't establish a stable property-rights regime" as if even unstable property ownership could not radically change social relations in society.[44] Timothy J. Colton and Stephen Holmes, and Steve LeVine, like Taylor, do not see big property ownership as a crucial factor in post-Soviet life.[45] Some other authors do not completely ignore the impact of new property relations on post-Soviet Russia, but they reduce its influence to exclusively affecting the growth of economic inequality.[46]

The Hatred of Private Property in a Totalitarian Society with Socialist Ideology

A better understanding of the role of property relations in contemporary Russian authoritarian society demands an excursion back to the place held by public and private property in Soviet society. In addition, our understanding of the power of property relations will be enriched by highlighting the differences between the Soviet and post-Soviet regimes.

42 Levitsky and Way, "Competitive authoritarianism," 51–65.

43 Taras Kuzio, "Regime type and politics in Ukraine under Kuchma," *Communist and Post-Communist Studies* 38.2 (2005), 167–90; see also the paper prepared for the conference "Mapping the great zone: Clientelism and the boundary between democratic and democratizing," Columbia University, April 4–5, 2003. (This is a revised version of a paper prepared for the Annual Meeting of the American Political Science Association, Boston, August 28–31, 2002.)

44 Brian D. Taylor, *State Building in Putin's Russia: Policing and Coercion after Communism* (Cambridge: Cambridge University Press, 2011), pp. 102, 107.

45 Timothy J. Colton and Stephen Holmes, *The State after Communism: Governance in the New Russia* (Lanham, MD: Rowman & Littlefield, 2006); Steve LeVine, *Putin's Labyrinth: Spies, Murder, and the Dark Heart of the New Russia* (New York: Random House, 2009).

46 Pridemore (ed.), *Ruling Russia.*

The Soviet totalitarian state (we view the totalitarian society as the most aggressive form of authoritarianism), with its mixture of socialist and nationalist ideologies (both champions of a powerful state), was deeply hostile to the existence of any property held outside the state sphere, whether large or small. The confiscation of big private property was the main goal of the Russian revolution and split society into victors and victims: those who enhanced their social status and those who became paupers through their loss of property. Obviously, those who lost their property (such as the grandfather of one of the authors, whose pharmacies in Kiev were confiscated) hated the revolution with all their hearts and were reasonably suspected by the Soviet authorities of being unswerving enemies of the new regime.[47]

After the establishment of the Soviet totalitarian society, its leaders – until the end of their reigns – were aware of the fact that private property posed a formidable challenge to their rigid ruling ideology. They were sure that private property and the ensuing corruption that unavoidably accompanies it would undermine the fundamentals of their totalitarian rule, helping the opposition. For this reason, they used an iron hand to destroy any practice they believed encouraged respect for private property or diminished the glorification and high esteem of public property as the essential institution of a socialist society. The Soviet leaders declared those who damaged state property to be enemies of the people and held that these adversaries of the nation deserved extremely cruel punishments.[48]

In order to save the country from total economic collapse after the period of the civil war and War Communism, private property and market relations were completely eliminated. Lenin introduced the NEP in 1922; this new economic policy allowed the ownership of small- and middle-sized property. However, it only took two or three years for the Bolsheviks to understand the threat a new class of property owners posed to their regime and to decide to abolish the NEP. The Communist leadership were completely correct in thinking that even small amounts of private property in Soviet society encouraged illegal economic activity and expanded corruption in the party and state apparatus. For these reasons, the regime fought hard against underground entrepreneurs and their illegal accumulations of money.

The Soviet leaders not only saw private property as a dangerous political enemy to their order, but also believed in the economic superiority of public property over private property, as well as of a planned economy over a market one. The Bolsheviks believed in the almost magical potential of public property and the planning system. Interestingly enough, seventy years later, many

[47] Timothy Ash, "Velvet revolution: The prospects," *New York Review of Books*, December 3, 2009.

[48] One of the most notorious laws (1932) to protect socialist property was the edict that sent many thousands of peasants to the Gulag for picking up grain left on the field after the official end of the harvest, during the time of the cruel famine.

of their grandchildren maintained similar pessimistic expectations regarding private property and the market in post-Communist Russia.

To the end, the Soviet system continued to fight any semblance of private property. Only great necessity forced Stalin to allow peasants (collective farmers and workers in state farms) to grow private plots in order to satisfy their basic needs and even to sell some of their produce on a free market, on the condition that they also fulfill their quota on the collective farm. This decision was of great historical importance, as it allowed for the survival of the peasants, who received virtually nothing for their work on collective and state farms.[49] Peasants could use a small patch of land as their private plot, but this was never considered their property; it could be withdrawn from them at any time. In addition, peasants were only permitted to raise a limited number of cattle. The Soviet system was always more or less hostile to private plots, viewing them as something alien to its nature, and regularly oscillated in its policy toward them. Khrushchev, for example, supported private plots in the beginning of his rule in early 1950s but reversed his position later. Support for this type of agriculture resumed in the mid-1970s, under Brezhnev.

Only during the 1960s did the Kremlin allow people to have personal property such as an apartment, house, or car. (It is also the case, though, that the Soviet authorities in the post-Stalin era were not able to exterminate the growth of underground fortunes and private property in a shadow economy, despite their draconian measures.)

As Richard Pipes underscored, it was amazing how easily the Bolsheviks were able to eliminate respect for private property from the public mind in the 1920s, though it had been quite strong in Russia for many centuries, even if it was not as secure as in the West.[50] The manufactured change in public attitudes toward big private property was so successful that the Soviet dogma about private property was even shared by refugees from the Soviet Union during World War II. Attesting to this, more than 80 percent of all respondents

49 In 1940, almost all of the food consumption by peasants was from their own plots: 86 percent of their meat, 98 percent of their milk, and 97 percent of their eggs. See V. Ostrovsky (ed.), *Lichnoie Podsobnoie Khosiastvo* (Moscow: Nauka, 1988).

50 Making the contrast between Russian and European history in the role of private property, Richard Pipes focused attention on the power of the Russian tsar to confiscate the private property of the nobility. Amazingly, however, Pipes ignored the evolution of property relations in Russia; he did not mention that from the end of the eighteenth century forward, cases of state intervention in the activity of landlords were quite rare. Neither did he pay any attention to the development of the typical bourgeois property in the country in the seventeenth through twentieth centuries. Even in the countryside, despite the communal traditions, many peasants had become private owners of land and other property before the revolution. Sharply underestimating the place of private property in Russia, Pipes, at the same time, wrote that "within two or three years of seizing power, Lenin abolished, in favor of the state, all private property except small landholdings," in Richard Pipes, "Private property, freedom, and the rule of law," *Hoover Digest*, 2 (April 30, 2001); Richard Pipes, *Property and Freedom* (New York: Alfred A. Knopf, 1999).

participating in the Harvard project on Soviet émigrés (1956) believed in the superiority of state ownership over private property ownership for "heavy industry" and "transport."[51] The dogmatic belief in the necessity of nationalizing heavy industry and transport was intact in the minds of the majority of the Soviet population during Perestroika, despite all of the attacks on socialist ideology. This idea was so strongly rooted in the mentality of the Russians that preference for public property persisted past the dismantling of the Soviet Union, and even into the 2000s, when no less than 30 percent of Russians continued to support it. This fact amazed a lot of Russian liberals, who were sure that respect for private property would quickly reemerge in the public mind, as soon as the people were freed from the restraints of the Soviet authorities. As became clear in the post-Communist period, this reversal did not take place.

Certainly, the positive attitudes of the Soviet people toward public property should be accepted *cum grano salis*. In fact, most Soviet people – the same as many people in the West – shared a sort of social democratic view on property: that a combination of public property in big industry and small private property in services is the best model of an economy.[52]

Many of the same deeply negative attitudes toward private property were held by all of the totalitarian communist regimes: Mao's China, Pol Pot's Cambodia, Vietnam before the unification, Castro's Cuba, and, of course, all of the Soviet satellite states in Eastern Europe. Nazi Germany, however, presents us with something of an exception. Because the Nazi regime rose to power struggling with communists and scaring Germans with Bolshevism, they touted themselves as defenders of private property, and German tycoons largely supported the Nazi movement. However, with the firm establishment of Nazi rule, the role of big capital was virtually nonexistent. For example, the steel dynasty heir Gustav Krupp and others like him were only managers at their companies and were entirely obedient to the orders of the leadership.

Liberal Ideology in Soviet Society: Ambivalence toward Private Property

It is remarkable that even the most courageous dissidents of the last two decades of the Soviet order were mesmerized by the dogma asserting the superiority of public property over individual ownership in industry or transport. They preached, as the economist Vladimir Venzher did, for private property only in agriculture. Not even Andrei Sakharov dared to raise the question of privatizing big industry, deciding rather only to lament the necessity of

[51] Raymond A. Bauer, Alex Inkeles, and Clyde Kluckhohn, *How the Soviet System Works: Cultural, Psychological, and Social Themes* (New York: Vintage, 1956).

[52] The public belief in the superiority of public property did not prevent the Russian masses from participating in the mass pilfering of goods from state enterprises and offices (see Shlapentokh, *Public and Private Life*).

allowing small private property ownership.[53] Even the advocates of market socialism in the USSR, like Gennady Lisichkin, Nikolai Petrakov, and Evsei Liberman, never, even indirectly, demanded the privatization of public property in heavy industry.

On the other hand, Mikhail Gorbachev, a reformer who virtually destroyed communist rule, did not express any positive thoughts about private property until one year before the collapse of the Soviet Union. He and other reformers substituted vague and often misleading euphemisms such as "cooperative property" and "life lease" for this term. It was only in 1991 that the all union and national parliaments passed laws that fostered privatization and private business activities.

It is important to note that members of the Soviet nomenclature, from top to bottom, could not even claim to be the owners of the apartments or country houses in which they lived; neither were they able to transfer these dwellings to their children when they died. Indeed, the secret acquisition of private property in any form was a high political crime and was punished with a degree of severity that changed from leader to leader during the course of the Soviet regime.

At the same time, in the last years of Perestroika, when the liberals could say what they wanted, they moved fast from one extreme to another – from a high respect for public property in big industry to the denial of public property in any sphere of social life. They created a mythology about the supremacy of private property, the likes of which has probably only recently been surpassed by the ideologues of the Tea Party and the beliefs of some libertarians such as Ron Paul. The economist Larisa Piyasheva wrote in 1990 that Russia, from the moment private property was established, would only need one year to become a strong and prosperous economy.[54] Another economist, Grigory Yavlinsky, predicted it would take five hundred days. They spearheaded a host of authors who demanded the privatization of everything in society – not only mines and factories but also institutions in education and science, as well as police and corrections.

When Yegor Gaidar became first deputy prime minister in 1991, he immediately gave a powerful spurt to the propaganda that preached privatization of the economy as the solution to all of the problems of society. He and his friends were also inspired by the idea that the rapid privatization and the creation of a class of big property owners would make the restoration of the Soviet order impossible. To the end of his life, he practically ignored the negative consequences of privatization in the Russian context (corruption,

53 Andrei Sakharov, *Progress, Coexistence, and Intellectual Freedom* (New York: Norton, 1968).

54 See, for instance, the article by Larisa Piyasheva "What shall our life be under market conditions?" *Literaturnaia Gazeta*, May 30, 1990. See her famous article on what would happen in "one year" after the "three presidential decrees" on "free enterprise," Larisa Piyasheva, "The freedom of private property and the unregulated prices throughout all of Russia," *Literaturnaia Gazeta*, March 13, 1991.

among other issues).[55] Many social scientists and cultural figures, Russian and Western, followed Gaidar's lead either by ignoring the effect of privatization on Russian society or, for instance, by shifting the blame for corruption to the masses. Andrei Shleifer, a Harvard professor of economics and an expert on Russia, in describing the changes that occurred in the postcommunist countries, named seven issues that deserved the attention of policy makers; he did not even use the word "corruption" in his analysis.[56]

In the aftermath of Perestroika, some liberals even went so far in their praise of private property as to contend that the Soviet economy was an almost total "shadow" economy. They believed that the economy was only formally based on public property, when in fact it was ruled by the owners of illegal private property; the nomenklatura was among them.[57] Others, like Gaidar, composed a false theory that the holders of power began grabbing state property even before 1985 and Perestroika.[58] This theory of Gaidar's was repeated without serious empirical argument by Michael McFaul in his book *Russia's Unfinished Revolution* (2003).

Big Property and Its Legitimacy in a Post-Soviet Society

In the early 1990s, the leadership of the Russian Federation demonstrated its faith in private property by enacting new laws and a new constitution. The new ideology not only legalized big private property, but also allowed the Soviet nomenclature to keep their personal assets, which were quite large by Soviet standards. This stood in great contrast to what happened during the violent revolutions in both Russia and China, when the old ruling class lost all their material assets, including their apartments, furniture, or jewels. Moreover, the new rules did not restrain the access of anybody in the party apparatus from the acquisition of big property. They allowed the nomenclature to use their positions (for instance, as a minister or the director of a big factory), as well as their rich social capital, to be among the first who could privatize state property for their own benefit. The large sums of money that started to flow to former apparatchiks made the old party privileges unimportant, and provided "new Russians" with benefits the likes of which were unthinkable in Soviet times, when the ruling elite could not even permit itself extravagances. It was

55 Yegor Gaidar, "Revoliutsia ostalas' v 20 veke, reformy prodolzhaiutsia v 21," *Izvestiia*, January 17, 2001; "Svoiu povinnost' otbyl," *Moskovskie Novosti*, July 23, 2001. See also his major books.

56 Andrei Shleifer, "Seven things I learned about transition from communism," February 5, 2012, http://www.voxeu.org/index.php?q=node/7593, accessed March 1, 2012.

57 Vitaly Naishul', *Vysshaia i posledniaia stadiia sotsializma: Pogruzhenie v triasinu* (Moscow: Progress, 1991); Igor' Kliamkin and Lev Timofeev, *Tenevaia Rossiia: Ekonomiko-sotsiologicheskoe issledovanie* (Moscow: RGGU, 2000).

58 Yegor Gaidar, *Collapse of an Empire: Lessons for Modern Russia* (Washington, DC: Brookings Institution Press, 2007); Gaidar, *Dolgoie vremia*.

the apparatchiks in Komsomol, the Young Communist League, among them Mikhail Khodorkovsky, who started the process first of accumulating finance as bankers and traders, and then acquiring state property. Later, they were joined by ministers such as Viktor Chernomyrdin and Rem Vyakhirev, mayors such as Yury Luzhkov, and other members of the nomenclature, as well as their relatives and friends.

Kremlin leaders and the people in the highest echelons of power realized almost immediately that they should take the privatization of the economy under their personal control. These powerful people figured out that access to the privatization of big firms, especially in the extracting industry, should be treated as a privilege they could hand to only those people who, as owners, would reciprocate with lots of money for them. This process is highly reminiscent of the beginnings of the feudal structure in the early Middle Ages, when the king distributed the land and peasants among those whom he trusted, turning them into his vassals.

The easy access of the nomenclature to private property and the illegal acquisition of production assets by people with ties to the party and the state apparatus explain why the old dominant class did not resist the new order. This was a major contrast to the behavior of the old classes when it came to the changes in property relations during the violent revolutions in Russia and China. However, the fast emergence of the new owners of the crucial resources of the country created a problem that will hover over Russian society for decades: the illegitimacy of the new owners in the eyes of the population. The relatively mild attitude of the masses toward rich people in Western countries is caused by the belief in the legal origins of their fortunes – no more than one-fifth of the people in the United States doubt the legality of a person's accrued riches in their country, while around four-fifths of Russians are skeptical about the existence of the same principle in their country. In January 2012, at the start of his presidential campaign, even Putin – who himself benefited a lot from "wild privatization" – deemed it politically necessary to condemn it.

Big Private Property and Corruption: Rent-Seeking Activities

The relations between big property and corrupted political power deserve the special attention of those who analyze Russian society. One of the most important instruments of big property is the corruption or co-option of a country's bureaucracy and its political leaders. It fosters a phenomenal rate of corruption, impossible to achieve without big fortunes seeping into the highest ranks of power. This phenomenon is evident in Western societies as well, where big business undermines political and economic competition.[59]

[59] See Vladimir Shlapentokh and Joshua Woods, *Feudal America: Elements of the Middle Ages in Contemporary Society* (University Park: Pennsylvania State University Press, 2011).

Corruption – the exploitation of political power for the private interests of officials – in contemporary society is a "normal" channel that makes the exchange of political privileges for money possible.[60] In economic terms, corruption can be seen as a quasi-legitimate product of rent-seeking activities, which is a typical behavior for corporations and rich people.[61]

Rent-seeking activities are usually defined as the political activities of organizations, groups, or individuals with big resources to extricate special monopoly privileges from the government by compensating officials in various ways. Rent seeking is not always illegal. The privileges that corporations or individual owners of big property receive include government contracts, which are especially valuable in the defense industry; the exemption from or lowering of taxes; "redistributive legislation" (laws favorable to corporations); concessions in regulations; immunity from judicial prosecution; speeding of registration processes; autonomy in management, including the waiving of national laws; licenses for foreign trade; easy credit; and the redistribution of property in the interests of companies that enjoy the protection of national or local leaders. Of course, the same companies enjoy the elimination of competitors during the sale of state property, which makes it easy to bankrupt one's rivals or block their entry into the market.[62]

Big Property in a Segmented Society

As was mentioned earlier, the impact of big property on the political process depends on the structure of the society. Indeed, in order to understand the role of big property in Putin's society, we need to abandon the idea that post-Soviet Russia, like any other society, can be described in terms of only one theoretical framework – authoritarian or liberal. In fact, post-Soviet society is deeply segmented; like most societies, it is a combination of three types

[60] According to Donald Treisman, corruption can be defined as "the misuse of a public office for private gain." See Donald Treisman, "The causes of corruption: A cross-national study," *Journal of Public Economics* **76** (2000), 399.

[61] See James Buchanan, Robert Tollison, and Gordin Tullock (eds.), *Toward a Theory of the Rent Seeking Society* (College Station: Texas A&M University Press, 1980); see also Robert Dahl, *A Preface to Democratic Theory* (Chicago: University of Chicago Press, 2006); Stein Ringen, *The Possibility of Politics* (New Brunswick, NJ: Transactions, 2006).

[62] Those who pursue rent-seeking activities (corporations and other big social actors) spend money and other resources in order to receive privileges from officials. The money used to bribe officials is considered a transaction cost, which reflects the expenditures of the firm on its public activities. Of course, transaction costs influence the price of goods and services. This transaction cost can be either fully legitimate and transparent – as when fees are written into a contract – or part of an unspoken agreement between businesspeople and officials, as is often the case in contemporary Russia (some Western fund managers working in Russia have even said, privately, that were bribery "institutionalized," as it is in some Middle Eastern countries, it would greatly improve the investment climate, since people would no longer have to guess how much to give to whom, nor worry about the legal repercussions).

of social organizations: authoritarian, liberal, and feudal. The relative role of each of these organizations changes from one society to another, and usually a society is labeled by the dominant organization within it. The predominance of liberal relations in the United States explains why American society claims to be liberal, even if two other elements – authoritarian and feudal – play an important role.

Soviet society was definitely mostly authoritarian, despite the existence of liberal and even feudal components. Contemporary Russia can also be considered a neofeudal society, with a very strong authoritarian and some liberal elements. One of the authors of this book was probably the first in the literature and media to characterize Russian society as feudal, as it emerged from the collapse of the USSR in the middle of the 1990s.[63] This characterization was later supported by several Russian experts, including Yulia Latynina, a prominent journalist with a strong knowledge of history.[64] Latynina's vision of Russia was, in turn, supported by Sergei Guriev.[65] In addition, the philosopher Erikh Solovyev talked about "the shopkeepers' feudalism."[66]

Those who insist on the leading role played by feudal elements in contemporary Russian society single out a key consequence of the feudal model: a weak Russian state unable to implement the principles of society, authoritarian or liberal. The weakness of the Russian state is generated by two causes, which often interact. One of them is the lack of resources necessary for running a central administration that can impose its will on national and local bureaucracies. Another cause is the Russian ruling elite's absorption with gaining personal enrichment. This self-first trend puts the country's national interests below the individual's quest to accrue and preserve personal power and fortune.

The weakness of the Russian state generates the high level of independence of the political and economic actors with big resources; the exchange between

[63] Vladimir Shlapentokh, "Four Russias," *Tocqueville Review*, vol. **XIX**, 9.1 (1998) 9–34; Vladimir Shlapentokh, "The four faces of Mother Russia," *Transition* **4**.5 (October 1997); Vladimir Shlapentokh, "'Normal' Russia," *Current History* no. **212** (October 1997), 331–6; Vladimir Shlapentokh, "Bonjour stagnation: Russia's next years," *Europe-ASIA Studies* **49**.5 (1997); Vladimir Shlapentokh, "Catastrophism on the eve of 2000: Apocalyptic ideology between Russia's past and future," *Demokratizatsia* 5 (Winter 1997); Vladimir Shlapentokh, "How Russians will see the status of their country by the end of the century," *Journal of Communist Studies and Transition Politics* 3 (September 1997); Vladimir Shlapentokh, "Moscow identity crisis," *Foreign Service* 4 (April 1997); Vladimir Shlapentokh, "Russia: Privatization and illegalization of social and political life in Russia," *Washington Quarterly* **19** (1996), 65–85; Vladimir Shlapentokh, "Russia after the election," *Transition* 4 (1996); Vladimir Shlapentokh, "Contemporary Russia: The best parallel to it – feudal Europe," *Europe-Asia Studies* (Spring 1996).

[64] Yulia Latynina, "Roi ili antibulochnik," *Novaya Gazeta*, January 25, 2010.

[65] Sergei Guriev, "Industrial'nyi feodalizm: Nizkaia geograficheskaia mobil'nost' trudovykh resursov sderzhivaet restrukturizatsiiu ekonomiki," *Ekspert*, April 10, 2001.

[66] Yulia Latynina, "Patent na blagorodstvo: Vydast li ego literatura kapitalu?" *Novyi Mir* 11 (1993), 191–5.

political power and money, and corruption and criminalization; the important role of personal relations; the existence of a private security society; and the personal domain of the leaders and the main members of the ruling elite, whose private interests prevail over national ones. Among the authors mentioned are those who we can consider as our "theoretical allies."

Our Allies

Indeed, a number of authors in the West and in Russia gravitate toward the segmented approach, even if they do not use our terminology. The first group pays special attention to the role of oligarchs and corruption in Russia, often using the term "corporatism" to characterize post-Soviet Russia. For example, analysts like Dmitry Travin[67] and Vladislav Inozemtsev[68] have this inclination, as do Russian historians like O. Gaman-Golutvina,[69] political analysts like Alexander Kostin,[70] and economists like E. Maiminas.[71] Several Western authors have joined them, such as Peter Rutland, who saw post-Soviet Russia as an oligarchic society.[72] But the oligarchic model falls short of explaining a number of developments in Russia, primarily by underestimating the role of the central administration, on one hand, and the existence of certain liberal institutions, on the other.

The second group of like-minded analysts such as Larry Diamond and several others[73] has directly abandoned the idea of one suitable systemic approach

67 Dmitry Travin, *Putinskaya Rossiia: Ot rassveta do otkata* (St. Petersburg: DELO, 2008).

68 As Inozemtsev writes, "Contemporary Russia is not a liberal society but it is also not an oriental despotic state and it is not also a new Soviet Union." It is, as he continues, "a new and particular society which is functioning on the basis of its original laws." See Vladislav Inozemtsev, "Chto sluchilos' s Rossiei," *Neprikosnovennyi Zapas* 6.74 (2010).

69 The historian O. Gaman-Golutvina wrote about the dominance of "the political financial oligarchy that was fighting with the bureaucracy in 2000." See O.V. Gaman-Golutvina, "Burokratiya ili oligarkhiya," in T.I. Zaslavskaya (ed.), *Kuda idet Rossia. Vlast'. Obshchestvo. Lichnost'* (Moscow: Moskovskaya vysshaya shkola sotsialnykh i ekonomicheskikh nauk, 2000), p. 162.

70 Aleksandr Kostin, *Petlya Putina: Razbor poletov za 10 let* (Moscow: Algoritm, 2010).

71 The economist E. Maiminas talked about "the system of bureaucratic or bureaucratic-oligarchic capitalism." See E. Z. Maiminas, "Sootnoshenie vlasti, obschestva i lichnosti," in T.I. Zaslavskaya (ed.), *Kuda idet Rossia. Vlast'. Obshchestvo. Lichnost'* (Moscow: Moskovskaya vysshaya shkola sotsialnykh i ekonomicheskikh nauk, 2000), p. 207.

72 See Peter Rutland, *The Politics of Economic Stagnation in the Soviet Union: The Role of Local Party Organs in Economic Management* (Cambridge: Cambridge University Press, 2010). See also a few other Western authors with the same view, for example, Simon Pirani, *Change in Putin's Russia: Power, Money and People* (London and New York: Pluto Press, 2010).

73 Diamond, "Hybrid regimes"; see also Steven Levitsky and Lucan A. Way, "Elections without democracy: The rise of competitive authoritarianism," *Journal of Democracy* 13.2 (2002), 51–65; Terry Lynn Karl, "The hybrid regimes of Central America," *Journal of Democracy* 6 (1995), 72–87; William Case, "Can the 'halfway house' stand? Semidemocracy and elite theory in three Southeast Asian countries," *Comparative Politics* 28, (1996), 437–64. To some degree, those political scientists who advocate "the graded approach" to authoritarianism and who try to

and operates, instead, with the concept of a "hybrid" society, which cuts close to our methodology. Some authors, including Dale Roy Herspring and his coauthors (2007)[74] and, in particular, Graeme Robertson (2011),[75] directly apply this concept to contemporary Russia. Still, our position is different from all of these. The proponents of the hybrid model, such as Graeme Robertson, look at society only in political terms, and for them a hybrid society is only a mixture of different authoritarian and democratic institutions, while our segmented approach supposes a combination of not only different political institutions, but also economic and social ones.

As strange as it may seem, it is reasonable to think of Vladimir Lenin as an advocate of the segmented approach, though he was clearly not drawn to this concept on theoretical grounds but by common sense, as he observed the Russian reality after the civil war. Indeed, in 1921, he talked about the coexistence of five "social structures" (*uklad*) in Soviet Russia: patriarchic, small commodity production, private capitalist, state capitalist, and socialist.[76]

Big Private Property and Big Money in a Feudal Context

Within the framework of the segmented approach, it is easy to understand the role of private property and big money in Russia, and to comprehend that the character of these elements depends on the weight of authoritarian and feudal elements in society.

The segmented approach is of particular importance to our analysis of the differences and similarities between the Soviet and post-Soviet regimes in Russia. When there are a weak state and many actors with big resources, the owners turn into influential feudal barons who are able to pursue their own narrow, private interests, which are often at odds with the public interest. Each office of an official is turned into a source of illegal income, in the same way as it was in the Middle Ages in France or in Russia. Russians described this phenomenon, both in the Middle Ages and in contemporary Russia, using the term *kormlenie*, or "feeding," which points to the fact that each position "feeds" its holder with illegal revenue.[77] In exchange for the fief, the holder grants his

measure the degree of democracy in society are close to the "hybrid" methodologists, sharing with them the same narrow perspective on the analysis of society; see K. Bollen and R. Jackman, "Democracy, stability, and dichotomies," *American Sociological Review* 54 (1989), 612, 618; Robert Dahl, *Polyarchy: Participation and Opposition* (New Haven, CT: Yale University Press, 1971), pp. 2, 8, 231–5; Robert Dahl, *Democracy and Its Critics* (New Haven, CT: Yale University Press, 1989), pp. 241, 316–17; and later Michael Coppedge and Wolfgang Reinicke, "Measuring polyarchy," *Studies in Comparative International Development* 25 (1990), 51–72.

74 See Dale Roy Herspring (ed.), *Putin's Russia: Past Imperfect, Future Uncertain* (Lanham, MD: Rowman & Littlefield, 2007).

75 Graeme B. Robertson, *The Politics of Protest in Hybrid Regimes: Managing Dissent in Post-Communist Russia* (Cambridge: Cambridge University Press, 2011).

76 Vladimir Lenin, *Collected Works*, vol. 43, (Moscow: Politizdat, 1955), p. 206.

77 This term can be found in contemporary Russian novels like *Germans* by a new literary star, Alexander Terekhov (Moscow: AST, 2012), as well as in articles describing various sides of

loyalty to the central administration, guaranteeing, for instance, the desired outcome of an election (the Soviet system resorted to the same social strategy, although less successfully, when it made one-third of the adult population "little bosses").[78]

But even more important is the fact that the possibility of the accumulation of wealth in a feudal context pollutes the whole system of incentives in a society. For example, the acquisition of big property and its permanent expansion, as well as an office for enrichment, became the main focus of Russian bureaucrats, who were supposed to be most concerned with the interests of the state and society.

There was no private property in Soviet society, and the role of money was relatively weak. This does not mean that money was not an important ingredient in Soviet social life. Even in Stalin's times, money played an important role in the economy and, particularly, in the everyday life of the Soviet people. The people, as employees of the state, received money in the form of salaries; everyone wanted to increase his or her income, even if one's social status was ultimately more important for receiving goods and services. The existence of a private market for food and other consumer goods illustrates that activities limited by regulations were also a stimulus for earning money, even for apparatchiks who had access to their closed stores.[79]

With money's limited role in Soviet society, it is understandable why the level of corruption was also minimal. Corruption was mostly concentrated at the lower levels of the state hierarchy. Ordinary people bribed low-level state officials and other people in the retail trade and service sectors. Bribe receivers were typically found among the local officials responsible for the distribution of real estate, the directors of stores and hospitals, low-ranking police officers, theater ticket distributors, and, sometimes, the heads of educational or research institutions. The informal economy had a special area of corruption, where the managers responsible for fulfilling state plans used bribes to get parts and raw materials. Overall, however, bribe giving was not highly prevalent in the Soviet Union. It was more common in non-Russian republics. We do not know of a single fact that showed evidence of even the slightest impact of money on

ordinary Russian life like Lev Moskovkin, "Sbol'noi golovy na zdorovuiu," *Moskovskaia Pravda*, April 10, 2012, or Yulia Krivoshapko, "Pravitelyistvo uchredit dolkhnosti glavnogo energetika Olimpiadi v Sochi," *Rossiiskaia Gazeta*, February 7, 2012.

[78] One must take into account the involvement of a little less than 20 million Soviet people as "little bosses" in official propaganda, which could only strengthen the Soviet regime. Read about "little bosses" in Soviet society in Shlapentokh, *Normal Totalitarian Society*.

[79] After 1953, the importance of the private market increased enormously. Several "colorful" markets emerged – "black," "gray," and "rosy," to use Aron Katsenelinboigen's terminology with respect to the free behavior of economic actors. See Aron Katsenelinboigen, "Color markets in the Soviet Union," *Soviet Studies* **XXIX** no. 1 (1976), 976; see also Galina Belikova and Alexander Shokhin, "Chernyi rynok: Liudi, veshchi, fakty," *Ogoniok* **36** (1987), 6–8.

political decisions or the selection of cadres, in either Moscow or the capitals and regional centers of the European Soviet republics.[80]

The level of bureaucratic corruption in Yeltsin's and Putin's Russia was much greater than that found in any contemporary democratic country. While corruption is a serious phenomenon in countries like the United States or France its scale is much larger in Russia. The difference is particularly apparent in the behavior of Russian and Western leaders. While politicians everywhere yearn for the continuation of their power and for personal enrichment, those in post-Soviet Russia were able to achieve power and riches beyond the wildest dreams of their counterparts in democratic countries. Yeltsin and Putin were able to make their private interests determine the domestic and foreign policy of their country. Almost every bureaucrat was able to turn his or her office into a fief, which became a source of enrichment not only for the individual but also for networks of his or her relatives and friends.

The Possibility of Fast Accumulation of Wealth and the Downgrading of Meritocracy and Morals in Society

The possibilities for personal enrichment through the use of one's position in a bureaucracy that uses corruptive processes dramatically change the moral compass of a society. Consider the influence of living in this sort of a society on the professional intentions of young people. One-third of Russian youth (48 percent among students) wanted to join the ranks of state employees in the late 2000s. Those who wished to become bureaucrats did not hide the fact that "the patriotic factor" played only a minimal role in their motivations. Most important in their thinking were purely material factors (social guarantees, privileges, the stability of the position, salary, and the opportunity to receive bribes and make deals) and "the connections." These data contrast with the prestige rankings of occupations in the Soviet Union in the 1960s–1980s, when jobs in the state apparatus attracted a small number of young people, while most dreamed of becoming scholars or engineers.[81]

The low demand for hard work and skills explains the low level of professionalism within the country, from the Kremlin down to police officers, pilots, intelligence officers, teachers, scholars, and doctors.

However, even more significant for contemporary Russian society is the fact that Russian professionals (particularly the young) have no chance, under the existing rules of the game, to become rich in Russia, as a result of the way big private property emerged in Russia and continues to expand mostly through

[80] See, for instance, Dimitri K. Simes, *After the Collapse: Russia Seeks Its Place as a Great Power* (New York: Simon & Schuster, 1999).

[81] Vladimir Shubkin, *Sotsiologicheskie opyty* (Moscow: Mysl, 1970); Vladimri Shubkin, *Trudiaschaiasia molodezh': Obrazovanie, professiia, mobil'nost'* (Moscow: Nauka, 1984).

illegal means. It is one of the major reasons contributing to the emigration of the cream of the crop among the Russian people, which has become a fixture of post-Soviet Russia.

Big Property and Criminals

The weak state and outburst of feudal elements in post-Soviet Russian society account for the deep ties between big property and criminal activity. Since the 1990s, these ties have been the stuff of everyday news. This is why Grigory Yavlinsky named Russian society a "corporate-criminal system."[82]

Whereas criminals tried to penetrate small enterprises in the Soviet economy, mostly in commerce and services,[83] criminal encroachment into the big Soviet industrial units (not to mention the Soviet bureaucratic structures) was simply unheard of. Murder of managers almost never happened, while it became a mass practice in post-Soviet Russia, at least up through the time of writing this text. Even during his short tenure, when Andropov wanted to find an example of criminal activity in the economy, he found many cases of corruption in the early 1980s (for instance, between the director of the Moscow supermarket Gastronom No.1 and the employees of other Moscow stores) but not one case of organized criminal activities. The situation was somewhat different in the Caucasian and Central Asian republics, but, even there, the penetration of criminals into the political system was very limited.

After the anticommunist revolutionary victory, the role of criminals in Russia changed radically and real mafias came onto the scene. As contended by the general and former head of the Russian branch of Interpol Vladimir Ovchinsky, in 2011, criminals encroached in all units of political power and business.[84] The emerging oligarchs – big business tycoons with inevitable ties to state officials – were some of the first to recognize these mafias as potential instruments in their battles with business rivals during the expansion of their new empires. Almost simultaneously, mafia outfits began to penetrate governmental offices, which by that time were interlaced with oligarchs. In addition to their usual means of persuasion (big money), oligarchs applied direct threats of violence to get things done. Vladimir Gusinsky, who, in a strange twist of events in 1999, became an icon of Russian democracy, publicly blackmailed people, threatening, among other things, to murder their children.[85] The deep connections between the managers of Avtovaz, a major car manufacturer based

[82] Grigory Yavlinsky, "Unizhennyie liudi ne sozdadut ekonomiku 21 veka," *Novaya Gazeta*, November 11, 2002.

[83] Simes, *After the Collapse*.

[84] "General-mayor MVD Vladimir Ovchinsky: Mafiya pronikla vo vse gosstruktury RF," *Newsru.com*, June 29, 2011, http://www.newsru.com/arch/crime/29jun2011/ovchinskymafiarf.html, accessed March 1, 2012.

[85] See Paul Khlebnikov, *Godfather of the Kremlin* (New York: Harcourt, 2000), pp. 152–3. Vladimir Shlapentokh received the same information from a private source who knew Gusinsky well.

in Toliatti, and a powerful organized-crime syndicate have been discussed in the media by several Russian and foreign authors.[86]

The governor of the Far East region from 2001 to 2010, Sergei Darkin, was known as both an oligarch and a criminal before he was elected in 2001.[87] It was also documented in 1999–2002 that Vladimir Butov, the governor of the Nenets district, has both a long criminal record and close ties to oil companies.[88] Even more notorious is the case of Anatoly Bykov, who combined his control over the aluminum industry with obvious involvement in crime and corruption, and an active role as a deputy in the local Duma in Krasnoyarsk.[89]

In 2000–2, big corporations – particularly in metallurgy and the oil trade – declared war on the criminal structures, which were too aggressive toward big businesses. But they resorted, once again, to turning local police into their own security forces, combining the police with their own army of guards, rather than using legal means. This is exactly how a medieval society behaved, with the individuals and institutions protecting themselves with their own forces, not by asking for official help from the state.[90] But by the early 2000s, criminal structures started to function – in some cases in coordination with mafias – as governmental structures, particularly those of the police and FSB, the security agency formerly known as the KGB. Therefore, corporations began turning to these criminalized governmental agencies to solve their problems more often than they had in the past. For instance, they used illegal raiding, or grabbing property occupied by their rivals with the use of force, in order to eliminate them from the market.[91] What is more, the murder of managers – often a joint action of criminals and the police – became a fixture of Russian economic life throughout the first decade of the twenty-first century.[92]

86 Mikhail Lamzov, "Zhiguli na krovi," *Argumenty i Fakty*, September 11, 2002.

87 Igor Korolkov, "Gubernator i Vinni Pukh," *Moskovskie Novosti*, July 9, 2001.

88 See Andrei Kolovangin, "Kriminal uvlasti," *Slovo*, July 5, 2002; Korolkov, "Gubernator i Vinni Pukh"; "Uvolen sobesednik Putina," *Kommersant daily*, July 3, 2002; Sergei Alekhin, Dmitry Doroshenko and Andrei Murashev, "Kuda propal gubernator Butov," *Rossiiskaia Gazeta*, June 29, 2002.

89 Alexei Tarasov, "Chisto na doverii," *Moskovskie Novosti*, February 10, 2003. The late Alexander Lebed, "The letter to president," *Nezavisimaia Gazeta*, April 4, 2002; see also Chuvashev, "Belyi kon dlia Anatoliia Bykova," *Nezavisimaia Gazeta*, June 24, 2002.

90 Konstantin Simonov, "Krupny bizness mozhet nas spasti ot kriminala," *Vek*, November 1, 2002.

91 The criminal structure in Bratsk was typical. This structure was headed by the former deputy of the State Duma, Vadim Maliakov. As was established in 2011, this criminal group was very active in the lumber business and, at the request of some businessmen, grabbed the property of their rivals. See http://www.newsru.com/crime/29jun2011/ovchinskymafiarf.html.

92 A few cases from the year 2002: Two prominent businesspeople – the director of the hotel Pekin and the director of a leading Russian advertising firm – were killed in Moscow in January–February 2002. In April, a local newspaper editor from Tolliatti city was gunned down. One month later, General Vitaly Gamov, the head of the border guards in Yuzhnyi Sakhalinsk, was killed (many Russians attributed his death to his battle against fish poachers in the Far East). After being seriously wounded by the first attempt on his life, Moscow's vice mayor, Iosif

Private Wealth and Political Leaders: Their Feudal Domain

The establishment of private property and the possibility of accumulating money without constraints in a society with few observing the law or little enforcement of it radically changed the behavior of the leaders in post-Soviet society, in comparison with the Soviet rulers. Indeed, Soviet leaders had practically no private property, as was clearly manifested in the fact that their children, just as with the offspring of those from the lower levels of the hierarchy, were unable to inherit almost anything from their fathers. Brezhnev's garage of several cars – mostly gifts from foreign leaders – was an extreme extravagance in Soviet times.

The post-Soviet leaders began building up their domains like feudal kings as soon as they got the keys to power. Yeltsin and Putin tended to ignore the distinction between the public and their own private interests. They also ignored the rights of rich people and considered their resources almost as their own. The Kremlin regularly ordered tycoons to provide them with the money necessary for some public project (for instance, the Olympic Games of 2014), for their election campaigns, or simply for their own enrichment and entertainment. In 2003, for instance, Putin accepted the invitation of the leading oligarch Oleg Deripaska to join him on a lavish ski trip in Khakasia, East Siberia.

This practice was typical of feudal monarchs and barons, who, in addition to getting money through official taxes, often "borrowed" money from merchants and factory owners. It is difficult to imagine Soviet leaders, even Stalin, similarly ordering their ministers or the director of a big factory to deliver a necessary sum of money.

The creation of private companies in Russia and, in particular, the transformation of state companies into mixed state/private firms made it very easy, and seemingly legal, to provide the leaders and their circles with corporate stocks. Several companies such as Gunvor, which is involved in selling oil, is widely seen as the joint property of Putin and his close friends, according to numerous reports.[93] Putin's alleged role was based not on the legal ownership of stock in his name, but rather on unwritten agreements with his friends.

Almost all members of Putin's presidential administration were either "elected" or "appointed by the government" to the boards of directors of the major oil and gas companies, including Gazprom, Rosneft, and Transneft. Of course, all such state appropriations or "raids" in Putin's Russia, including the persecution of Mikhail Khodorkovsky and the confiscation of his firm Yuykos, were the results of a convergence of factors. Besides the Kremlin's willingness

Ordzhonikidze, narrowly escaped death during a second attempt in June. In August, hitmen gunned down Duma Deputy Vladimir Golovlev; the deputy chief of the Moscow city government's railway system, Sergei Paristy; and the vice governor of Smolensk, Vladimir Prokhorov. This is only a partial list of the high-profile killings of 2002.

[93] Yulia Latynina, "Putin. Itogo," *newsland.ru*, January 1, 2012, http://www.newsland.ru/news/detail/id/867316, accessed March 1, 2012.

to take direct control over Yukos, Putin considered Khodorkovsky as an increasingly formidable threat to his monopoly on power through aggressive participation in national politics through his purchase of seats in the Duma. Of special importance to the leaders and their friends was the blending of foreign and Russian companies, which opened up an avenue that allowed them "legally" to launder money in the West. Putin and his close friends went as far as merging Russian semistate companies with foreign corporations that promised them either direct or indirect ownership of legitimate Western stocks. Far from being unique, this practice, wherein officials ensure their interests in other countries, parallels the actions of many leaders of contemporary authoritarian regimes in Central Asia or Africa.

Bureaucracy: Office as a Private Property

The emergence of private property in a society with strong feudal characteristics made it possible to turn each public office into a fief – a private source of illegal income, or "feeding office." The result, as in the Middle Ages, was that each position in the bureaucracy, including membership in national and local parliaments, became an object for commercial bargaining. A Russian author tried to estimate the value of each office from a rent-seeking perspective. As an indicator, he used the amount of revenue produced by companies that were under the given office's control. The highest score was given to the head of the presidential administration, who supervised the activities of companies with revenues amounting to more than $10 billion a year. Second place belonged to a federal minister who controlled roughly $1 billion. The next place went to directors of some departments in the federal ministry ($100 million). Other high officials in the ministry handled companies with revenue streams between $1 million and $10 million. This list of offices was similar to a king's ranking of the most and least wealthy areas in a country in the Middle Ages. The king would charge a vassal or a claimant for the position of tax collector ("tax farming") in a given area in accordance with this ranking.

It is certainly predictable that the transformation of public office into a sort of private property stimulated the proliferation of nepotism to a scale unknown in liberal or totalitarian societies. Of course, the elements of nepotism were not alien to the Soviet system.[94] But in post-Soviet Russia, nepotism became a regular feature of society. Innumerable data show how almost all members of the bureaucracy extended various privileges to their relatives, close and remote, including second and third cousins.[95]

94 The Kaganovich family was a textbook example. Before the war, in addition to Lazar Kaganovich, who was a member of the Politburo, two of his brothers were ministers, while other relatives also held some positions in bureaucracy. Still, there were so many similar cases in Soviet society that this was not the exception.

95 See, for instance, what happened in the late 2000s–early 2010s in the Omsk region, where Governor Leonid Polezhayev's "clan" was composed of all his relatives – a typical phenomenon

The possibility of accumulating wealth radically changed the behavior of all of the law enforcement agencies: police, courts, and the Federal Security Service. Officials in these agencies turned their positions into a source of illegal income, as did other apparatchiks. The highest officers gained possession of big fortunes, accounts in foreign banks, and real estate abroad.

Even during Brezhnev's times, the KGB people had a reputation, even among the dissidents they arrested, as honest individuals. In post-Soviet Russia, particularly in Putin's times, the FSB – the heir to the KGB – turned into the symbol of corruption. In fact, Putin, himself a former KGB agent, placed hundreds of his former colleagues, as well as many army generals, in key governmental jobs and encouraged them to enrich themselves, creating the praetorian guard, which is personally faithful to him. These people were the first beneficiaries of property redistribution in the 2000s. (For more about the corruption in the FSB, see the chapter on that group in this book.)

Big Property and Democracy

Big property, which means big money, has played an ambivalent role in history with respect to democratic institutions. On one hand, authoritarian and, even more so, totalitarian regimes have been hostile toward big property. In Western society, big property plays an important, often positive role in politics by helping to sustain political pluralism in society, for instance, through magnates who finance media corporations with different ideological perspectives. On the other hand, as mentioned earlier, big property also undermines the principles of democracy because the use of big money in the election process destroys a sacred fundamental tenet of democracy, that is, the equality of all people in the voting process. Collusion with the government also allows corporations to have a great impact on the selection of cadres, which undermines the meritocratic principle of promoting those people with the most merit to important offices.

In a nondemocratic society, the political role of big property is even more uncertain than in Western-type societies. Let us consider Russian history and bourgeois property. (Being landed – owning property – in Russia, as in many other countries, was the bulwark of the authoritarian state – with England as a possible exception, where, in fighting against the monarchy, the lords were an important catalyst for establishing democracy.) In prerevolutionary Russia, the bourgeoisie, unlike most of the Russian intelligentsia, were very cautious in their support of the liberalization process. Still, some rich people financed liberal and leftist activities in the country. However, at the same time, the bourgeoisie were always afraid of revolution and mass disturbances, such as those

in most Russian regions, including small administrative units such as small cities and villages (see Georgy Borodiansky, "Mozhno zaiavit' s uverennost'iu, sem'ia gubernatora Polezhaeva ne voruet vozdukh," *Novaya Gazeta*, August 4, 2011).

that happened during the first Russian revolution in 1905, when big capital took the side of the monarchy, which cruelly crushed the rebellion.

After 1905, some members of the bourgeois class supported the party of Cadets (constitutional democrats), which strove to build a democratic society in Russia; another part of the bourgeois was represented by the Oktobrists, the party that wanted to have a constitutional monarchy and only reluctantly participated in the monarchy's removal in 1917. It was only during the short period of the February revolution that most of the Russian bourgeois showed they were indeed on the side of democracy.

Post-Stalin Russia did not have people with underground wealth who tried to help the budding liberal movement, even indirectly, by financially supporting the arrested dissidents and their families. Even if there were, none of them achieved the reputation of the prerevolutionary Russian capitalist Savva Morozov, who aided the revolutionaries.

In post-Soviet Russia, the role of big property was negative, with respect to democracy. It is well known that a few new capitalists, like Konstantin Borovoy, helped Yeltsin in August 1991. Later, however, the position of the new Russian magnates toward democratic values essentially changed. The cause lies in the fact that most of them made their fortunes through collusion with the obviously nondemocratic government. In supporting the nondemocratic regime, the oligarchs rewarded Yeltsin and his family with gigantic sums of money for selling them big chunks of state property at ridiculously low prices in the loans for shares program – a widely disputed scheme by which oligarchs such as Mikhail Khodorkovsky obtained their state holdings in exchange for bailing out the state with cash.

It is not very shocking that oligarchs were ready to run the country using the same nondemocratic methods. In the middle of the 1990s, they even installed their own partial control over the bureaucracy, particularly in the selection of people for crucial state positions, ignoring both the parliament and public opinion. This period was described as *semibankirshchina*, or rule by "seven bankers" – a play on the sixteenth-century term *semiboyarshchina*. The label was used to describe a group of bankers who supported Yeltsin's regime in return for major assets. In 1996, the group of the oligarchs who published the notorious "Letter of 13" tried to cancel the presidential election (it is a funny coincidence that the title of Simon Johnson and James Kwak's book (2010) is *13 Bankers*[96] – about the American financial moguls responsible, in the authors' opinion, for the Great Recession). Having failed, the oligarchs helped Yeltsin to win the election, which violated many democratic procedures and was, ultimately, rigged. In no way were the Russian oligarchs fazed by Yeltsin's reputation on the eve of the election, as "Tsar Boris" held the division of powers in deep contempt.

[96] Simon Johnson and James Kwak, *13 Bankers: The Wall Street Takeover and the Next Financial Meltdown* (New York: Pantheon Books, 2010).

The Russian tycoons' activities had the same effect on the next parliamentary election in 1999. The media empires of Berezovsky and Gusinsky violated all rules of honesty in their attempts to discredit Yeltsin's two opponents, Evgeny Primakov and Yury Luzhkov. These practices were sufficient evidence that neither of their stations could be regarded as true champions of democracy.[97] The parliamentary election arranged by the oligarchs, like the presidential election of 1996, negatively impacted Russian democratic institutions, particularly the elections in the regions, which looked similar to the Soviet-style elections of old.

The next step undertaken by the oligarchs was no less deleterious to Russian democracy. Headed by Boris Berezovsky, they helped Yeltsin to install Vladimir Putin, a former KGB man, as the next Russian president, with no concerns about the future of liberalism and democracy in Russia. (Later, already in emigration, Berezovsky repented of his crucial role in the installation of Putin as president, while in the aftermath of his death in March 2013 those liberals who reflected on his life considered his alliance with Putin as a mortal sin with respect to Russian democracy. Berezovsky's fight against Putin after his flight from Russia in 2000 under democratic slogans aroused skepticism and mistrust in those who remembered his political behavior before he fell out of favor with Putin, who refused to allow him to continue his role as power broker in the Kremlin.)[98] Having entered Putin's era, oligarchs either fled Russia as Berezovsky and Gusinsky did, or started to cooperate with the regime, whose hostility toward democracy increased exponentially, in comparison with Yeltsin's time.

The Russian tycoons (with the probable exception of Alexander Lebedev, a banker with a KGB past, who sponsored the critical *Novaya Gazeta*) did not try to help; nor did the independent media. As one Russian author noted, "Russian

[97] During the campaign, two major Russian TV stations literally spent hours each day denigrating Primakov and Luzhkov in the most aggressive ways. The stations combined some real facts with crass fabrications. As a rule, the stations never gave the two politicians a chance to answer the allegations. Sergei Dorenko and Mikhail Leontyev (dubbed the "TV Killers" by the Russian media) were two journalists for the television station ORT. In serving their boss, they rudely maligned the seventy-year-old Primakov by focusing on his age and physical ailments. The patriotic card, the Chechen war, and acrimonious anti-Western propaganda were actively employed by these journalists to denounce anyone who refused to give full loyalty to Putin. Dorenko and Leontiev labeled Putin's two main rivals as enemies of Russia, traitors, and agents of the West. See how the Russian public perceived its media in the late 1990s in the article by Yury Zaynashev, "The fourth power is becoming the second oldest profession," *Moskovskii Komsomolets*, August 12, 1997.

[98] Boris Berezovsky boasted that he "shaped the developments" in Russia ; see his interview with *Novaya Gazeta* (December 14, 1999); see also Alexander Budberg, "Zabudet li Putin svoikh roditelei," *Moskovskii Komsomolets*, January 27, 2000; Natalia Gorodezkaia, "Obida oligarkha," *Vremia MN*, December 23, 1999.

oligarchs do not stay in line in order to help Russian investigative journalists who are regularly harassed and even murdered across the country."[99]

Khodorkovsky, who tried to stand up to Putin as an independent figure, was a clear exception. His democratic credentials, however, aroused some later suspicions. He openly financed both the liberal parties that were advocates of a Western style of democracy and the communists who did not hide their contempt for this democracy. There were those who thought that the major goal of the mogul was to acquire personal control over parliament.[100]

Big business in Russia cannot boast that it helped to promote civil society. After all, even in the more liberal times of Yeltsin's regime, it did not do a lot in this area. Moreover, the oligarchs transformed several NGOs (nongovernmental organizations) into their "instruments." The oligarchs worked with the Kremlin to manufacture faux-independent NGOs. In August 2001, with the endorsement of the Kremlin, big companies such as Lukoil and Yukos devised "the Association of Trade Unions of National and Transnational Companies." The association pretended to defend the interests of workers but was really under the strict control of the big companies.[101]

Russian oligarchs' records of charitable activities or support of science and culture are not very extensive. In this arena, Khodorkovsky once again stood out as a sort of maverick among Russian oligarchs. In his attempts to make his oil company not only transparent but also socially responsible, he created a network of schools equipped with computers together with computer training centers for teachers in the early 2000s.[102] Other oligarchs made investments in some public endeavors, like the Olympic Games project (2014), but only under the direct command of the Kremlin. At the time this book is being written, there are eight hundred endowment funds functioning at various universities and colleges in the United States; there are only twenty such institutions in Russia. Society treats the charity activity of corporations with suspicion, viewing it as one of the channels corporations use to avoid taxes and bribe officials. According to the data of VTSIOM, only 17 percent of twelve hundred CEOs and owners of companies in 2009 evaluated themselves and their level of their activity in the sphere of charities as quite high.[103]

99 Yelena Novoselova and Yelena Yakovleva, "Kormilitsa s bol'shim appetitom," *Rossiiskaia Gazeta*, March 16, 2011.

100 See a few recent books on Khodorkovsky, such as Richard Sakwa, *The Quality of Freedom: Khodorkovsky, Putin, and the Yukos Affair* (Oxford: Oxford University Press, 2009); Martin Sixsmith, *Putin's Oil: The Yukos Affair and the Struggle for Russia* (New York: Continuum International Publishing Group, 2010).

101 Marina Solntseva, "Pod krylom u oligarkhov," *Obshchaia Gazeta*, August 23, 2001.

102 Sergei Lebedev, "Podaite na nuzhdy obrazovaniia, a to khuzhe budet!," *www.ps.1september.ru*, http://ps.1september.ru/article.php?ID=200307701, accessed March 1, 2012.

103 "Blagotvoritel'nost' u nikh i u nas," *soc-pr.livejournal.com*, July 6, 2010, http://soc-pr.livejournal.com/9529.html, accessed March 1, 2012.

We have no data showing that rich people and corporations helped to finance, even moderately, the protest movement in Russia that sprang up in dissent against rigged elections from December 2011 to February and March 2012. What is more, on the eve of a protest rally (February 4, 2012), Russian businessmen expressed their disquiet with the liberal protest movement. Boris Titov, the chairman of the lobby group Delovaya Rossia, reminded the Russian public of the position held by the Russian bourgeoisie in 1905, suggesting that the leaders of the movement should be more pragmatic and wary of ushering in a period of chaos. He reproached the protest leaders for making "the sort of demands that [you know] in advance [the authorities] will not agree with."[104]

Russian oligarchs have actively incorporated themselves in the authoritarian system. In 1995, Boris Berezovsky was given the position of deputy secretary of the Russian Security Council. Khodorkovsky held many positions in the government in 1991–2000, including the position of deputy minister of fuel and energy and a member of various governmental committees. Roman Abramovich was elected to the State Duma in 1999, then was appointed as the governor of Chukotka region in the next year. He kept this position until 2008, when he was elected as the chairman of the legislative chamber in the same area. Alexander Khloponin was even more active in his bureaucratic endeavors than Abramovich. His list of positions includes the governor of the gigantic Krasonoyarsk region (2002–10), deputy premier minister, and presidential emissary in the North Caucasian district. Another tycoon, Vladimir Potanin, head of a big financial empire, served as deputy prime minister in 1996–7 and headed various governmental committees while an oligarch. Sergei Pugachev asserted himself as a senator in the Tuva Republic in 2002, and Andrei Klishas, director of the giant corporation Norilsky Nickel, was appointed as a senator in 2012. He was also was included by the Kremlin in the Public Chamber, a body that, despite evidence to the contrary, claims to be independent of the government.

Prokhorov's Case: A Mogul at the Service of the Regime

Prokhorov is a perfect example for refuting the dogma about monied people loving democracy. In Putin's Russia, political power has manipulated the wealthy as it wished. Indeed, Mikhail Prokhorov, one of the richest men in Russia, was actively used by the presidential administration as a pawn in the game to suggest to the Russian and international public that Putin's regime is indeed democratic. The regime tried to exploit the myth about rich people as staunch defenders of democracy.

Despite the importance of Putin and Medvedev as the main actors and central focus, the show's authors deemed it necessary to include other actors, in order to add to the show's intrigue. Indeed, as any Hollywood fan knows,

[104] Howard Amos, "Businessmen cautious about protest," *Moscow Times*, February 2, 2012.

a good show requires the addition of fresh personalities from time to time. Thus, in May 2011, Mikhail Prokhorov, a famous mogul who was close to Putin, was introduced as a new "supporting actor." Prokhorov presented himself as an independent man who decided to be the leader of the bogus "Right Cause" Party, which apparently had to represent liberalism in the State Duma for propaganda purposes. But when Prokhorov tried to introduce independent politicians into the party, he himself, to his own surprise, was ousted by the Presidential Administration. This move baffled many people in Russia, who continued to believe that Prokhorov's wealth protected him from humiliation and from serving as a political lackey to those who held political power. The public could only compare Prokhorov's behavior with that of another mogul, Oleg Deripaska, who, during a labor conflict in Pikalyovo in 2009, suffered public humiliation by Putin in a scene that was shown on federal TV stations – in the manner of a Soviet apparatchik berating his secretary. To the surprise of the Russians, however, not only did Prokhorov refrain from expressing his displeasure about the disrespectful behavior of the Kremlin, he even accepted another role in Putin's political show a few months later. He allowed Putin's myrmidons to include him in the list of candidates for the presidential election. He had no hope of winning the election; there was only one purpose behind this move: to create the appearance of true competition. Indeed, with 8 percent of the vote in the real election, Prokhorov did not present any threat to Putin. At the same time, though, he helped to create a façade of democracy.

Conclusion

The transformation of the Soviet economy away from centralization eased the way for the emergence of big private corporations in post-Soviet Russia. It takes a lot of time to create a big company in a normal capitalist economy, but in the 1990s it was relatively easy to transform a former ministry into a new big private company, as the Russians did when the Ministry of Gas smoothly evolved into the gigantic corporation "Gazprom."

The heritage of the centralized Soviet system strongly influenced the structure of the post-Soviet economy. Most of the big Soviet companies were not split among new owners; they retained their size and simply changed the label. By 2009, Russia continued to be a country with one of the highest concentrations of property. While almost half of the U.S. labor population worked in small business (defined as fewer than five hundred people in one firm) in 2010, less than a quarter of Russian labor worked for small firms.[105] In the extraction industry, small businesses contributed only 1 percent of all production in 2009; it was only 10 percent in manufacturing and just 8 percent in transport and communications. The dominance of big businesses in the economy explains

[105] Surinov (ed.), *Rossiiskii statisticheskii ezhegodnik, Federal'naia sluzhba gosudarstvennoi statistiki* (Moscow: Rosstat, 2010); statistics about business size (including small business) from the U.S. Census Bureau, available from http://www.census.gov.

why Russia places thirtieth of fifty-three countries in their friendliness to small businesses.[106]

It is evident that the Russian economy simply could not function in the modern world without big corporations. The idea of splitting big Soviet industrial complexes into small businesses, even if it has circulated at times, was completely shattered by commercial and technological requirements. However, the impact of big property, which emerged after 1991, stretched far beyond just the economic realm. As we have tried to show, big property, in the context of feudal and authoritarian relations, influenced political and social life in the country and shaped its foreign policy to a great degree.

The existence of big private property made the behavior of the ruling elite, and the leadership of society in particular, radically different than it was in Soviet times. Promoting universal corruption, big property created a new type of bureaucracy that turned out to be very different from the nomenclature. Private property in a contemporary Russian context demoralized society, lowered the professionalism in the country, and encouraged the emigration of the best minds in Russia.

In the political sphere, and against the expectations and dogmas of Western political science, big property in post-Soviet Russia became a tool of the authoritarian regime in its fight against liberal principles, rather than a bastion of democracy. Big property's contribution to Russian democracy has been very modest so far.

Still, private property in post-Soviet Russia is also a force that has introduced democratic elements into Russian society. In the 1990s, when magnates controlled the media companies, the level of pluralism in Russian media was much higher than it was later, in Putin's times. Private property, while entrenching autocracy, has also succeeded in mitigating it – creating a degree of freedom that would be nonexistent without it.

[106] Geoff Lewis, "Who in the world is entrepreneurial? We scan the globe to uncover which countries are the most – and least – friendly to small business," *CNN Money*, June 1 2007, http://money.cnn.com/magazines/fsb/fsb_archive/2007/06/01/100049637/index.htm, accessed March 1, 2012.

2

Ideology and Public Opinion in a Centralized Society and in a Fragmented Society

One of the chief differences between the Soviet and post-Soviet regimes lies in their relative treatment of official ideology. Only the distance between the Soviet and post-Soviet economic orders may have been as dramatic as the one between the public ideologies of the two systems. These regimes differed from each other in the content of their public ideology, in the attention the regimes paid to ideological activity, and in the impact of their ideologies on the minds and behavior of the masses. These differences were caused by the transition from a centralized Soviet society to a post-Soviet society that was fragmented; from a society where money played a minimal political role to one in which money determined all aspects of social life, including the political and ideological.

A Fragmented Society and the Interests of the Elites

The fragmented character of post-Soviet society, and especially of Putin's regime, accounts for its deeply eclectic official ideology. It had to adjust to all three segments of society – authoritarian (or statist), feudal and liberal – which are in conflict with each other. For this reason, Putin's official ideology contains three separate components that are mostly incompatible with each other. The first, the authoritarian /nationalist, consists of the cult of the state and patriotism, respect for the Soviet past, and dislike of the West. The second component, the oligarchic or feudal, commends the accumulation of wealth, assumes the right of officials to collect revenue by any means possible, and supports the free movement of rich people, their money, and their relatives abroad. The third, liberal segment praises democratic institutions, private property, the free market and human rights.

These three components of Putin's official ideology are connected by the regime's attempt to use each of them for its legitimization. In supporting the goal of legitimizing the regime, the liberal component offers democratic procedures (mainly elections), the authoritarian/nationalist component offers a description of the regime as the single antidote against anarchy and as a powerful instrument in protecting Russian national interests in the world, and the feudal, or oligarchic, component depicts the regime as the guarantor of the prosperity of big corporations and fast economic growth.

Was Soviet Ideology Eclectic?

From the 1930s, when Stalin infused Russian nationalism into society, superficial observers wrongly perceived Soviet ideology as deeply eclectic. From the victory of the Bolshevik revolution until the early 1930s, official Soviet ideology was formally based on the tenets of Lenin's style of Marxism. This ideology praised the dictatorship of the proletariat and the leading role of the Communist Party; it insisted that the might of the state should be the major goal for all Soviet people; it also commended collectivism and social equality, state property and a planned economy, internationalism and the cordial relations between people of different ethnic groups.

However, in the early 1930s, the Bolshevik ideology developed into a crossbreed of two major trends in twentieth-century Russia: socialism and Russian nationalism. These parallel trends were combined into an ideology that dominated society and legitimized the system in the eyes of the people. In Stalin's interpretation, socialist ideas and Russian nationalism were not antagonistic but rather were germane to each other, mostly because they were both based on the cult of the state. Indeed, under the guise of "the dictatorship of the proletariat," the cult of the totalitarian state began to develop almost immediately after the seizure of power in 1917. The leadership quickly abandoned all of the democratic elements of the socialist idea, such as the active role of the masses in governing society and political freedom of choice (elements regarded as vitally important by Western Marxists).The formal inclusion of the nationalist component in the ideology in the early 1930s only magnified the cult of the state in society. In fact, the cult of the state united Russian Marxists and nationalists because they both needed the totalitarianism to achieve their goals. The amalgam of both elements was also revealed in the fact that, since the 1930s, they had both insisted on the superiority of Soviet Russia over the West, with one element believing in the preeminence of Russia as possessing the best social order, and the other in the supremacy of Russian moral values and culture over their Western counterparts.

During the war with Germany, Stalin clearly placed nationalist values and Russian patriotism in a leading role in his official ideology. Despite some fluctuations in public ideology after Stalin's rule, nationalist values continued to be used as crucial guidance for Soviet society in pursuing the central goals of the USSR – military parity with the West, and the protection and expansion of the empire.

Soviet Russia was not the only country to have used an ideological blend of socialism and nationalism. Nazi Germany also used it, although their ideology advanced different perceptions of socialism. The Nazis' ideology was strongly hostile toward Marxism, the class struggle, and internationalism. Instead, it focused on the unity of all German people, whatever their status, and wanted to diminish inequality through the cooperation of the different classes under the total control of the supreme leader. The marriage of socialism (in one of its many versions) and nationalism was also very popular almost in all underdeveloped countries of the twentieth century (China and India, among others).

With the natural wedding of totalitarian socialism and nationalism, Soviet ideology appeared quite cohesive to the Russians. There was some discordance, however, brought on by the thesis of the leading role of the Russian nation and by the important role played by state anti-Semitism in society. Yet, both of these parts of the official ideology were fully accepted by the absolute majority of Russians, who did not see any contradiction between nationalism and socialist principles.

Contrary to Soviet ideology, which managed to blend both of its major parts quite effectively, Putin's ideology did not; all of its three components – state-nationalist, feudal (oligarchic), and liberal – were in deep conflict with each other. Let us analyze the place of each of the three components in Putin's official ideology and show how the Kremlin tried to adjust all of them to their real politics.

Playing with Liberal Ideology: The Formal Allegiance to Western Democratic Principles

Soviet ideology, starting with Stalin's constitution (1936), included the recognition of some democratic principles (direct voting for the national parliament, universal participation in voting, a booth for individual private voting, etc.). However, in keeping with Lenin's tradition of praise for the Soviet system of self-government as being superior to bourgeois democracy, Stalin's ideology continued openly and consistently to praise Soviet democracy over Western democracy. Soviet ideology never pretended that the Soviet political order was similar to the Western political system. Soviet ideology and practice did not assume that the leader of the country had to be elected by the population. Instead, it considered it normal for the leader to be endorsed by only a tiny group of people, and for his appointment to be for life.

This ideology publicly refused either to permit the existence of many parties or to have more than one candidate on the ballot in an election of any type (e.g., the election of the national parliament or the election of the members of a trade union in a small shop). Soviet politicians and ideologues almost never made concrete comparisons of Soviet elections with Western ones. Soviet people could not even entertain the idea of inviting Western observers to watch elections in the Soviet Union.

Putin's ideology, on the other hand, was mostly based on the assumption that the political system in post-Soviet Russia was as democratic as that of any country in the West.[1] Remarkably, Putin's frontal attack against the West, made during his notorious Munich speech in February 2007, did not discard Western democracy as being irrelevant to Russia (whereas, in similar circumstances, all of the Soviet leaders said exactly this) but insisted that the level of democracy in Russia was higher than in the West. He talked with weakly veiled contempt about those "who teach us democracy but do not want to learn it themselves" (he clearly had the United States in mind).[2] What is more, Russian politicians of every ilk, even communists and nationalists, when looking for arguments to support their positions, regularly made references to the American or the Western political system in general as examples to imitate. Ironically, even Putin, who systematically foments anti-Western and anti-American sentiment in the country, justified his draconian laws against political opponents in 2012 by referencing Western nations that offered a model of how government can maintain order in society.

The Technology of Imitation Democracy

Putin's administration fashioned the complicated mechanism of a false imitation of democracy, which in such a developed form was essentially unknown in past international practices. While making United Russia the absolutely dominant party in the country (the party plays the same role as the Communist Party did in the Soviet Union), the Kremlin regularly invented false parties that imitated an oppositional political force. Formally, Russia's State Duma has three opposition parties – the Communist Party, the Liberal Democratic Party, and A Just Russia. While the two former parties formed spontaneously in the early 1990s, they were quickly co-opted by the presidential administration, which all but fully reined them in during Putin's administration. A Just Russia is a slightly more complicated case. Engineered in the presidential administration as a social-democratic party that also incorporated several nationalist groups,

[1] It is true that the Kremlin made some attempts to protect the obvious dissimilarities in the political practices between the two worlds. The concept of "sovereign democracy" advanced by Vladislav Surkov, which suggests a principal difference between Western and Russian democracies, claimed to repeat the Soviet thesis about the incomparability of the bourgeois and proletarian democracies. The motto about "the special historical road of Russia," even if it only received limited visibility in the talks of the leading members of the ruling elite, was used also as a new version of the Soviet gimmick, which supposedly had to prevent an undesirable comparison between Putin's and the Western political order. However Surkov's subterfuge and the claim for Russia's special case in history could not subvert the general tenor of Putin's ideological framework, which continued to be based on the idea of Russian devotion to Western democratic principles, and even on Russian superiority in observing these principles better than the United States or Western Europe.

[2] See Putin's speech at the Munich Conference on Security at http://www.securityconference.de/konferenzen/rede.php?sprache=en&id=179, accessed September 30, 2008.

it has deputies who have demonstrated the greatest degree of independence in all of the oppositionist parties. During the protest movement of 2011–12, many of its members, including Gennady Gudkov; his son, Dmitry Gudkov; Ilya Ponomaryov; and others, joined the leadership of the protest movement. However, they came under severe pressure for their participation. Gennady Gudkov was ousted from the State Duma in 2012, while pressure began to mount on Ponomaryov and Dmitry Gudkov to leave the party. The party's chief, Sergei Mironov, is a close ally of Putin – and while he has demonstrated some ideological opposition in the past, he firmly backed the crackdown by calling on the oppositionists to leave the party in February 2013.

Another example of the Kremlin's role in engineering political parties was its creation, in 2011, of Right Cause, a purported neoliberal party. While there was evidence that it was created in order for the then Finance Minister Alexei Kudrin, a leading liberal and a key Putin ally, to head the party, it was eventually handed over in May 2011 to Mikhail Prokhorov, a famous mogul and a man clearly doing Putin's bidding. The party was apparently created to represent liberalism in the State Duma – but the moment Prokhorov began demonstrating any modicum of independence by drawing real oppositionists into his party, he was squeezed out. This happened in September 2011, in what he called a "raid" by the Kremlin's chief ideologist at the time, Vladislav Surkov.[3] Right Cause never managed to garner enough votes to make it into the State Duma. Nevertheless, Prokhorov, in an agreement that was apparently mediated with the Kremlin through Kudrin, was allowed to run for president in March 2012.[4]

The Case of the Tandem as a Surrogate for Pluralism

In order to imitate democracy, Putin's administration put on some very complicated performances that would have been hard for Soviet bureaucrats to pull off. While the Stalin regime was not completely foreign to performances showing political pluralism in society, it was rare for them (or their successors) to resort to them. In 1936, Stalin organized open national debates. Even today, some Sovietologists believe these debates, which were about crafting the constitution, were genuine[5] (one of the authors, as a teenager, vividly remembers how

[3] In some ways, Putin's Kremlin repeats the experience of the Soviet satellites in postwar Eastern Europe, which, with the permission of Moscow, arranged the functioning of a few supposedly independent political parties, together with the leading Communist Party. In Communist Poland, for instance, there were two minor parties – the United People's Party and the Democratic Party. Of course, they were fake organizations and nobody inside or outside the country took them seriously.

[4] In 2008 the Kremlin also created the party Civic Force, which was headed by Putin's official Mikhail Borshchevsky; it only lasted a year, leaving hardly any footprint.

[5] See Lewis Seigelbaum, *Making Workers Soviet: Power, Class, and Identity* (Ithaca, NY: Cornell University Press, 1994).

one of these meetings was organized by the authorities on his residential block in Kiev, in a climate of growing mass terror). According to official Soviet data, 623,334 meetings were held; more than 42 million people attended them; and some 169,739 proposals, comments, and prospective amendments were generated. Stalin did not use these debates to show the Soviet people and the world the existence of diverse opinions within the country, however; all of the proposals under debate were absolutely loyal to the regime.

Stalin's PR skills pale in comparison to Putin's technique in deceiving the Russians and international public opinion. Since Putin was constantly obsessed with retaining and enhancing his legitimacy, he did not risk changing the Constitution so that he could legally remain on for a third consecutive presidential term after serving back-to-back terms (2000–08). In order to get the legal right to regain the presidential position in 2012, he chose Dmitry Medvedev, a lawyer and a loyal subordinate, as the keeper of the presidential seat and appointed him president in 2008. Putin also allowed Medvedev to pursue fledgling liberal reform during his four years in the Kremlin, in order to persuade the public of the existence of democratic tendencies in Russia. Putin's democratic facade needed someone with obvious liberal credentials, a person who could appeal to the Russian intelligentsia. Unlike Putin, who had an established reputation as a hoodlum during his childhood – something that not even his official biography denied – Dmitry Medvedev's pedigree consisted of growing up in a professorial family who socialized with refined St. Petersburg intellectuals. In addition, he had a penchant for using the latest electronic gadgets to communicate with people (he was the first Russian politician to wield an iPhone, and bureaucrats using iPads at their desks and having accounts on Twitter and Facebook became a fixture during his term). Thus, Medvedev's mild-mannered, ironic, and self-deprecating style was an ideal contrast to Putin's abrasive and commanding ways.

As the member of a highly educated family, Medvedev was expected to avoid the locutions used in gang slang in his speech, offering citations of famous scholars instead, including the seventeenth-century Dutch law authority Hugo Grotius and Seymour Lipset, the twentieth-century American political scientist. Would it even have been possible to see Putin speaking with great warmth about a subtle author such as Anton Chekhov? Is it possible to imagine Putin adorning his site with a long proverb, not in Russian but in Latin ("Quid bonum, felix, faustum, fortunatumque sit!" or "Be good, happy, lucky, and fortunate!")? It is unlikely that any Western leaders, knowing how snobbish it would make them appear, would even dare to publish something like this in their public documents, for fear of looking ridiculous. Dmitry Medvedev fit this role perfectly as a man widely appealing to Russia's intelligentsia.

Essentially, Medvedev began to perform his role as soon as he was designated to be the intermediate, figurehead president. He presented himself as a political maverick, one who would sever the country from its old ways. Indeed, he immediately started to profess his love of freedom, democracy, law, and modernization. For example, on February 18, 2008, he declared, to the stupefaction of the whole country, that "freedom is better than non-freedom." From then on, Medvedev regularly announced "Urbi et Orbi" as a way of showing his admiration for liberalism. For instance, in September 2010, he solemnly declared at Yaroslavl's forum that "there is no democracy if man personally feels non-freedom and injustice."

He was, supposedly, in favor of liberal pragmatic initiatives like reforming the legislative system, transforming courts into independent bodies, liberalizing elections, and creating conditions to fight corruption. In addition, he gave empty directives to various governmental institutions to work efficiently for the public, not to steal, to be kind to people, to cure patients in hospitals, to support young families, to strengthen the defense of the country, to battle terrorism effectively, and so on. He was known, for example, sternly to reprimand officials, demand investigations, and issue recommendations to improve "government responsiveness" after national disasters (e.g., in the aftermath of the fires during the summer of 2010, the sinking of a pleasure boat on the Volga River in 2011, and acts of terrorism). In a speech he made at the economic forum in Petersburg in July 2011, he was so critical of the government that one journalist sarcastically noted that he would not be surprised if the president fired the premier minister; while this would have been a good gesture for a "reality show," it was not for this show.

On the eve of the presidential election campaign of 2012, the Kremlin created a false drama of political competition between Medvedev and Putin. Keeping the audience interested in the confrontation between the two leaders required them to appear to be of the same political weight, in the same way gripping sports events are contested by equals. This occurred despite conventional wisdom in Russia that Putin was the boss and Medvedev no more than his obedient subordinate. Thus, according to the requirements of the script of this fake political rivalry, the major TV channels (basically, the single source of information for the majority of Russians) were obliged to give each leader equal representation. Equal representation pertained to other matters as well, such as the portraits hung in the offices of officials, where both men were prominently displayed.

To deepen the intrigue of the show, its architects did something that would rival a John Le Carré spy novel. On the one hand, the script focused on a fissure between the two leaders, by showing their differences through official declarations, press conferences, meetings with various people, official sites, blogs, and Twitter posts. On the other hand, the script also included the leaders' declaring that there were no substantial differences between them.

Only shows like the long-running TV series, like *The Sopranos,* can claim superiority in holding an audience's attention. The spellbinding nature of Putin's show can be credited to Medvedev's critiques of Putin's policies; some were openly defiant, but most were thinly veiled. Each one of those statements intensified the drama of the show, since it immediately generated a new wave of debates in Russia and abroad, regarding the size and depth of the growing fissure between the two leaders.

A particularly useful device for the show were Medvedev's nearly direct confrontations with Putin. These often revolved around foreign relations. Within a showdown, Medvedev would take a friendly position toward the West, while Putin would take an aggressive, almost xenophobic, position. Such a confrontation played out over the war in Libya, as Medvedev supported Western actions against Muammar Gaddafi, while Putin vehemently did not.

The Kremlin was able to keep the world in suspense over who would be the presidential candidate for the 2012 election. Since the beginning of 2010, there had not been one press conference or public meeting where the leaders had not touched upon this uncertainty, despite the flurry of issues that could be addressed regarding the state of the country. Following the logic of a good detective novel, the authors of the script suggested that both actors avoid direct answers and, instead, gave cryptic hints and gestures, thus raising curiosity. Several interpretations and theories would emerge from these highly publicized events. The artificially-created frenzy regarding which of these two men would be the future ruler of Russia left practically no room for journalists to ask questions about other opponents, or about how elections were going to be fair and honest, or about the numerous problems of Russian life.

Initially, Putin's show produced the intended results. Indeed, those who yearned for a democratic Russia had largely accepted the idea that their hero would rise up to fight the dragon. Even some liberal Moscow analysts accepted this charade. In the last two years, Radio Ekho Moskvy, the most critical outlet in Russia, has devoted a lion's share of its programs to the interminable guessing game of who will be president. Such a seasoned journalist as Dmitry Muratov, the editor of the liberal newspaper *Novaya Gazeta,* for four years saw in Medvedev an icon of progress. Before Putin's reelection in 2012, such prominent liberals as Igor Yurgens and Evgeny Gontmakher, the director and leading economist of the Institute of Contemporary Development (INSOR), which was considered to be Medvedev's think tank, gave talks and published articles full of aggressive criticism against Putin, while praising Medvedev as a Russian reformer who would save Russia from Putin's morass.

In addition, Russian intellectuals implored Russian citizens to believe in Medvedev's mission and support him. In their "Letter of the intelligentsia," published in *Novaya Gazeta* in July 2011, they begged Russians not "to permit" Medvedev's departure from the political scene, seeing him as the savior of democracy. A host of top-ranked intellectuals fervently tried to persuade their readers that "Medvedev's departure would cancel and reverse his long-term initiatives," as if the authors of the letter could cite even one example of Medvededv's real actions, and not only empty words, in favor of democratization.

Most of the Western media, including prestigious newspapers such as the *New York Times* and *Le Monde,* also accepted the show – hook, line, and sinker. Indeed, they regularly published articles that scrutinized the words and actions of the two leaders, in order to divine who had a better chance of controlling Russia in the coming years.

The facade was made so believable that when Medvedev announced in September 2011 that he would step aside to allow Putin to run for president, the clearly orchestrated switch came as a deep blow to the intelligentsia, many of whom interpreted it as a betrayal. The mass protests that spilled into the streets in December 2011, following the parliamentary elections, can be attributed to this sense of betrayal, rather than the fact that the elections were rigged – previous parliamentary elections were rigged, and it was the 2011 ballot that drew an unprecedented number of election observers from the ranks of the middle class and the intelligentsia, in a clear reaction to the facade that was exposed when Medvedev backed Putin for president.

Indeed, when Putin was reelected as president in March 2012 Medvedev abruptly forgot his liberal activity, which in fact produced zero change. He even openly declared that he was not a liberal but a conservative politician.[6] Medvedev showed the same hostility to the mass protest movement in Russia in the first half of 2012 and made no move to stop the harassment of its participants or to object to Putin's draconian laws violating rudely the rights of assembly and freedom of speech in summer of 2012.

The success of Putin's deception with Medvedev was in fact enormous. Indeed, he was able to mislead the sophisticated Russian intellectuals and first-rank Western journalists for four years.[7]

The Conflicting Status of Private Property in Putin's Ideology and Practice

While most elements of the liberal order run counter to the way decisions in Putin's administration are actually made, one very important element of that order has indeed played a significant role in Putin's ideology and practice. It is private property. We have already discussed this issue in the first chapter. Indeed, private property is very precarious in Putin's regime and the confiscation of the property of the opponents of the regime in one way or another is a regular practice in Russia. The Kremlin at will orders big business to spend

[6] http://www.novayagazeta.ru/columns/52389.html.

[7] Of course, there are many people in Russia who do not believe that Medvedev is an independent crusader. Rather, they are confident that Putin is in firm control of the country. They believe that Medvedev is Putin's puppet. Thus, the imaginary conflict between the two leaders is merely a ploy to pave the way for Putin's return to the presidency. Those who do not take the fabricated political drama on official TV channels at face value are mostly ordinary people, alien to the political sophistry of Putin-Surkov. In July 2011, 68 percent of them were confident that Putin is the real master of the country. In contrast, only 19 percent of Russians cherish the view, together with the intellectuals, that Medvedev is an independent politician.

money. It is also true that the bureaucracy controls business in its activity. Still private business makes up a very important part of Russian life, a radical contrast with the Soviet past.[8]

The Play with Communist Ideology and the Inconsistency of Putin's Ideology

At the same time, communist ideology, with its many elements, is dear to the Kremlin. The cult of state and the empire, social equality, the glorification of the Soviet past and Stalin, the denial or downplaying of mass repression, and the support of anti-Americanism are important parts of the "statist ideology" that the Kremlin has espoused since Putin's achievement of power. Putin, like Gennady Zyuganov, the leader of the Communist party, never expressed his criticism of the Soviet political system, and neither he nor his ideologues denied accusation that Putin's political system was similar to the Soviet regime in many respects. Of course, they both praised the KGB and its predecessors.

On those occasions when Putin has criticized the Soviet past, his criticism focused on lack of market economy. He has frequently been confronted about the benefits of the Soviet system by Gennady Zyuganov. On one occasion in April 2012, Putin lashed out at the Communist Party, saying that the Soviet economy could never produce enough meat.[9] (By the way, while all Soviet leaders before 1985 praised the Soviet political system, none of them was satisfied with the Soviet economic order and all tried to improve it.)

In this case as with liberalism, Putin's regime was again ambivalent: accepting several communist postulates, the regime hid its deep animosity to some of the important elements of communist ideology, first of all its support of social equality and its hostility to private property.

Stalin and Mass Repressions

The Russian Communist Party after 1991 unswervingly praised the Soviet past and Stalin, and denied, justified, or downplayed the mass repressions. Indeed, the treatment of mass repressions even among Stalin's apologists is far from uniform. Some of them prefer simply to deny that the mass repressions occurred. Close to them are those who simply ignore the repressions as much as possible, reducing any account of them to a few lines. Some of Stalin's sympathizers found that a better way to achieve their goal was to justify the terror as necessary. Others recognize it, but hold everybody except Stalin responsible. We have labeled these deniers of the terror as "Stalin's defenders," while others are called "sophisticated apologists." As a matter of fact, the handling of

[8] http://expert.ru/2012/01/30/rol-gosudarstva-izmenitsya/

[9] A. Arutunyan, N. Doff. "Putin's speech beset by tensions." *The Moscow News*. April 12, 2012. http://www.themoscownews.com/politics/20120412/189623196.html.

Stalin's repressions in the dominant ideology is a perfect illustration of the complex technology of historical falsification.[10]

The leading forces among Stalin's defenders are the Communists and some nationalist groups, who influenced the post-Soviet official ideology's attitude toward the repressions. Gennady Zyuganov has never mentioned the mass repressions. He said only that "there was some bitterness and difficulties" during Stalin's time, but he did not elaborate on them.[11] In 2005, he called for Stalin's full rehabilitation and revision of the decision of the Twentieth Party Congress.[12] "The name of Stalin," Zyuganov declared, "is tightly linked with the history of our country ... in many respects it represents the 20th century ... during which the civilization moved several steps forward."[13] Pursuing the party line, the majority of communist newspapers tend to avoid the issue of the mass repressions.[14] Most Russian nationalists, such as Dmitry Rogozin, are also among Stalin's defenders.[15]

Putin basically followed the Communist Party position on Stalin. He said almost nothing negative about Stalin when he talked inside the country. (Another case is when Putin talked to foreigners. Then he was often critical of Stalin.)[16] Putin used several occasions to mention Stalin in a positive light.[17] For instance, he cited Stalin as a leader who knew how to stimulate the activities of Soviet academics, which was necessary for industrialization.[18] Putin's presidential Web site was full of materials that praised Stalin unconditionally.[19]

[10] See Vladimir Shlapentokh and Vera Bondartsova, "Stalin in Russian ideology and public opinion: Caught in a conflict between imperial and liberal elements," *Russian History* 36.2 (May 2009).

[11] Gennady Zyuganov, "Ia schitaiu, chto Stalin byl glavnym stroitelem Sovetskoi derzhavy," March 5, 2008, available at http://kprf.ru/personal/zyuganov/foto/55447.html, accessed June 2, 2007.

[12] *Vesti Nedeli*, April 17, 2005, see also "O 125-letii I. V. Stalina," *Vestnik organizationno-partiinoi raboty*, No. 4, 2004; see G. A. Zyuganov's book devoted to I. V. Stalin at http://kprf-org.ru/archiv/vestnik6/vestnik6–2004.htm, accessed June 2, 2007.

[13] Maksim Artemyev, "Neveselyi iubilei," *Novaia Politika*, December 17, 2004.

[14] According to our content analysis, 60 percent of articles in the two major Communist newspapers published in 2006–7 did not mention the issue of repressions.

[15] Dmitry Rogozin, "Dukhovnyi lider dlia Rossii," available at http://echo.msk.ru/programs/proverka/52209/, accessed June 2, 2007.

[16] "Interviiu pol'skoi gazete 'Gazeta Vyborcha' i pol'skomu telekanalu TVP," January 15, 2002, available at http://www.kremlin.ru/text/appears/2002/01/28773.shtml, accessed April 23, 2008.

[17] "Stenograficheskii otchet o vstreche s tvorcheskim kollektivom gazety," *Komsomolskaya Pravda*, March 9, 2005, available at http://www.kremlin.ru/text/appears/2005/05/88557.shtml, accessed April 23, 2008; "Stenograficheskii otchet zasedaniia Rossiiskogo organizatsionnogo komiteta 'Pobeda,'" March 9, 2005, available at http://www.kremlin.ru/text/appears/2005/03/86104.shtml, accessed April 23, 2008.

[18] "Stenograficheskii otchet zasedaniia Soveta po realizatsii prioritetnykh natsional'nykh proektov i demograficheskoi politiki," September 13, 2007, available at http://www.kremlin.ru/appears/2007/09/13/2351_type63378type63381_143866.shtml, accessed April 23, 2008.

[19] See, for instance, "SMI o Prezidente. Vladimir Putin prodolzhil Kurskuiu bitvu," August 8, 2003, available at http://www.kremlin.ru/text/publications/2003/08/50863.shtml, accessed April 23, 2008.

Putin talked about the bad things that happened in "Stalin's time," but, to a domestic audience, never suggested Stalin's responsibility for the atrocities.[20] The restoration of such powerful symbols as the Stalinist hymn and the flag of the USSR in the army was, of course, indicative of Putin's attitude toward Stalin. Russian TV regularly shows old Soviet movies that glorify Soviet history and in particular the KGB and its predecessors.[21] However, in the same spirit of ambivalence the Kremlin permits movies that describe the Soviet past never blaming Stalin (but often describing Khrushchev as a caricature) as a combination of positive and negative elements. In such a spirit two semidocumentary movies were made in 2012 about Marshal Georgy Zhukov and Minister of Culture Yekaterina Furtseva.

Putin's people, naturally, described Stalin in the same way as their boss. Boris Gryzlov, the leader for many years of the United Russia Party and speaker of the State Duma in 2003–11, praised Stalin in connection with the 125th anniversary of his birth and recognized only some "distortions" in his domestic policy.[22] A high school history textbook by Alexander Filippov and Leonid Polyakov (*A Modern History of Russia, 1945–2006: A Manual for History Teachers*), which has been endorsed by the Kremlin, is another illustration of this tactic. Almost ignoring the repressions, the book refers to Stalin as "one of the most successful leaders in the USSR." The book considers the repressions of 1937 and the creation of concentration camps as a way to develop the country after the crisis – a necessary measure to build a great country and mobilize the administrative cadres. According to Filippov and Polyakov, Stalin's "revolution from above" was similar to the reforms of Peter the Great and was based on the "responsibilities of all classes before the government." They write that "this goal was achieved by political repressions among other means that were used for the mobilization of not only regular citizens but also the administrative elite."[23]

Vitaly Tretyakov, a well-known political observer and journalist, also chose this tactic. He suggested that before Putin there were only three great Russian leaders: Peter the Great, Catherine the Great, and Joseph Stalin. All these leaders, as Tretyakov wrote, belong to the same group, because the characteristics

[20] He equated the mass terror in the Soviet past to any other negative development in history, such as the invasion of foreign countries or the dropping of nuclear bombs. See the interview of Putin and Schroder with the newspaper *Build*, May 7, 2005, available at http://www.kremlin.ru/text/appears/2005/05/87603.shtml, accessed May 11, 2008.Putin declared that Russia was not the only country with "black pages" in its history and highlighted the fact that the United States used the atom bomb on Japan and conventional bombing in Vietnam. He went on to insist, "We can't allow people to force a sense of guilt on us. Let them think about themselves." Russian TV, Channel 1, June 21, 2007.

[21] Vyacheslav Kostikov, "Isaev protiv Shtirlitsa," *Argumenty i Fakty*, December 6, 2009.

[22] Kira Latukhina, "Partbossy priznali Stalina 'vydaiushchimsia gosudarstvennikom,'" *Nezavisimaia Gazeta*, December 12, 2004.

[23] Alexander Filippov and Leonid Polyakov, *Noveishaia istoriia Russii 1945–2006* (Moscow: Prosveshchenie, 2007), 87–8.

of their reigns included "victorious deeds, omnipresent power and an increase of Russia's might and territories." He said nothing about the repressions.[24]

Juggling the Soviet past while struggling to avoid challenging common sense, Putin recognized the ordeals of the Russian people under Stalin; however, he did his best to dedramatize this period, suggesting that the histories of other nations were the same or even worse. Giving an address at a conference in July 2007 before teachers in his countryside residence, Putin acknowledged that Stalin's repressions of 1937 (1.5 million people were imprisoned and 700,000 were killed, according to official statistics) were horrific, but he added that "in other countries even worse things happened."[25]

Russian Nationalism and the Church for Putin

Despite the Kremlin's overtly eclectic ideologies, one of the major ideological trends that emerged toward Putin's third presidential term was his increasing closeness with the Orthodox Church.

In the past, Putin, like the Communist Party, has demonstratively espoused some form of moderate nationalism. Putin and Communist leader Gennady Zyuganov have both described themselves as the protectors of Russian society, its culture, traditions, and religion, against destructive Western forces.[26] Both men have espoused Russian patriotism as the most important value for their countrymen, praised the notorious KGB as being a highly useful organization for Russia, and consistently spoken of Russia's glorious history. Putin repeated in the 2000s the major postulate of the Soviet ideology as well as of contemporary Communism when he talked about "Russian cultural dominance" and asserted that "the Russian people and Russian culture" are "the core of a unique civilization." But similarly to Soviet leaders he also insisted that all national groups in Russia should enjoy the same rights, including Jews, who were the object of special hatred in the USSR (we will discuss the details of this later). The eclectic character of his ideology made it easier for him than for Brezhnev to combine mutually exclusive views.[27] Putin and Zyuganov liked to call attention to Russia's role in saving the world from the Nazis, as well as from Genghis Khan and Napoleon.[28] They both considered the collapse of the Soviet empire as Russia's biggest tragedy, and both men are intent on restoring the geopolitical role of Russia.[29]

24 Vitaly Tretyakov, "Inoguratsiia," *Rossiiskaia Gazeta*, April 29, 2004.

25 "The times: uchebniki v Rossii budut rasskazyvat' o velikoi strane Stalina i Putina," July 30, 2007, available at http://www.newsru.com/russia/30jul2007/obrazovanie.html, accessed on October 4, 2007.

26 Gennady Zyuganov, *My Russia*, edited by Vadim Medish (Armonk, NY: M. E. Sharpe, 1997), 9–10.

27 Vladimir Putin, "Rossia: natsionmalnyi vopros," *Nezavisiamia Gazeta*, January 23, 2012.

28 "G. A. Zyuganov na vstreche s molodymi inostrannymi zhurnalistami v Obschestvennoi palate," available at http://kprf.ru/rus_soc/71605.html, accessed December 25, 2009.

29 Gennady Zyuganov, *Postizhenie Rossii* (Moscow: Mysl', 2000). Putin, "Rossia: natsionmalnyi vopros."

It is also remarkable how close both politicians are in their attitudes toward the Orthodox Church. Putin treats the Church as his major ally and assures that it is the beneficiary of numerous privileges, and Zyuganov also takes every opportunity to show his respect for the Orthodox Church.[30] The strong public shift toward religion and Russian nationalism by Zyuganov and other leaders of the Russian Communist Party make their ideological proximity particularly close with Putin, who once declared himself (and Medvedev) as a "Russian nationalist."[31]

Putin's closeness with the Orthodox Church grew significantly toward his third presidential term. Patriarch Kirill virtually blessed Putin for the presidency when he declared in February 2012 that Putin's rule had been a "miracle of God" for Russia. Most of all, this was underlined with Putin's persecution of the punk group Pussy Riot, who protested the closeness between the Kremlin and the church by dancing and singing an obscene song on the ambo of Christ the Savior Cathedral that same month. In one of the most high-profile trials of the decade, three of the members of the group were arrested, convicted of hooliganism motivated by religious hatred, and sentenced to two years in a penal colony in August 2012 (a third was later released). Putin vigorously supported the sentence, even while as much as a third of the population considered it too harsh.[32]

Indeed, the Pussy Riot trial and particularly Putin's outspoken condemnation of the group marked a shift in the Kremlin's ideological identification: from its eclectic policy of "sovereign democracy," it began visibly moving toward religious traditionalism. The reemergence of various nationalist and ultrareligious groups who argued for church-state harmony, and, indeed, an official statement in April 2012 by the church spokesman Archpriest Vsevolod Chaplin that separation of church and state is a "fiction," are evidence of this trend.[33]

Hatred of the West and the Nostalgia for the Empire

Both Putin and Zyuganov regularly expressed their hatred for the West, particularly the United States.[34] They rivaled one another in their invectives against

[30] Gennady Zyuganov, "The speech at the Party meeting 2009–10–19," *Pravda*, October 29, 2009; Gennady Zyuganov, "Ob otnosheniiakh gosudarstvennoi vlasti i tserkvi v techenie 70 let sovetskoi vlasti," August 11, 2008, available at http://kprf.ru/rus_soc/58997.html, accessed December 25, 2009.

[31] Regarding Putin's meeting with Angela Merkel in Samara in March 2008, see "Vladimir Putin: Medvedev ne men'shii russkii natsionalist, chem ia," March 3, 2008, available at http://news.mail.ru/politics/1646187, accessed December 25, 2009.

[32] According to an opinion poll by the All-Russian Center for Public Opinion, conducted in August 2012. http://wciom.ru/index.php?id=459&uid=112988.

[33] See Blythe, Kristen, "Religious radicalism in Russia: hell, heaven and the state." *The Moscow News*. Feb. 4, 2012. For Chaplin comment, see: Simon Shuster, "The priest who beat Pussy Riot: The Orthodox point man with the Kremlin." *Time*, Aug. 20, 2012. http://world.time.com/2012/08/20/the-priest-who-beat-pussy-riot-the-orthodox-point-man-with-the-kremlin/.

[34] Truscott, Peter. *Russia First: Breaking with the West* (New York: I. B. Tauris, 1997).

America, and both portray the United States as a money grabbing country that aims for world domination.[35] They both believed that the United States was responsible for the collapse of the USSR and is currently plotting to destroy the Russian Federation. There is no question in either Putin's or Zyuganov's mind that the Orange Revolutions in the post-Soviet republics were backed by the West through its secret services, particularly through the anti-Russian forces in the United States.[36] Furthermore, they vehemently preached the necessity of the restoration of the Soviet Union, at least as a union of Russia, Ukraine, Belorussia, and Kazakhstan.[37] Putin and Zyuganov have been hostile toward the actions of any foreign organizations inside Russia, operating under the assumption that any foreign enterprise might plot to undermine Russian security and order.

At the same time, it is important to note that both Putin's official ideology and the ideology of the Russian Communist Party practically abandoned an essential component of the Soviet ideology (and to some degree, of the prerevolutionary monarchist ideology) – the slogan about the social and cultural superiority of Russia over the West. In fact, this thesis was replaced by another, much milder one about Russia's special path in history. At the same time, Putin's eclectic ideology allows him also to tell the Russian people many positive things about the West, such as Hollywood's experience in inculcating audiences with decent moral values.[38] This allows some of Putin's critics, particularly from the Left, to criticize him as a pro-Western politician.[39]

Contempt for Perestroika and Yeltsin's Time

The Communists and current Russian leaders are all in agreement in their negative attitudes toward Khrushchev and his "thaw," as well as toward Perestroika, the anti-Communist revolution of August 1991, and the collapse of the USSR. During his November 2009 interview in *Spiegel*, Medvedev refused to give a positive appraisal of Gorbachev "because the time of his leadership coincided with the breakup of our state and a considerable portion of our people associate the demise of our country with his activities."[40] It is notable that on November 1, 2009, Medvedev awarded a special medal to the former Soviet defense minister Marshal Dmitry Yazov, a leading figure among the conspirators who sought the restoration of the Communist regime and who were

35 Regarding Zyuganov's meeting with young foreign journalists, see "G. A. Zyuganov na vstreche s molodymi inostrannymi zhurnalistami v Obschestvennoi palate," available at http://kprf.ru/rus_soc/71605.html, accessed December 25, 2009.

36 Vera Kholmogorova, "Krasnyi otvet," *Ekspert*, March 30, 2009; Gennady Zyuganov, "Vlasti postsovetskikh stran ne sposobny reshit' stoiaschie pered nimi problemy," October 24, 2009, available at http://kprf.ru/international/72385.html, accessed December 25, 2009.

37 Evgeny Kolyshev, "The report at the Party meeting," *Pravda*, October 29, 2009.

38 Putin, "Rossia: natsionmalnyi vopros."

39 http://avv71.livejournal.com/5948.html.

40 Interview of President of Russia Dmitry Medvedev with *Der Spiegel* on the twentieth anniversary

arrested after their failure.[41] Putin and Zyuganov are very closely aligned in their assessment of Yeltsin's rule and either personally or through spokespeople referred negatively to Yeltsin's regime and "the arrogant 1990s."

Some Disagreements on Economy and Private Property

Putin's regime supports the strong intervention of the state in economic affairs and does so systematically. Formally, the state corporations created by Putin's regime (among them the corporations that administer the export of weapons, technological innovation research, economic development, and several other enterprises) are almost independent economic actors as private companies; however, with Putin's people as the members of the board of directors of major state corporations the Kremlin in fact fully controls their activity. The same is true about mixed state-private companies like Gazprom, the biggest corporation in Russia and the monopolist in the production and distribution of gas. Still, with all their common elements, Putin's and the Communist ideologies are on opposite poles in their attitudes toward private property and market regulation.

Anti-Semitism in Soviet and Putin's ideology

Putin and the Communists have radical differences in their attitudes toward private property and market regulation. While Russian Communists continued their traditional rejection of private property as the "means of production" and demanded renationalization of many sectors of the economy with the restoration of a planning system, Putin's ideology had in general positive attitudes toward private property and market regulation, which indeed make it different from Soviet ideology as well as from the ideology of contemporary Communists.

There is one point in which Putin's ideology is very much opposed to Communist ideology in the Soviet Union and in the post-Soviet era – attitudes toward anti-Semitism.

If Putin were a dogmatic leader, he would have included anti-Semitism in his public ideology. Anti-Semitism was introduced in the ideology of the Soviet Union in the late 1930s. The Soviet state's anti-Semitic policy of the 1940s–1980s made it difficult and sometimes impossible for Jews to enter the best colleges or get positions in the party apparatus, the army, or managerial jobs at a high level in the economy. In media, novels, and movies, Jews were almost never shown in a positive light. A Jewish name could only appear in a negative context.

The open propaganda against Jews jarred with Lenin's heritage and internationalism. For this reason, the Soviet authorities replaced the term "Jews" with

of the Berlin Wall's fall, available at http://www.isria.com/pages/7_November_2009_1.php, accessed December 25, 2009.

[41] "Staryi ne durak," November 2, 2009, available at http://www.grani.ru/Politics/Russia/President/m.161524.html, accessed December 25, 2009.

"Zionists." Since Zionism was a "legitimate" enemy of socialism, it became possible to carry out an anti-Semitic campaign in the guise of the fight against it. The hatred of Jews was so high that the Soviet propaganda tended to describe Zionism as a greater evil than the United States.

However, even more important than the state's policy toward Jews was the transformation of anti-Semitism into a strong emotional component in the ideology created for the masses and party elite. The involvement of an individual in an ideology is high only if he or she shows allegiance to its elements in private conversations, in the family or in communications with friends. As we know from various sources of information, such as memoirs, movies, and novels, people's private conversations at home or parties almost totally ignored Soviet dogmas, such as the leading role of the working class or the importance of social equality.

Of course, anti-Americanism was a very important element of Soviet ideology, but it did not play an important role in the emotional life of the political elite in the 1960s–1980s. (It was later, under Putin, that anti-Americanism became an essential element in the minds of the Russian elite.) Anti-Semitism, on the other hand, represented a different case. It was indeed a part of the emotional life of the Soviet ruling class. In private communications, most apparatchiks talked with enthusiasm about Zionist plots, about the hidden Jews in the bureaucracy, or about the treacherous behavior of Jewish intellectuals. As a matter of fact, the hatred of Jews and Zionism cemented the ideology of the party and state apparatchiks. We already raised this issue when talked about the role of anti-Semitism in the post war KGB. The traditional anti-Semitism, honed by Stalin over many years, was seen by his successors who dared to make reforms as a fundamental aspect of the Russian psyche, which they had to avoid for the sake of liberalizing society. In his four-volume memoir, *Time, People, Power* (1999), which he dictated after his dismissal as the party leader, Khrushchev talked a lot about Stalin's anti-Semitism. However, he did not risk even indirectly mentioning Stalin's anti-Semitic policy in his public reports to the party congresses in 1956 and 1961, when he harshly denounced his former boss.

Putin had grounds to believe that a demonstration of negative attitudes toward Jews could enhance his position in the country. Indeed, the anti-Semitic feelings in the country in the early 2000s, as illustrated by the data from the most prestigious public opinion firms, including the Levada-zentr and the Fund of Public Opinion, were running high, even if they were weaker than anti-Chechen or anti-Azerbaijan sentiments. There are strong xenophobic and anti-Semitic elements in the Orthodox Church, a new and very important Kremlin ally. Even indirect support from Putin for these feelings would contribute to the Kremlin's relationship with the church. What is more, many nationalist movements in the country, which Putin sees as a sort of hidden constituency that could be important to him in a critical situation, are deeply anti-Semitic and actively spread anti-Semitic literature. Putin, however, did the opposite of what almost everybody expected. He expressed respect for all ethnic groups in Russia, particularly Muslims, who make up almost 20 percent of the population. He appointed many Germans to high positions in the country to rectify the injustice done to them during the Soviet period. Most surprising was Putin's positive attitude toward Jews. In 2005, he began a harsh anti-American campaign. Meanwhile, there was a popular view in Russia that anti-Americanism and anti-Semitism always go together. For this reason, most analysts did not pay attention to Putin's "Jewish anomaly." None of the authors (inside or outside Russia) who have recently written about Putin drew attention to this remarkable fact.

Taking all of Putin's publications, meetings, and speeches since 2000 into account, he said more positive words about the Jews than all the Russian leaders before him, with Lenin as the only exception.[42]

During his stay in the Kremlin Putin meets regularly with representatives from Russian Jewish communities and various Western Jewish organizations. In October 2007, he met with a representative of the European Jewish Congress, attended many Jewish religious celebrations (for instance, Hanukkah in 2001), and regularly sent congratulations to the Russian Jews in connection with Rosh Ha-Shanah, the Jewish New Year, and Hanukkah. Speaking in Krakow on January 27, 2005, in connection with the sixtieth anniversary of the liberation of Auschwitz, Putin urged other nations to consider the lessons learned from the Holocaust and warned against anti-Semitism, racism, and xenophobia worldwide. No Russian leader after 1945, including Gorbachev and Yeltsin, had even remotely or indirectly mentioned the Holocaust. Such a reference was forbidden in Soviet media. Putin was also the first Russian leader who expressed his regret that many Jews left Russia and expressed a hope that some of them would return to the country. He sent a special message to the Congress of Russian-Speaking Jews (2002). What is more, he also noted the existence of anti-Semitism in Russia, a statement that none of the Soviet leaders after Lenin dared to make. Putin was also the first Russian leader who visited Israel (the last time in 2012).

On November 30, 1936, when Stalin was already in the process of making Russian chauvinism a pillar of his ideology and taking his first hidden moves toward an anti-Semitic state policy (one of the first anti-Semitic documents

[42] With a high degree of warmth, he described a Jewish family who lived with his family in the same communal apartment in Leningrad. He talked about his Jewish wrestling coach Anatoly Rakhlin as a person who "probably played the crucial role in my life." The coach had attracted him to serious sports and drew him away from a dangerous life on the streets. Putin showed special sympathy toward his high school teacher, who has an apparently Jewish name, Vera Gurevich. Among other things, he publicly invited her to his birthday party. As suggested in *Komsomolskaya Pravda* in October 2007, Putin bought a new apartment in Tel Aviv for his old schoolteacher Mina Yuditskaya. In his memoir, *An Astonishingly Frank Self-Portrait by Russia's President* (2000), Putin did something that no other Russian leader has done.

was circulated at the Central Committee in 1938, according to the book *State Anti-Semitism in the USSR, 1938–1953*, 2005), he published a letter in *Pravda* to a Jewish organization in the United States, in which he strongly condemned anti-Semitism as "the most dangerous remnant of cannibalism" (in fact, it was written in 1931).

However, contrary to Stalin's hypocrisy, in no way can Putin's numerous positive statements about Jews be treated as propaganda. Anti-Semitism in Russia today is lower than it was in the last seven decades. Despite the negative developments we have noted, at no other time has the Kremlin treated Jews as well as it treats them today.

At the same time, the eclectic character of Putin's ideology made its strong imprint on the Kremlin's policy toward the Jewish issue. While showing loyalty to Jews, Putin's administration, however, found some niche for anti-Semitism in its propaganda. One of the most aggressive anti-Semites, Maxim Shevchenko, is a leading speaker on the main official TV channel. There is still a possibility, however, that the Jewish card could be played if the danger to Putin's elites from Russian nationalists increased. In this case, the Kremlin, without any compunction, could deprive its opponents of their powerful weapon, anti-Semitism, and resort to moving the regime even closer to that of Stalin. Putin's speech at the Forum of Supporters in Moscow on November 21, 2007, was full of hatred not only for foreigners, but also for his own compatriots whom he identified as his opponents; he characterized them as "jackals." This speech, which showed an obvious escalation in Putin's hostility toward his opponents, is a bad omen not only to liberals, but also to non-Russians, even if it was free of any ethnic slurs.

The memory of state anti-Semitism is quite fresh in the minds of Russian Jews and many of them are psychologically prepared for a tragic course of events. It is evident that Putin will resort to state anti-Semitism only under very pressing circumstances. In any case, the West is dealing with a very flexible and pragmatic Russian leader. Given his obsession with maintaining political power in the country, he is open to various options in domestic and foreign policy.

Radical Differences between Soviet Communist and Putin's Ideologies – the Role of the Future

The role of the future emerges as a key aspect that separates Putin's ideology from Soviet ideology. The future was the essential part of the Soviet official ideology. The future world revolution was a key element of Lenin's ideological writing. Stalin's plan to build his country in the near-future as a powerful socialist state was the core of the Soviet propaganda until the war. After the war this propaganda depicted a future in which the USSR would permanently strengthen its geopolitically dominant role in the world with the task of crushing American imperialism as the single obstacle to the dominance of the USSR. In his speech at the Nineteenth Party Congress in 1952 Stalin depicted the future as a world in which the Communists, obedient servants to Moscow, would be the leading political force in their countries.

While Khrushchev abandoned Stalin's dream of world dominance, he made ideology the focus of future life in the USSR. He declared at the Twenty-second Party Congress that "by 1980, the next generations of the Soviet people will live under Communism"; the idea, as Grushin's survey showed, did not look absurd to many people in Russia, particularly the youth.[43] Brezhnev's regime dedramatized somewhat the role of the future in its propaganda but was far from reducing its important role. During Brezhnev's time the media incessantly talked about economic plans not only for five years, as was a fixture in previous Soviet periods, but for fifteen and twenty years. Almost all scholarly units were involved in the 1970s in the preparation of the various versions of these plans, which obviously appeared to their designers (including one of the authors of this book, who worked then in the Institute of Sociology) as a purely propagandistic, even if important, action. The ideology of Gorbachev's regime was also permeated with the promises for the future, and first of all, the building of a true democratic society.

Putin's regime stands out as one whose ideology is almost fully deprived of futuristic elements, particularly in relation to politics and social relations. In fact, Putin approached the future only in relation to various individual programs such as the necessity to accelerate technological progress or to increase the number of skilled jobs in the economy, as well as the importance of providing the army with modern weapons or enhancing the work of various governmental bodies. In his seven newspaper articles (*Izvestia, Nezavisimaia Gazeta, Kommersant, Ekspert, Vedomosti, Moskovskie Novosti, Rossiiskaya Gazeta)* on the eve of the presidential election campaign of 2012, there was nothing even remotely of the romantic spirit of the Soviet ideology that promised Russians a life radically different from that which they have now.[44]

The Oligarchic Component and Putin's Ideologies – A Big Overlap

Of the three components of Putin's official ideology the oligarchic one is the most hidden. But as a matter of fact it is exactly this ideology that reflects the leading role of feudal relations in Putin's Russia that is the closest to his Weltanschauung.

First of all, Putin's elite and the oligarchs have a common contempt for ordinary people, as well as for social equality. They all are sure that ordinary people cannot be trusted to run society and choose officials in honest elections. Putin has demonstrated his attitudes toward real democracy many times. In some cases, such as during the protest activity in Moscow in late 2011 and

[43] Boris Grushin, *Chetyre zhizni Rossii v zerkale oprosov obshchestvennogo mneniia. Epokha Brezhneva* (Moscow: Prigress-Traditsia, 2001).

[44] http://izvestia.ru/news/511884; https://mail.msu.edu/cgi-bin/webmail?index=1.

early 2012, he could not restrain himself from talking about the protesters in the most contemptuous ways. In December 2011 he named the participants of the demonstrations "bandar-logs" (chattering monkeys from Kipling's *The Jungle Book*), "contraceptives and cheeps."[45] The oligarchs, when they felt themselves "the masters of the universe" in the 1990s, revealed what they really thought about "the masses." Alfred Koch, one of the best-known Russian oligarchs in this period, was blunt in his assessment of the Russian people: "This long suffering people suffers for their own guilt. Nobody occupied them, nobody subjugated them. They snitched on each other (in the Soviet times) and nobody herded them into prisons and they shot each other at the firing squad." He claimed that Russians had turned into "homo soveticus who does not want to work but keeps his mouth open all the time and wants bread and entertainment."[46]

It is to be expected that Putin and the oligarchs, with their contempt for the masses, would have little regard for democracy. Putin's regime showed its real attitude toward democracy in countless ways after 1999. But oligarchs, too, revealed what they thought about democracy; Boris Berezovsky headed a group of thirteen oligarchs who used their media assets and their influence to skew the elections in favor of the widely unpopular Boris Yeltsin.

With their common disdain for democracy, Putin (at least until 2012 when he started to talk about corruption and to imitate a real fight against it) and the oligarchs were united in their determination to ignore corruption in Russian society.[47] They all endorsed privatization in the 1990s, widely regarded with its open violation of law as criminal, and were against the revision of its results.

Both Putin, maintaining the position of his predecessor, and the oligarchs in Russia fuelled the cult of money and the right of rich people to conspicuous consumption. Indeed, Putin's attitudes toward the "high life" were the same as those of the oligarchs'.[48] During his thirteen years in power Putin never uttered even one word of condemnation of the glamorous lifestyle of wealthy people, including officials, with their many galas, anniversary receptions, weddings of their children, consumption of expensive foods and liquors, the newest luxury automobiles, private jets and yachts, and trips to the most expensive casinos and foreign resorts. At the Russian economic forum in London in May 2006, there was a discussion of "luxury as a Russian national idea." The editor of *GQ*, a magazine addressed to the richest segment of the population, talked about "the emergence of a class of 'golden collars' for which the consumption

45 http://www.aif.ru/society/news/104390.

46 See the text of this unusually revealing speech in Alexander Minkin, "Vlast' i sovest,'" *Novaya Gazeta*, November 2, 1998.

47 Oleg Deripaska, a great friend of Putin, argued that public officials could not survive on the "miserable official salary," and therefore the money they received from corporations should not be seen as corruption, but as a normal part of their income. (See Oleg Deripaska's interview with *VIP-bulletin "Vremia Evrazii,"* No. 2, 2006).

48 For more about the Putin's attitudes toward corruption see Chapter 3 in this book.

of luxury goods became a priority." As an argument, he mentioned that "Putin's love of luxury goods is well known."[49]

An important example is Mikhail Prokhorov, a mogul with close ties with Putin, who played an active political role during the presidential election in 2012. Prokhorov was arrested in France in January 2007 under suspicion of entertaining guests with prostitutes. This gentleman hardly used the prostitutes for himself, but it was alleged that he supplied sixteen young women from Russia for his guests. Prokhorov was released after a few days of detention, but his case showed the whole world how rich Russians "s'amuse" (entertain themselves, in French).[50] Another oligarch, the metals and media tycoon Vladimir Potanin, also from Putin's circle, attracted the interest of international media because he invited the British pop singer George Michael to a private New Year's Eve party in Moscow to perform an hour-long concert and paid him $3 billion.[51]

The major differences between the oligarchic and Putin's official ideology lie in the attitudes toward state and bureaucracy. While Putin shares with the Communist ideology the cult of the state, oligarchs usually hold negative attitudes toward a powerful state machine. In this case, we are dealing with a typical conflict between the ruler in a predominately feudal society, or "a feudal monarch," and his barons. While in Yeltsin's time the barons prevailed, in Putin's it is "the feudal monarch" who has had the upper hand, recognizing, however, the power of the barons and accommodating them. The ideological fight between the feudal monarchs and the barons, in our cases, oligarchs and governors, was quite intense. In the middle of the 1990s Boris Berezovsky could openly declare that the country should be run by "the kings of business," and not by the president or the masses.[52] In the 2000s Putin subdued oligarchs as well as governors who challenged his power and created a new system of relations, consisting of full obedience of Putin's oligarchs to the Kremlin but at the same time keeping intact their freedom to be involved in corruption schemes with impunity and maintain full control over trade unions in their empires.

Ideological Work in Both Regimes

The Soviet regimes saw in their cohesive and strong ideology, supported by the fear of repression, a powerful means of maintaining and perpetuating their power and devoted considerable resources to it. The ideology, eclectic and torn by internal contradictions, played a rather secondary role as a means for

[49] See Natalia Rostova, "Glamour kak natsional'naia ideia," *Novaia Gazeta*, May 17, 2006.

[50] Dmitry Loginov and Alina Travina, "intim s privkusom nikelai," *Moskovskie Novosti*, January 25, 2007.

[51] Steven Lee Myers, "Russia's extended winter holidays: A binge of drinking and spending," *New York Times*, January 8, 2006.

[52] http://www.molva.ru/bibl/bereza/article1090.html.

sustaining Putin's regime. In Putin's regime it was big money that compensated for the weakness of its ideology. Big money allowed for the maintenance of a relatively decent standard of life for many Russians. What is even more important, big money allowed the regime to reward generously those who serve in the army, police, and FSB. As already mentioned, only in 2012 did Putin increase the salary of military personnel by three times.[53] The same money gave the regime the opportunity to suborn the intelligentsia, which is a key actor in the ideological battle, and blunted its criticism of the regime. Indeed, Soviet leadership considered ideological control over the population to be almost as important as the systematic enhancement of the military strength of the country. Soviet leaders systematically talked publicly on ideological matters. All of them included in their reports to the party congresses a big section about the ideological work of the party and some ideological issues. The party official who was responsible for ideology was the second highest ranking person in the Central Committee of the Communist Party of the Soviet Union (CPUS) as well as in all party committees at lower degrees in the party hierarchy. Mikhail Suslov, who held the position of secretary of the Central Committee for ideology for almost a quarter of a century until his death in 1982, was one of the most influential politicians in the country. His status rose a lot in Brezhnev's times, when he was the second person in the country to have the nickname of the "Gray Cardinal" because it was in his power to denounce "ideological deviations" in the views of any official and in this way terminate his or her career.

The ideological work in the country was under the supervision of the department of propaganda at the Central Committee. Several other departments of the body were also directly involved in ideological work, even those that were apparently far removed from ideological work, like the department of heavy industry. The party committees at all levels of hierarchy imitated the structure of the Central Committee. The editors of all periodicals in the country – from *Pravda* to a factory newspaper with low circulation – were responsible for the ideological purity of their publications as well as for their active role in propaganda.

The state apparatus was also fully involved in ideological work. The minister of higher education, the minister of culture, the minister of cinematography, and the state committee of the publishing industry, from their headquarters in Moscow down to their units in villages, played important roles in the ideological indoctrination of the population. Besides, each professional who dealt with the people or with ideological issues, such as a teacher of history in a rural school or a senior fellow in the academic institute of history or philosophy, had to be cleared by a party committee before starting to work.

The system used for ideological work used not only party cadres and officials but ordinary people. Some 20 million people in 1985 were involved in

[53] http://www.nextrus.ru/interes/405-putin-bytj-silnymi.html.

ideological work. This number included full- and part-time workers, professors, teachers, and an army of agitators and propagandists. By the end of the 1970s, 480 million copies of newspapers and magazines containing official propaganda were produced each day.[54]

The control over the mind of the people was one of the major tasks of the KGB. In fact, with its network of informers, the KGB literally monitored the mind of each active person in the country – not only party and state officials but also all members of the intelligentsia, in particular, the so-called creative intelligentsia (scholars, writers, journalists, movie and theater figures), as well as high-skilled workers and peasants. By all accounts, speaking about the domestic activity of the KGB, the lion's share of its resources was directed at finding cases of deviation from the official ideology. In fact, the cases of real anti-Soviet behavior were quite rare. According to Andropov's analysis of anti-Soviet activity, between 1967 and 1975, 50 percent of the punishable offenses against the state were categorized as "calumnious or politically damaging statements." The second category in importance (about 8 percent) comprised people who "produced and spread calumnious or politically damaging documents"; the third group (about 6 percent) included people who "participated in antisocial actions imitating hippies." The people who committed the most terrible deeds were those who "attempted to contact or contacted anti-Soviet centers abroad." The actions against these offenders were only 0.4 percent of all repressions by the KGB between 1967 and 1977.[55]

It would be wrong to say that Putin's regime totally neglected ideological work. However, it is true that Putin never talked at length or published long texts on ideological matters. In not one of the seven articles that he published on the eve of the presidential campaign in March 2012 did he try to describe the ideology of his regime, its major social and political goals.

The presidential administration that replaced the apparatus of the Central Committee deals with propaganda on a daily basis. The operatives of this administration regularly convene meetings of directors of TV channels and newspaper editors in order to instruct them about how to cover certain issues. However, with all this, Putin's regime lacks the powerful ideological network of the Soviet leaders and is unable to control the ideological position of the "creative class" as the Kremlin did in the past.

Take, as an example, social science. Under Putin it had much less official supervision than it had in Soviet times. Indeed, in the past no scholarly work even remotely relevant to ideology could be published without passing several levels of censorship. The publications of one of the authors of this book in Soviet times had to be endorsed by his colleagues in the research institute where he worked, then by the head of the institute, by the editors of his texts in the publishing house, and finally by the official censors (the notorious Glavlit).

[54] Vladimir Shlapentokh, *Soviet Public Opinion and Ideology* (New York: Praeger, 1986).

[55] Vladimir Bukovsky, *Judgment a Moscou* (Paris: Robert Lafont, 1995).

(Without censors nothing could be printed or copied. Xerox was out of the reach of senior fellows in the research institute and copies were made only with the permission of the director and the "special" (or KGB) department by workers assigned to do it.)[56] Even the draft of a questionnaire for a survey had to be approved by three to four levels of censors.[57]

The situation was very different under Putin. Formally state censorship as an institution disappeared. Hundreds of publishers are ready to publish anything. However, the regime could still use its resources to control social science as well as the media without resorting to formal censorship. Most sociological research centers in the country, such as the Institute of Sociology or the Institute of Social and Political Research (both of the Russian Academy of Science in Moscow), are directly controlled by the state. Several centers of public opinion studies like VTSIOM (the national center of public opinion studies) and FOM (the fund of public opinion studies) are openly financed by the Kremlin, and the heads of both – Valery Fedorov and Alexander Oslon – openly showed their loyalty to the Kremlin and without claiming neutrality as heads of public opinion firms, regularly published articles supporting official policy. Both are members of governmental bodies. Fedorov accepted the position as director of VTSIOM after Yury Levada, the founder of this firm and famous Russian sociologist, was unceremoniously expelled from the firm. In 2008 he was awarded a government medal and in the same year a special certificate for his participation in the presidential election, which had a reputation as essentially dishonest. Oslon was a member of Putin's election headquarters in 2000. In 2012 he was appointed by the Kremlin as a member of the board of public TV.[58]

The Kremlin uses enormous money to suborn directly not only social science but all other spheres of intellectual activity. The list of the five hundred people who agreed to be Putin's campaign delegates ahead of the 2012 elections contained numerous cultural figures who openly declared that they were grateful to Putin for his financial support of their institutions (for example, the famous actors Oleg Tabakov and Gennady Khazanov were grateful for Putin shoring up the theater, and the outstanding directors Valery Gergiev and Yury Bashmet were obliged to the Kremlin for buttressing the orchestra).

Besides money, fear was an instrument of the Kremlin to control intellectuals. The mass repressions of Stalin's times and the more moderate ones in post-Stalin Russia are certainly absent in the political system built up by Putin. Putin realized that the politics of terrorizing people in Soviet times was often

[56] Free access to Xerox machines was one of the greatest joys of one of the authors when he arrived in the United States in 1979.

[57] On the role of censorship in sociological work see Vladimir Shlapentokh, *The Politics of Sociology in the Soviet Union* (Boulder, CO: Westview Press, 1987).

[58] See the debates about trust of polling firms in Russia, http://lenya.livejournal.com/157910.html.

accompanied by "overkill." The same results could be achieved through much smaller actions, such as the repressions that took place after the mass protests in the spring of 2012, when dozens of activists were arrested after their participation in a violent protest rally on May 6. The murder of a few journalists and politicians combined with an obvious unwillingness to discover the true perpetrators were enough to sow the seeds of fear among many prominent intellectuals.

Suslov and Surkov

The differences between the status of ideology in both societies, Soviet and post-Soviet, illustrate the comparison between two ideological gurus, Mikhail Suslov and Vladislav Surkov. One represented a cohesive and strong ideology, the other – eclectic and weak. The "gray cardinal of the Kremlin" was the epitome of the archaic Soviet ideologists, who were absolutely impervious to flexible propagandistic devices. Not only he but the people who worked as his subordinates, such as Boris Ponomarev or Leonid Illyichev, were the same type of ideological curmudgeons as their superior. A few officials in the department of agitation or propaganda with more liberal views, such as Georgy Smirnov or Alexander Yakovlev, also only moderately educated people, had to conceal their thoughts and cater to the opinions of their boss.[59]

Vladislav Surkov, a deputy of the chief of the presidential administration in 1999–2011, was an absolutely different person. He claimed to have read Joyce's *Ulysses*, a serious feat for even the most educated people. His office in the Kremlin, according to people who visited it, was full of the most refined books. He has also written lyrics for rock groups and authored journal articles about art. In 2009, under the pseudonym Natan Dubovitsky, he published the novel *Close to Zero*. With his thoughtful and educated approach, this work showcased the author's ability to understand the true state of Russia in the 2000s.[60] How very different were Suslov's and Surkov's personalities: the first carrying considerable political weight in the Kremlin and the other only an ideological servant to Putin.

Ideology and the Selection of Cadres

Aside from the priority of the military issues for each party and state body, only the selection of the cadres could compete with ideological work in the agenda of those who ruled Soviet society.

Ideological and cadre issues were always intermingled in the work of the apparatus because ideological purity, aside from political loyalty to the regime, for a candidate for any more or less significant position was the absolute

[59] On the role of Suslov see *The Diary of Anatoly Chernyaev, National Security Archive Electronic Briefing Book No. 192*. http://www.gwu.edu/~nsarchiv/NSAEBB/NSAEBB192/index.htm.

[60] See the description of Vladislav Surkov in Yelena Tregubova's *Tales of a Kremlin Digger* (Moscow: AdMarginem, 2004)

condition for his or her endorsement by the party committee, at the national or local level. The party policy from the very beginning of the Soviet system conspicuously preferred ideological fealty along with personal allegiance to the regime and its leader to competence and professionalism. A "red manager" was always better than a "competent manager" even if the latter was ready to work for the regime. The rule was violated only once, during the civil war, when Leon Trotsky recruited white officers to the Red Army. Stalin released from the gulag some army generals such as General Konstantin Rokossovsky or engineers like Andrei Tupolev, who, as Stalin was aware, continued to be ideologically loyal to the regime and to him personally despite their sufferings in the camps. (In any case, neither privately nor publicly were these people critical of the regime, neither inside the concentration camp nor after their release.) Post-Soviet leaders were a little milder toward the ideological deviations of the people whom they considered as useful for military purposes.

Brezhnev, for instance, did not fire those mathematicians who signed protest letters against the trials of the dissidents in 1968; however, during his regime ideological allegiance to the regime was an iron condition for selection and promotion of cadres.

Putin's regime also selected those officials who were loyal to it, however, with much less interest in their ideological views, as is quite logical if we take into account the eclectic character of the official ideology, which allows everybody to choose an ideological line. With this ideological indifference among Putin's entourage we could see people whom he nominated as deputy prime minister in various periods: a hawk of the Communist style of Sergei Ivanov, as aggressive a nationalist as Dmitry Rogozin, as moderate a liberal as Alexei Kudrin, as Communist a person as Sergei Glazyev, as committed a liberal as Andrei Illarionov. Among those who defended Putin's regime in media were also people of all ideological colors. Each of them used the arguments from his or her ideological arsenal to prove that Putin was the best leader for the country, usually berating the Russian people for their antidemocratic and xenophobic tendencies. Leonid Radzikhovsky, a journalist with a reputation as a liberal, argued in his articles and talks on radio *Ekho Moskvy* that the protest movements against Putin can produce chaos in society.[61] The nationalist Maxim Shevchenko suggested that only Putin's regime can defend the interests of ethnic Russians of the country.[62] Alexander Prokhanov, a Communist, saw in Putin the only hope to restore "the red empire."[63]

Ironically, the eclectic character of the official ideology to some degree countervails the tenor of Putin's regime and allows and even encourages the

[61] See as an example his article "Zavinchenie" in *Rossiiskaia Gazeta, July 17, 2012*. http://www.rg.ru/2012/07/17/zavinchivanie.html.

[62] See, for instance, his talks in the program "Osoboie mnenie" on radio *Ekho Moskvy* in 2012 http://www.echo.msk.ru/guests/7198/.

[63] See, for instance, his 2012 movie *The Soldier of Empire*, full of the glorification of Soviet imperial policy, http://www.youtube.com/watch?v=o-nTzbsWGvg.

coexistence on TV, in some cases, of opposing description of the past. In summer of 2012 the official TV channel NTV showed two such movies, one made in 2012 by Alexander Ustyugov, *I Serve the Soviet Union*, another, an old Soviet movie, *The Fall of Berlin*, made in 1949 by a director notoriously loyal to Stalin, Mikhail Chiaureli. The first movie aroused the wild anger of those who considered themselves patriots because while hailing the patriotism of the Soviet people in the first, tragic, days of the war, it depicted the Stalin regime as deeply terroristic.[64] The second, deeply deceptive film with its unprecedented (even by Soviet standards) groveling before Stalin as the father of the victory was for a long time the laughingstock of the Russian public.[65] The showing of both movies at the same time (July 2012) on the same governmental TV channel baffled Russian journalists, who obviously underestimated the eclectic character of Putin's ideology.[66]

The Fight with Ideological "Allies-Enemies" Undermines Putin's Propaganda

This weakness of Putin's official ideology can only be enhanced by the necessity for the elite to fight against those political forces in Russia that claimed to be the true representatives of each part of the official ideology.

It is well known that the major threat to political power often stems not from the adversary who holds diametrically opposite views, but from the rivals who share almost the same ideological position. The closer the ideological position is of a rival, the more intense the competition. If we were to address Soviet history, we would find quite a number of examples that illustrate this idea. Lenin despised the Mensheviks, who were Marxists, much more than the Socialist-Revolutionaries, who were not. He detested those who were advocates of the revolution much more than the Constitutional Democrats (Kadets), who were reformists. Lenin was much more furious about the Cadets than about the monarchists who supported the regime. Trotsky and Stalin shared the same leftist views on industrialization, particularly collectivization. In fact, with his brutal collectivization in 1929, Stalin followed Trotsky's precepts while expelling his archenemy from the country in the same year.

Similarly, the main ideological opponent of Putin's official ideology is liberal ideology, represented by the views of the liberal community and international public opinion, which accuse the Kremlin of fake democracy, of being authoritarian, corrupt, and nationalist. The second set of opponents are Communists or nationalists who charge the regime with fake statism, with promotion of inequality; with groveling before the West and Jews; and with neglecting the

[64] http://www.rg.ru/2012/06/20/zapret-site.html.

[65] Dmitry Shlapentokh and Vladimir Shlapentokh, *Soviet Cinema in 1918–1991: Ideological Conflict and Social Reality* (New York: Aldine De Gruyter, 1993).

[66] See Slava Taroshchina, "Kogda nas v boi vedet tovarishch Markin," *Novaya Gazeta*, July 8, 2012.

ethnic Russians. The third opponents are the oligarchs, who profess to represent business and who accuse the Kremlin of state intervention in the economy and unwillingness to protect business from corrupt state officials.

Fighting each of its three ideological opponents – liberals, Communists, and oligarchs – Putin's regime was forced to contradict itself regularly and confuse the masses. Indeed, confronting the liberals, Putin's ideologues raised the issues of state stability and downgraded the role of democratic procedures. But opposing Communists, even mildly or indirectly, the regime highlighted the importance of private property and self-regulation in the economy. In the polemics with nationalists the Kremlin highlighted the significance of ethnic peace in the country as well as the necessity to maintain business relations with the West. Arguing against the oligarchs the Kremlin pointed to the social responsibility of business, moving close to socialist phraseology.

Compare these ideological jugglings with the serene-in-simplicity ideological stance of the Soviet leadership, which brainwashed the population much more efficiently. Only for a short period after the divulging of Stalin's atrocities at the Twentieth Party Congress was Soviet ideology in a state of confusion, which, however, was soon left behind. As Boris Grushin's surveys in the late 1950s showed, most young Russians were deeply influenced by official ideology and took Khrushchev's slogan about the building of communism in the next decade very seriously.[67]

The Impact of the Soviet Ideology on the Masses

There is no doubt that the impact of Soviet ideology on the masses was uneven in the various stages of Soviet history. It was rather low in the aftermath of the revolution, during the civil war, and even in the 1920s up to the beginning of the war. In fact, in these periods, the real believers in the official ideology were Communist Party members and the young generations of all groups of the population, in particular the children of workers and peasants. Big chunks of the Soviet population were very deeply hostile to the new system, as was revealed in the first two years of the war with the mass flight from the Red Army and the mass exodus of people (Ukrainians, Russians, and others), who retreated along with the German troops. (This issue became prominent in Russian public opinion because of the books of Mark Solonin, who, refuting the thesis about the unpreparedness of the Red Army for the war, explained its defeat in 1941 by the hostility of the soldiers and officers toward the regime and their unwillingness to fight.)[68]

However, by the end of the war the majority of the Russian population accepted most elements of the official propaganda, such as the Soviet successes in various areas or even the advantages of the planning system and state property.[69] However, the real peak of the impact of the official ideology on

[67] Grushin, *Chetyre zhizni Rossii v zerkale*.

[68] See Mark Solonin, *22 iunia. Anatomia katastrophy* (Moscow: Eksmo, 2008).

[69] However, even among these people the Soviet ideals were quite popular. The data obtained by

the population fell at the end of the war. The power of public ideology was high many years after the war. Certainly, the erosion of ideology, in particular among educated people, that started after Stalin's death in 1953 was a serious development; however, it could not undermine it significantly.

Indeed, by 1985, the majority of the Soviet people supported a variety of official dogmas, including Soviet and Russian patriotism, the supremacy of socialism, social equality, the obligation of the state to guarantee the basic needs of the people, social and moral superiority over the West, the superiority of public property over private property, the central planning system as superior to a market economy, and Soviet-Russian cultural and moral superiority over the West.[70] In 1989 according to polls from the Levada Center, answering the question of what the Soviet people lack in their life, only 14 percent mentioned "political rights" (56 percent pointed to the "low standard of living"). Asked about the main task of the country in 1989, only 19 percent mentioned the building of a democratic society. Again, only 12 percent of the residents of Moscow and Leningrad endorsed the idea of private property. Of the respondents 77 percent thought positively of Stalin as the greatest man in history.[71]

More importantly, as Shlapentokh's surveys of the readers of the central newspapers in 1960–70s showed, the Russians accepted the images of the world that the leaders imposed on them. The leadership controlled the images of the past as well as the images of foreign countries. In spite of their criticism, the people trusted the leadership and strongly supported almost all of its domestic and foreign policies. Most Soviet people, at least according to their responses in opinion polls, backed the invasions of Czechoslovakia in 1968 and Afghanistan in 1980, and such actions as the shooting of a Korean Boeing in 1983. The absolute majority of people either ignored or condemned the behavior of dissidents.

Our own data collected in the 1960s and 1970s from the national surveys suggest that no less than 80 percent of the population supported the major postulates of the official ideology and no less than 90 percent the ideological position of the government toward foreign countries, the West in particular. Even the Russian intelligentsia, the most critical part of society, essentially supported

the Harvard project – which was based on the surveys of people who fled the Soviet Union during the war, or who, as German prisoners of war, did not want to return to the USSR – shed light on the mind-set of Soviet people before the war. Of all respondents in the Harvard project, 80 to 90 percent supported state ownership of "heavy industry" and "transport" as well as the "cradle-to-grave welfare program." Alex Inkeles and Raymond Augustine Bauer, *The Soviet Citizen: Daily Life in a Totalitarian Society* (New York: Atheneum, 1968) p. 243.

[70] Two-thirds of Russian emigrants in the 1970s advocated Soviet educational and health services. The majority (70–80 percent) voted for a "basic socialist economy as in the NEP period," while only about 5–28 percent voted for "capitalism." See Alex Inkeles and Raymond Augustine Bauer, *The Soviet Citizen: Daily Life in a Totalitarian Society*.

[71] Yury Levada, (ed.), *Prostoi Sovetsdkii chelovek* (Moscow: Interxentr, 1993) pp. 46, 69, 176, 187.

the main elements of the Soviet ideology and Soviet order and demanded only softening of the regime, dreaming about "socialism with a human face."[72] The Soviet beliefs resisted rather successfully the offensive against them during Perestroika. In any case, public opinion studies show that in the early 1990s, after the anti-Communist revolution, many Soviet dogmas still enjoyed great support among a considerable part of the population.

It is remarkable that many American Sovietologists, in particular those who saw Soviet society as "abnormal," ignored the attitudes of the Russians toward the system, probably because the mass support of the Soviet order was not compatible with their views of the USSR as an "evil empire."[73]

The Efficacy of Ideological Work: The Major Preoccupation of the Soviet Regime and the Indifference of Putin's Team

The Soviet leadership paid enormous attention to the enhancement of ideological work in the country. In the 1960s–80s dozens of research institutes, and in particular the Academy of Social Science at the Central Committee of the CPUS, had to provide the party apparatus with data about the efficacy of propaganda. It is true that many of the works in this area were purely ritualistic, often absurd, but in any case they sustained alertness in the ideological apparatus of the party and helped to enroll many thousands of educated people in the ideological business, making them conscientious keepers of the regime.

Nothing like this happened in Putin's Russia. There is no organization in Putin's Russia that studies the efficiency of the official propaganda. To some degree, the former center of the study of propaganda was replaced by PR experts (or "political techonologists," as they are named in post-Soviet Russia), who, with their numerous minuscule research units, elaborated the election strategy for the Kremlin, the governmental parties, and individual candidates with minimal research resources. As a matter of fact, the regime and its operators did not feel it necessary to spend much effort on the study of public opinion besides the ranking of leaders. They displayed the same indifference to serious sociological studies as the Soviet leaders, as one of the authors of this book was told in the 2000s by his friends and colleagues Boris Grushin, Yury Levada, and Vladimir Yadov.[74] As a matter of fact, Putin and his circle

[72] See the diaries and the memoirs of the committed enemies of the Soviet regime who all witnessed the popular support of the regime: Raisa Orlova, *Memoirs* (New York: Random House, 1983); L. Kopelev, *Khranit' Vechno* (Ann Arbor, MI: Ardis, 1975); L. Kopelev, *Sotvorim Sebe Kumira* (Ann Arbor, MI: Ardis, 1978); Petro Grigorenko, *Memoirs*. New York: Norton, 1982); Ulanovskaya, M. and N. Ulanovskaya, *Istoria Odnoi Sem'i*. (New York: Chalidze, 1982); see also Shlapentokh, *Soviet Intellectuals and Political Power*.

[73] Richard Pipes, *Russia under the Bolshevik Regime* (New York: Vintage Books, 1995) p. 511; Malia, *The Soviet Tragedy*; Martin Malia, *Russia under Western Eyes* (Cambridge, MA: Harvard University Press, 1999).

[74] A curious and remarkable fact: by the late 1970s Vladimir Shlapentokh had at his disposal unique data about the political attitudes of the Soviet population based on his large scientific

returned to the deep conviction of the Soviet apparatchiks – and it was far from groundless – that the mind of their subjects was mostly regulated by the governmental media and therefore they did not need sociological data to know this. To this belief Putin's ruling class added the belief that big money, as far as it is at disposal, are able to produce loyalty to the regime – first of all in behavior such as voting and nonparticipation in protest – not only among the intellectual elite but also among a large chunk of the population such as retired people and state employees.

Significant in this respect is Putin's replacement of Vladislav Surkov in 2012 with the less sophisticated apparatchik Vyacheslav Volodin as the first deputy chief of staff and the de facto ideologue of the Kremlin. Volodin's style, as was demonstrated with massive Soviet-style support rallies for Putin ahead of the 2012 elections, gave up Surkov's intricately orchestrated PR for a simpler, more propagandistic approach. This approach has merged with the increasing support of nationalist, religious, and statist groups and has led to the emergence of more conservative ideologists, such as Sergei Kurginyan.

Polarization of Public Opinion in Putin's Russia

Focusing only on the behavior of the Russians, Putin's Kremlin in fact was indifferent to what people were thinking and what they told the members of their family, friends, or colleagues. In fact, with the eclectic character of official ideology – with the lack of a so-called national idea – Putin's regime could not achieve the same level of penetration into the minds of the Russians as the last Soviet regimes did. Indeed, in the Soviet times the official media with their uniform ideological position were the single authority for the masses. The one newspaper that was liberal by Soviet standards – *Literaturnaya Gazeta* – never dared to challenge directly even one dogma. Foreign radio in the 1960–70s, which was critical of various elements of Soviet society, reached 10–20 percent of the educated class, according to studies conducted by Shlapentokh at the time, but could not greatly influence the mind of the majority. Only when critique of Soviet ideology from the Kremlin and official media occurred during Perestroika did the Soviet people start to rethink major elements of their propaganda.

At the same time, the eclectic character of Putin's ideology, along with the important role of the Internet and social networks, made it weak in its impact on the population. In each community – almost in each family – people have different ideological views.

polls of the readers of the major national newspapers. He was never invited to the Central Committee to report his findings. Probably three of his "merits" – not a party member, Jewish ethnicity, and liberal reputation – outweighed the eventual utility of these data for the ideological gurus in the Kremlin at that time. This fact was impossible to digest for the people from the State Department and CIA when he told about it in 1980, after his immigration to the United States, because in their opinion it was against common sense to ignore data supposedly useful for running such a complex society as the USSR. See Shlapentokh, *The Politics of Sociology*.

If we can contend that 80–90 percent of Russians were on the side of the Soviet system under the Soviet Union, today the population is ideologically very much fragmented. Practically, it is not easy to find an ideological issue that can garner the support of more than 50 percent of the population. Aside from mostly universal values, such as "patriotism" or "family," Russians are strongly divided on most new post-Soviet values. Only a minority of the Russians in the 2000s endorsed private property for large companies, particularly in areas of the economy close to the country's natural resources.[75] Russians are also split on the value of competition. According to the World Values Survey, 43 percent of Russians strongly support competition (30 percent showed moderate support).[76] Russians are deeply split when they compare the socialist and capitalist systems. Among Russians 53 percent supported "an economic system based on state planning and distribution," compared to 34 percent who preferred "an economic system based on private property and the market."[77]

The polarization of Russian society on political issues is no less acute. In 2010, 55 percent of Russians regretted the collapse of the Soviet Union; the rest did not or abstained from answering. A total of 58 percent positively assessed the October Revolution; the rest assessed it negatively or abstained from answering. The role of Stalin in Russian history was positively evaluated by 51 percent; the rest did not evaluate it positively or abstained. Yeltsin's time was considered by 59 percent negatively; by the rest, positively or they abstained. Among Russians 55 percent considered their country as a "great power"; the rest did not or abstained. A total of 60 percent thought that their country needs democracy; the rest did not or abstained. A total of 44 percent voted for the special "Russian" democracy; the rest supported other versions of democracy or abstained. A total of 47 percent denied that Russia is now a democratic country; the rest held the opposite view or abstained.

It is important that even those Russians who on the surface are not under the ideological control of the Kremlin voted for Putin and "the United Russia." They still behaved as conformists, even if not so emotionally loyal to the regime as the Soviet people. Indeed, many Russians in the past as the "true Soviet people" emotionally believed in the official propaganda and even often behaved accordingly (for instance, defending the prestige of the motherland in their contacts with foreigners, even if they were absolutely safe from surveillance). In other words, the conformist in Soviet times and the conformist in Putin's era are different personalities: The first think and behave as loyalists to the regime while the second only behave loyally by avoiding protest actions but think rather poorly of the leadership.[78]

[75] ROMIR. *Monitoring*. July 2003.

[76] Ronald Inglehart, Miguel Basanez, and Alejandro Moreno, *Human Values and Beliefs* (Ann Arbor: University of Michigan Press, 1998).

[77] Levada-zentr, *Press vypusk*, March 19, 2004.

[78] On two types of conformism see Vladimir Shlapentokh, "The study of values as a social phenomenon: The Soviet case" *Social Forces* 61.2 (December 1982), 403–17.

What is more, most people who are loyal on the surface to the regime are practically indifferent to any public ideology and even to any social actions and in fact are deeply antisocial, while, as Boris Grushin mentioned in the early 2000s, analyzing his surveys from the early 1960s, "the level of socialization of the Soviet society was very high."[79] Indeed, most observers of Putin's Russia note the extreme atomization of Russians, a fact that, of course, has to be ascribed not only to the weak and eclectic ideology but also to several other factors.[80]

Conclusion: Expediency and Eclectic Ideology

Putin has shown himself to be one of the most cynical, and at the same time, pragmatic politicians in Russian history. Stalin, who is closest to Putin in terms of ideological flexibility, still appears to be a person with some values, as Stalin was concerned about the power of the state and Russia's geopolitical role in the world. Unlike Putin, Stalin was obviously concerned during the postwar period with the long-term perspectives of the Russian army, science, and economy. Putin, however, has demonstrated little interest in the future of Russia. It is enough to cite his apathy toward the status of science in the country to corroborate this idea. No other Soviet leader after Stalin, including Brezhnev, has been as cynical about his personal power as Putin. Khrushchev, Andropov, and even Yeltsin seem to be almost idealists in comparison.

It is only logical that as a politician, Putin is poised to embrace an eclectic ideology while refusing to be completely faithful to any one postulate. However, this assorted and unstable ideology is one of the weaknesses of his regime and the governing United Russia party. As long as oppositional forces are effectively muzzled, ideological cynicism is not a big problem for the ruling elite. But the situation can drastically change in the event of a resurgence of a politically conscious country, which might be expedited in cases of political crisis or a number of other circumstances.

[79] Boris Grushin, *Chetyre zhizni Rossii v zerkale*. See Vladimir Shlapentokh's comments on Grushin's book "Sovietskie liudi v nachale 60kh godov: Razmyshlenia po povodu knigi Borisa Grushina," *Monitoring obshchestvennogo menia* 4.54 (2001), 42–8.

[80] See Ovsei Shkaratan, "Perezhivaet li Rossia sotsial'nyi krisis," http://ecsocman.hse.ru/data/687/643/1219/033.shkaratan.pdf.

3

Corruption, the Power of the State, and Big Business in the Soviet and Post-Soviet Regimes

The twenty-five-hundred-year-old Indian manuscript *Arthashastra* demanded that the king fight corruption. We dare to suppose that the author of this text would agree with the definition of corruption used by both laymen and experts: the abuse of public power for personal gain. In the contemporary world, corruption is rampant – in the democratic United States as well in more authoritarian societies – although there is a big difference in the magnitude and scope of corruption across the modern societal landscape.[1]

The universal character of corruption ultimately lies in having a monopoly on power that provides even a modicum of control over "others." The monopoly on power can be relatively long-term, like that of the president of a university, or temporary, like that of a traffic policeman. Whatever the longevity of the position, its ability gives its holder power over others and extracts additional benefits, or rent. Similar to private corruption, a monopoly on a public office, short or long term, grants its holder access to public money as well as to various additional, or even extra-legal services, at the expense of the state.[2]

Only a few authors who operate with the concept of corruption recognize that corruption is, by definition, based on the monopoly of power over people

[1] See Annette Y. Lee-Chai and John A. Bargh, *The Use and Abuse of Power: Multiple Perspectives on the Causes of Corruption* (Philadelphia: Psychology Press, 2001); A. Jain, (ed.) *Economics of Corruption* (Dordrecht: Kluwer Academic, 1998); Andrew Wallace-Hadrill, *Patronage in Ancient Society* (New York: Routledge, 1989); Ronald Wilson, *Ancient Republicanism: Its Struggle for Liberty against Corruption* (New York: Peter Lang, 1989); Susan Rose-Ackerman, *Corruption: A Study in Political Economy* (New York: Academic Press, 1978); Paolo Mauro, "Corruption and the composition of government expenditure," *Journal of Public Economics* **69** (1998), 263–79; Edward Banfield, "Corruption as a feature of governmental organization," *Journal of Law and Economics* 18 (1975), 587–605.

[2] See, for instance, Mauro, "Corruption and composition."

who depend on the holders of power in one capacity or another.[3] Most attempts made by a society, through its ideology and ethics, to encourage people to forsake the opportunities their positions afford them to exploit their monopoly of power will fail when external control enforced by the state machine or public opinion is absent or weak. Internalized values, even in a deeply democratic society, are useful in sustaining honesty and respect for law in society but are not enough to restrain an official from the abuse of power and to make public opinion an effective instrument for preventing corruption.

A telling example: in the Soviet society, where a shortage of all consumer goods was a perennial problem, ordinary salesmen and saleswomen had the freedom to choose their customers. They could deny a good piece of veal to one buyer and could sell it, for additional money, to another. The ordinary salespeople had a monopoly on goods in shortage and could extract additional revenues, which people would have to pay in order to be allowed to purchase the goods. The Soviet authorities tried many methods to combat the abuse of power by salespeople – from increasing their salary (it was a widespread idea that it was the low level of a salesperson's official income that drove him or her to violate the rules) to providing special ideological training sessions (it was supposed that an insufficient level of ethics allowed salespeople to behave in this way). However, nothing helped to mitigate the abuse of power by salespeople who enjoyed their monopoly on scarce commodities, until the introduction of free prices in 1992 eliminated the phenomenon of deficit goods.[4]

Among the legions of people who abuse their power, the main abusers and beneficiaries of corruption are those who hold offices in the governmental machine. In addition to receiving bribes, they have opportunities to embezzle public money and to exploit their position to receive various illegal services at the expense of the state. While the office as a source of illegal income is a universal phenomenon, it is particularly significant in a society with feudal elements, one in which the state is weak, or in which the rulers delegate a part of their power to various actors. In such a society, each office has its own price paid to the government by claimants. The practice of buying an office, which

[3] It is terribly wrong to treat corruption as the "illegitimate reminder of the values of the marketplace (everything can be bought and sold) that in the age of capitalism increasingly, even legitimately, permeate formerly autonomous political and social spheres," as John Girling and Richard Sakva suggest. See John Girling, *Corruption, Capitalism and Democracy* (New York: Routledge, 1997); Richard Sakva, *Russian Politics and Society*, 4th ed. (New York: Routledge, 2008). Even more arguable is the theory that supports an expert on Russia such as Marshall Goldman in linking corruption to "resource abundance." In fact, corruption is a phenomenon whose roots lie not in the market but in the existence of a monopoly on scarce resources, which is why it spreads in any type of society. See Marshall Goldman, "Russian energy: A blessing or a curse," *Journal of International Affairs* (1999), 74; see also Ike Okonta and Oronto Douglas, *Where Vultures Feast: Shell, Human Rights, and Oil* (New York: Verso, 2003).

[4] A Russian TV serial (2012) about the famous Moscow supermarket, *Grocery store No.1*, described in detail how the shortage of food allowed its director to manipulate the highest party officials in the 1980s.

could "feed" its holder (this term was used in Russia in the Middle Ages), was and is widespread in any society with strong feudal elements (e.g., contemporary Italy, Mexico, or Russia).[5]

Every society is aware of the possibility that those in a favorable position will abuse their power. For this reason, various systems of control are developed, aimed at preventing or, at the very least, mitigating this problem. All societies have used state structures for this purpose, while liberal societies also rely on democratic and state institutions: free elections, which can oust corrupt bureaucrats from power, and, of course, public opinion and the free media, which see the exposure of corruption in society as one of their main missions. As history shows, efficiency in curbing corruption primarily depends, even in a democratic society, on the harshness of punishments levied upon people for acts of corruption, which, in turn, depends on the determination of the government to decide, and to have suitable resources available, to fight corruption. Since a weak government is an essential part of a feudal model of society, corruption flourishes in feudal societies. In fact "the ideal corruption" is a purely feudal phenomenon because it is a form of using personal power that is not controlled by either the state or the market for personal benefit. As will be shown later, the outburst of corruption in Russia after 1991 was a direct result of the feudalization of the post-Soviet Russian society.

At the same time, the ability of the state machine to fight corruption in a feudal society is limited because the bodies assigned to curb corruption can also be infected by corruption. This makes a hierarchy of governmental bodies that supervise each other necessary, a system that complicates the fight against corruption and tends to increase the size of bribes (with an increase of supervision and the risk of being caught, bribes need to be larger to be effective). The system of control over corruption, in the Soviet Union, for example, was vertical as well as horizontal. There were special units at the local (a city or big village), regional, and national levels, for the supervision of officials inside both the state apparatus and the party apparatus. In addition, ten million Soviet volunteers, members of "the system of people's control," worked as supervisors.[6] As history tells us, not even the multiple layers of the state mechanism created for fighting corruption were able to accomplish their tasks effectively.

Attitudes toward corruption, as it developed in post-Soviet Russia, vary greatly. They are strongly affected by one's relations with the regime (its support or its critique), as well as by one's views on Russian culture and history. These attitudes have oscillated between denying that there is extensive corruption in

[5] It is wrong to name the use of office for personal enrichment as "tax farming," as did Mark Galeotti. See Mark Galeotti (ed.), *Russian and Post-Soviet Organized Crime* (London: Ashgate, 2002). In fact, the manipulation of taxes is only one means – and, in contemporary Russia, obviously not a leading one, used by Russian bureaucrats and other holders of office for their enrichment.

[6] See more about it in Shlapentokh, *Normal Totalitarian Society*.

post-Soviet Russia and declaring Russia to be a corrupt and criminal country, between the belief in corruption as a typical Russian phenomenon that is practically the same in all regimes and the belief that corruption in Putin's Russia is mostly a product of the Kremlin's policy. And, of course, Russian society has been polarized between those who condemned corruption and demanded to fight it by all means and those who either endorsed corruption or considered it a "normal phenomenon" that is useless to combat.

The Ignoring (or Denial) of Corruption

The Russian liberals were the first in the country to bluntly deny the existence of the gigantic amount of corrupt activity taking place during Yeltsin's regime or to dismiss its existence as a nonessential element of a new society. Yegor Gaidar was a typical representative of these liberals in that he totally disregarded corruption in post-Soviet society in his numerous publications and speeches.[7] Rejecting accusations that Yeltsin's regime was reluctant to prosecute people involved in corruption, Russian liberals suggested that holding trials of such people would mean a repetition of Stalin's show trials of the 1930s.[8]

The advocates of Putin's regime continued to deny the large scope of corruption in Russia. Putin himself, until the middle of 2012, generally avoided the subject or only talked about it briefly and superficially without using the names of any officials involved in corruption. He did not even mention the issue in his article in *Komsomolskaya Pravda* in February 2012. In his report to the State Duma on the government's performance in 2011, he only mentioned it quickly, without giving it any serious attention.[9] It was only during a meeting with the editors of foreign (non-Russian) newspapers on March 2, 2012 – on the eve of the presidential election – that Putin agreed to discuss this problem. Here, he downplayed the seriousness of corruption in Russia, equating it with corruption in America and Germany. He refused to discuss corruption at the highest echelons of power and contended that the fight against corruption was quite effective under his watch. He, like liberals in the 1990s, asserted that harsher measures against people suspected of corruption would mean a repetition of Stalin's terror.

At the same time, he tried to discredit people like Alexei Navalny, who had gained a reputation as a crusader against corruption in 2011. In June 2012, speaking at the Petersburg Economic Forum, Putin suddenly made a confession

[7] Gaidar, *Dolgoie vremia*; Gaidar, *Anomalii eknomicheskogo rosta;* see also his "Revolutsia ostalas v 20 veke, reformy prodolzhautsia v 21," *Izvestiia*, January 17, 2001; "Svoiu povinnost otbyl," *Moskovskie Novosti*, July 23, 2001. See also Shlapentokh, *Privatization and Illegalization*.

[8] This argument was used by Otto Latsis, one of the most famous Russian liberals in the 1990s, in conversation with me.

[9] See the report of Prime Minister Vladimir Putin on the government's performance in 2011 to the State Duma, April 11, 2012, http://premier.gov.ru/eng/events/news/18671, accessed June 1, 2012.

for the whole country, again without making any specific statements. Putin acknowledged that countering corruption "is a difficult task, of which there has been a lot of talk recently." He then asserted, as if he were speaking of a new problem for his regime, "This problem is not easy to resolve, but pretending that it does not exist is not possible either. We have to talk, search for, and make a decision."[10]

Dmitry Medvedev, as president in 2008–12, spoke about corruption much more often than his mentor and proposed various measures to fight it. However, nothing came of his activity. Recognizing this in a meeting on Russian TV on April 26, 2012, he avowed that his anticorruption drive was stymied because "officials do not want anyone to meddle in their affairs." In this way, he, like Putin, avoided talking about corruption; again, like Putin, he never even mentioned the name of Alexei Navalny.[11]

The Endorsement of Corruption by Some Supporters and Some Enemies of the Regime: The Cultural Approach

The simplistic denial of severe and widespread corruption, and of a high level of criminality in the country, was not accepted by either the sophisticated advocates of the regime or its critics. Some members of both camps attribute the robust presence of corruption to cultural forces; the critics of the regime have used this explanation as a justification for why their efforts to change the situation have not worked. This approach focuses on the specific character of Russian culture and its traditions. Lev Timofeev, a brave journalist who denounced corruption in the 1960–70s, later descended into the camp of those who saw corruption as a normal phenomenon in Russian society.[12] Ascribing the origins of corruption to Russian traditions, some sociologists – like Lev Gudkov from the Levada Center of Public Opinion Studies – insisted that "our whole society rests on bilateral, two-way corruption."[13] Similar to Gudkov, the St. Petersburg sociologist Yakov Gilinsky also saw corruption as a "normal" social institution in Russian society, even as an "element of control," that is "of great importance in the structure of society."[14]

It was not only liberals who played with the cultural theory of Russian corruption, using it as the main argument to substantiate both their pessimism

[10] http://vz.ru/news/2012/6/21/584838.html Interfax, June 21, 2012,; http://premier.gov.ru/events/news/18323 accessed June 1, 2012.

[11] See Ellen Barry, "Medvedev, unscripted, admits disappointments," *New York Times*, April 27, 2012.

[12] Lev Timofeyev, *Institutsional'naia korruptsiia: Ocherki teorii* (Moscow: Rossiiskii Gosudarstvennyi Gumaniratnyi Universitet, 2000).

[13] Lev Gudkov's interview with *Gazeta*, January 18, 2007.

[14] Yakov Gilinsky, "Korruptsiia: teoriia i rossiiskaia real'nost," *Saratovskii Tsentr po Issledovaniu Problem Organizovannoi Prestupnosti i Korruptsii*, http://sartraccc.ru/print.php?print_file=Pub/gilinsky%2830-06-05%29.htm, accessed May 1, 2012.

about the future of Russia and their refusal to oppose the regime. The advocates of the regime were also quick to use it, clinging to the cultural explanation of why Putin's regime had failed in its "fight" against corruption. They suggested that post-Soviet regimes were no more corrupt than the USSR or the tsarist monarchy, and that even the totalitarian regime was unable to fight corruption.[15] This was the exact position held by the famous film director Stanislav Govorukhin, who, as the head of Putin's team of election delegates, asserted that "corruption is a normal phenomenon" and that it also existed in tsarist Russia.[16] Culturologists like Govorukhin shifted the blame for corruption away from the highest echelons of power, falsely contending that the government cannot eradicate corruption from the top but that changes must begin on a local level – attitudes toward bribery must change at the grass roots. This position aroused the anger of the real fighters of corruption like Kirill Kabanov, the chairman of the unofficial National Anti-Corruption Committee, who, in February 2012, while not denying the passivity of the population, insisted that effectively fighting corruption can only start at "the top."[17]

It is amusing that the famous poet Joseph Brodsky was also engaged in the defense of corruption. The future Nobel Prize winner, still living in the Soviet Union and fresh from his exile in northern Russia, mused about his experiences in a totalitarian society in a poem. He proposed the idea of dividing rulers into two categories: "looters" and "slayers." The poet expressed his preference for the looters, who seemed more humane than the murderers and torturers of the KGB.[18]

The Functionalist Approach – Corruption Is Good

While many officials and oligarchs, as well as the journalists serving them, have denied the existence of immense corruption in the new, post-Soviet Russia – particularly in the highest echelons of power – some supporters of the regime have chosen, instead, to laud corruption as a necessary and useful mechanism of society. They follow the logic of the functionalist approach, which tends to suggest that almost any social phenomenon that exists performs some useful function.[19]

Some enemies of the regime joined with their political adversaries in their appeal to recognize corruption in Russia as a positive phenomenon. Despite being deeply pessimistic about the willingness and ability of the Kremlin to fight

[15] See Igor Klyamkin and Lev Timofeyev, "Tenevaia Rossia nakanune vybora," *Nezavisimaia Gazeta*, December 8, 1999.

[16] See interview of Stanislav Govorukhin, *Trud*, February 10, 2012.

[17] http://sobesednik.ru/politics/kirill-kabanov-korruptsiya-delaet-rossiyu-afrikoi.

[18] Joseph Brodsky's poem "Letters to the Roman Friend" (1972).

[19] See one of the most recent works on functionalist theory in sociology by Anthony Smith, *The Concept of Social Change: A Critique of the Functionalist Theory of Social Change* (New York: Routledge, 2010).

corruption, they, in fact, shared the same view and tended to see widespread corruption as a necessary evil in a criminalized society where law is ignored. In the opinion of these liberal pessimists, corruption should be considered as the single real basis for the interaction of people, who, in the climate of lawlessness, have had to solve their problems with bribery. As we will show later, most Russians gravitate to this view. In this context, people need the stability found in the rules of corruption, or in the constancy of the size of bribes. People also need information about who can do what they want.

As an explanation, the functionalist approach is not completely absurd. Indeed, the concentration of money in private hands inexorably generates corruption. As soon as big business emerges, the scope of corruption tends to increase in any type of society. Therefore, to those who believe in the superiority of a market economy with big business to a centralized economy with state property, big corruption might seem to be an inevitable consequence of the transition from one sort of society to another, like an element of the transaction cost for making a new type of society. Anatoly Chubais, who was the father of privatization and viewed as a corrupt politician by the people, defended corruption as a normal and useful by-product of privatization.[20]

Even while recognizing corruption as a necessary cost in the transformation of Soviet society to a more capitalistic and democratic post-Soviet society, it is important to determine whether this cost could be a radical obstacle to the formation of an efficient market economy as well as a genuine democracy. These fundamental considerations are ignored by the advocates of the functionalist approach to Russian corruption, both in Russia and in the West.

The functionalist approach to corruption evolved, in the minds of both experts and the general public, into the denial of corruption on a theoretical basis. If it was accepted that post-Russia was in a state of lawlessness, then the concept of corruption, along with many crimes, lost its grounds for consideration. Indeed, corruption implicitly supposes the violation of law; therefore, in a case in which the law does not exist or is not functional, any action that in other societies would be defined as corruption could not be named as such. Corruption is nothing but an alternative mechanism for the interaction among actors at all levels of society. It creates its own rules and norms, and, therefore, a society where corruption is universal like Russia or Mexico is not anarchistic, as it appears to be to outsiders. It is interesting, in this regard, how the European Middle Ages were seen by different authors. According to the popular view, feudalism meant chaos in society. However, few historians saw that France, around the year 1000, was an orderly society that was simply ruled by other laws and norms that were dominant in the country before the victory of feudalism.[21]

20 "Corruption," said Chubais, "depends very little on the authorities. It depends on the people" (see Anatoly Chubais's interview with *Moskovskie Novosti,* July 29, 2002).

21 See, for instance, Georges Duby, *Feudalism* (Paris: Presses Universitaires de France, 1998).

Gavriil Popov, as mayor of Moscow, was enmeshed in corruption and could be considered the lead author of the positive perspective on Russian corruption. He was one of the first in Russia to contend that corruption is necessary to overcome archaic laws and promote economic growth.[22] Mikhail Khodorkovsky seconded Popov and explained his participation in various corrupt schemes that made him fabulously rich in the late 1990s by citing the lack of laws prohibiting those criminal actions. As Khodorkovsky and many other successful oligarchs contended, economic progress would be halted without these illegal activities. Khodorkovsky's explanation of his success in Yeltsin's times – "finding and taking advantage of legal loopholes" – became famous.[23] In addition, in 2006, Ruslan Grinberg, the director of the Institute of Economics of the Russian Academy of Sciences, saw corruption as a way to do for ordinary people what legal means did not allow; this, he said, "diminished the social tension in society."[24] Certainly, among the arguments in favor of corruption, the view that it helped to correct the unfair salaries of state employees was as visible in post-Soviet Russia as it was in Soviet times.[25]

Corruption and the State in Russian History

Russian history provides us with a sufficient number of examples to corroborate the thesis that, in a nondemocratic society, the state apparatus is the only institution able to fight against corruption, whether or not it does so effectively.[26]

The authoritarian government in the prerevolutionary monarchy was far from able to eliminate corruption, which was well described in the Russian literature as one of the important elements of society.[27] However, the monarchy was strong enough to contain corruption. The laws adopted by Alexander II were much more aggressive against corruption than those of Putin's regime. During the reign of Alexander II, the government started to publish data accessible to the general public on the material well-being of officials. What is more, the monarchy did what Putin's administration has not been able to do: officially categorize bribes to include money or gifts given to the wife, children, relatives, and/or acquaintances of the officials. Officials could not enter into

[22] See Boris Kagarlitsky, "'Political capitalism' and corruption in Russia," *Links* 21, May–August 2002; see also Victor Polterovich, "Faktory corruptsii," *Ekonomiko-matemathicheskie Metody* 34.3 (1998).

[23] See, for instance, his interview to *Spiegel* when he was a prisoner on August 9, 2010, http://www.spiegel.de/international/world/spiegel-interview-with-mikhail-khodorkovsky-i-had-no-interest-in-being-an-enemy-of-the-kremlin-or-a-martyr-a-710844-2.html.

[24] See interview with Ruslan Grinberg in *Moskovskii Komsomolets*, March 31, 2006.

[25] http://rus.kg/news/vlast/2891-yavlyaetsya-li-nizkaya-zarplata-v-silovyh-strukturah-opravdaniem-korrupcii.html.

[26] On corruption in Russia, see Oleg Karpovich, *Corruption in Present Day Russia* (Bloomington, IN: AuthorHouse, 2008).

[27] Nikolai Gogol *Revizor* (s.l.: s.n., 1836); *Mertvye Dushi* (s.l.: s.n., 1842); Aleksandr Sukhovo-Kobylin, *Delo* (s.l.: s.n., 1861).

any outside contact with people who had business with the office where these officials served. Corruption hit Russia at the lowest levels of bureaucracy, whereas high officials only rarely took bribes. During the Russian-Japanese War (1905–7), when there was an upsurge in corrupt activity, the government drastically increased the punishment for bribery. Amazingly, the Provisional Government and its commission, despite their efforts in trying to expose the tsarist government, could not substantiate the numerous accusations that members of the tsarist government were engaged in corruption. Alexander Zviaginstev and Yury Orlov, who studied the biographies of all thirty attorneys general of the Russian empire since 1722, found only one who was implicated in corruption.[28]

The Soviet state was much more powerful than the tsarist one, and it was able, even without democratic institutions, to curb corruption quite effectively. It is true that there was a surge of corruption during the New Economic Policy (NEP) in the 1920s; this corruption was well described in Soviet literature of that time.[29] However, Leon Trotsky's prognoses about corruption's bringing about the fall of the Soviet system were wrong. It turned out that Stalin's regime was quite successful in curbing corruption, which probably reached its lowest levels in Russian history. Under Mussolini, much the same happened in Italy, which was known for its corruption prior to that period.

With the softening of the Soviet system after Stalin's death, corruption obviously increased, but it never affected the highest echelons of the Soviet bureaucracy.[30] It is true that the various chronic diseases of the Soviet system worsened in the 1970s.[31] At this time, corruption and semilegal and illegal activities penetrated all spheres of Soviet life.[32] In Brezhnev's era, the apparatchiks became

[28] Alexander Zviagintsev and Yury Orlov, *V epokhu potriasenii i reform. Rossiiskie prokurory 1906–1917* (Moscow: ROSSPEN, 1996); A. Zviagintsev, *Pod sen'iu russkogo orla. General-prokurory Rossii* (Moscow: "Dovgan," 1997); A. Kirpichnikov, *Vziatka I korruptsiia v Rossii* (St. Petersburg: Alfa, 1997); see also Andrei Zubov, "Slugi verticali i kultura vziatochnichestva," *Novaya Gazeta*, March 30, 2012.

[29] See, for instance, Ilia Ilf and Evgeny Petrov *Zolotoi Telenok* (s.l.: s.n., 1931), Mikhail Zoschenko *Slabaia Tara* (s.l.: s.n., 1932), Andrei Platonov *Gorod Gradov* (s.l.: s.n., 1927).

[30] Of course, corruption existed even in Stalin's times. Zara Witkin's memoir *An American Engineer in Stalin's Russia: The Memoirs of Zara Witkin*, 1932–1934 (Berkeley: University of California Press, 1991) described his impressions of postrevolutionary Russia in the early 1930s. Witkin believed that the Soviet economy was plagued by the same bureaucratic inertia, incompetence, corruption, duplicity, and inefficiency that would later be regarded as newly acquired features in the post-Stalin period. See also a book by another American engineer who worked on the construction of the metallurgical complex in Magnitogorsk in the 1930s – John Scott, *Behind the Urals: An American Worker in Russia's City of Steel* (Bloomington: Indiana University Press, 1989).

[31] Regarding chronic diseases of the Soviet system see Shlapentokh, *Normal Totalitarian Society*.

[32] Regarding corruption in the USSR, see John Kramer, "Anti-corruption research concerning Eastern Europe and the former Soviet Union: A comparative analysis," Technical Note No. 2, Center for Governmental Integrity, Washington, DC: Management Systems International, 1999. Available at http://www.nobribes.org/documents/kramer_anti-corruption research report-tech2.doc;

increasingly involved in various forms of corruption. They not only ignored the interests of the state, but often made decisions that were clearly damaging to it. However, the level of corruption in the party apparatus, particularly in the Slav and Baltic republics, was quite low (if the level is measured by the standards of post-Soviet Russia) and was kept under control by the leadership. In the early 1980s, the Kremlin undertook a series of actions against corrupt officials; this was a serious anticorruption campaign, with high bureaucrats arrested and sentenced, compared to the post-Soviet Kremlin's refusal to prosecute officials of high rank who were evidently steeped in the most heinous activities. As much of a problem as corruption was, it did not threaten the Soviet state, even if its citizens regarded it as omnipresent and believed that corruption reached its peak during Brezhnev's years. Soviet people in the 1970s and 1980s could not have imagined that the problem would only grow worse in post-Communist Russia.

Konstantin Simis, who was a lawyer in the Soviet Union before emigrating, named his book on Soviet society – which he published in the United States in 1982 – *The Corrupt Society*. In this book, he asserted that "the Soviet Union is infected from top to bottom with corruption," a condition he attributes to the "totalitarian rule of the Communist party."[33] It is evident now, when we compare Soviet and post-Soviet societies, that Simis strongly exaggerated the scope of corruption in the USSR. However, his perception was shared by the majority of Soviet people, including the authors of this book: corruption appeared to have reached its peak at that time. How wrong were Simis and all of us!

The scope of corruption in Russia changed radically after 1991. One of the most important developments in post-Soviet Russia was the eruption of feudal tendencies, which immensely diminished the willingness and ability of the government to fight corruption.

While corruption, according to many sources, is one of the most important problems for Putin's Russia (some say it is the gravest problem), the Russian

John Kramer, "Political corruption in post-Communist Russia: The case for democratization," paper presented at the XVIIth World Congress of International Political Science Association (IPSA) held in Seoul, Korea, on August 17–21, 1997; Michael Johnston, *Syndromes of Corruption: Wealth, Power, and Democracy* (New York: Colgate University, 2005).

33 Konstantin Simis, *The Corrupt Society* (New York: Shuster, 1982). In the book, Simis treated corruption very broadly. He, as many other authors of texts on Soviet society have done, tended to consider any illegal activity of officials – like embezzlement, apparatchiks' privileges, and the illegal means used by managers for getting parts necessary for the fulfillment of production plans – as corruption. The necessity of getting parts or raw materials, always in shortage in the Soviet economy, forced the managers to try to fulfill the production plans by any means, indeed, even bribing those who distributed the scarce resources in the economy. However, this activity, along with bribing officials in order to decrease the production quotas for a factory or a state farm, can hardly be treated as cases of corruption because "bribe givers" did not obtain the direct benefits for themselves. See Vladimir Shlapentokh, "Standard of living and public discontent," in Mikhael Ellman and Vladimir Kontorovich (eds.), *The Destruction of the Soviet Economic System* (Armonk, NY: M. E. Sharpe, 1998) pp. 30–40.

public and experts diverge in their beliefs about the size and origins of Russian corruption. We discuss corruption in Putin's Russia in more detail later.

The views of Russians on the character of corruption in their country vary greatly. Attitudes toward Yeltsin's and Putin's regimes have strongly influenced individual positions on this issue. Defenders of the post-Soviet regimes have claimed that corruption is an organic part of society, that it was the same in the past as it is now, and that there is no chance it will ever be eradicated.[34] The critics of the current regime contend that corruption has never been as high in the country as now.

The Eruption of Corruption in Post-Soviet Russia: A Result of the Feudalization of Society

These authors join those analysts who consider the corruption in post-Soviet Russia to be much higher than in any period of Russian history since the emergence of the Russian state.[35] There are different estimates of the extent of the corruption in Russia. According to some estimates, the cost of corruption totals no less than 20 percent of the Russian GNP.[36] The large size of the shadow economy (up to 35–40 percent of the GNP) is also a direct result of corruption.[37] By the end of the first decade of the 2000s, at least half of the Russian population had some experience in bribing officials. In the corruption

34 An interesting detail: a former aid to Yeltsin, Georgy Satarov, became a major fighter against corruption under Putin. However, despite his conspicuous hatred of corruption, he never, in any of his numerous publications, mentioned the role played by Yeltsin and his circle in the massive expansion of corruption in the 1990s. (See, for instance, Satarov's reflections on Yeltsin's period in "Predvaritelnye itogi," *Nezavisimaia Gazeta*, November 1, 2001, and his "Maska dlia prezidenta," *Moskovskii Komsomolets*, January 2, 2002.)

35 About corruption in post-Soviet Russia, see the publications of Georgy Satarov and his collaborators in the project undertaken by *Fund Indem* [qqq]fin 1999–2012, such as Satarov (ed.), *Diagnostika: Rossiiskaia korruptsia* (Moscow: Indem, 2002), published online at www.anti-corr.ru. For more about the project, see a series of articles entitled "Vlast i dengi" [Power and money], *Novaya Gazeta*, August 5 and 12, 2002; see also Georgy Satarov, "Otdelnyi razgovor. Delo o $400 milliardakh," *Novaya Gazeta*, July 29, 2002; Sergei Valiansky and Dmitry Kaliuzhnyi, "Nuzhna li vlasti borba s korruptsiei" [Does power need the fight against corruption?], *Literaturnaia Gazeta*, August 2002; Vladislav Vorobiev, "Tsentr. INDEM – kuda idem...," *Rossiiskaia Gazeta*, June 29, 2002; Irina Rinaeva, "Ni dnia bez vziatki," *Moskovskii Komsomolets*, May 22, 2002; Maria-Luisa Tirmaste, "Rossiiskoi korruptsii postavlen unikalnyi diagnoz," *Kommersant-Daily*, May 22, 2002. See also the report by B. Nemtsov, V. Milov, V. Ryzhkov, and O. Shorina (eds.) *Putin. Corruption* (2011), http://www.putin-itogi.ru/putin-i-korruptsiya, accessed May 1, 2012; and the report by B. Nemtsov and V. Milov, *Putin. Conclusions. 10 years,* (2010), http://www.putin-itogi.ru/doklad/, accessed May 1, 2012; Edward Skidelsky, Moskovskaia shkola politicheskikh issledovaniĭ, Centre for Post-Collectivist Studies Moscow School of Political Studies, 2001.

36 Satarov (ed.), *Diagnostika: Rossiiskaia korruptsia*. For more about the project, see a series of articles entitled "Power and money" (Vlast i dengi), *Novaya Gazeta*, August 5 and 12, 2002.

37 See Vladislav Zhukovsky, "Raspil s uskoreniem," *Novaya Gazeta*, April 25, 2012.

category, Russia, according to Transparency International, was ranked 143rd least corrupt of 180 countries.[38]

Feudal Tendencies and Big Money as the Roots of Corruption in Post-Soviet Russia

The root of post-Soviet corruption mainly lies, in the opinion of the authors of this book, not in a Russian tradition of disrespect for the law but rather in the emergence of a feudal order, which has replaced the strong authoritarian (or totalitarian) state, in which feudal elements were very weak. The drastic increase of feudal elements after the collapse of the Soviet Union put an elite group in power who could not, and did not wish to, preserve a strong state. Lacking the necessary resources, the new central elite were unable to create a state apparatus able to maintain order in society. For this reason, the post-Yeltsin elite had to acquiesce to the emergence of new centers of power: persons with big money and those who, even temporarily, governed regions. At the same time, the weakening of the state encouraged and helped lead to both the mass enrichment of the elite and the immense expansion of corruption. Corruption in politics reached its highest level in 1996, on the eve of the presidential election campaign. The Kremlin sold shares of stock in some of Russia's most valuable state enterprises at very low prices, in exchange for loans offered by the oligarchs and used by Yeltsin and his circle for their political and personal needs.

The powerful push toward corruption in post-Soviet society accompanied market expansion and the increasing role of money, although corruption functions even in a society in which the role of money is very limited. To suborn officials in primitive societies, people used material objects of all kinds as "gifts" – such was the label for bribes then. The same thing happened in the Soviet Union, where using money for bribes was relatively rare. The officials from "the South" took boxes of cognac or fruits and, in some cases, jewels to their superiors.[39] The emergence of the market economy and big business increased the possibilities for corruption in post-Soviet Russia enormously.

To a very great extent, the expansion of corruption in Russia is also due to the personalities of Yeltsin and Putin. They were both tainted by corruption themselves and were unwilling to fight against it in their regimes. Putin's history of corruption began when he worked as an aide to Sobchak, the mayor of St. Petersburg in the 1990s.[40] The next step in Putin's burgeoning corrupt

[38] http://transparency.org/whoweare/contact/org/nc_russia/2.

[39] One of the authors of this book, Vladimir Shlapentokh, has to confess that as the superior of graduate students from Armenia and Moldova, he too was a perpetrator of corruption, having accepted a few bottles of cognac from them.

[40] See the materials published by a well-known politician, Marina Salie, who studied Putin's activities in executing her duty as a comptroller, http://www.putinavotstavku.org/author.php?id=4D81C9B782B35, accessed May, 2012.

activity occurred with his machinations around the association "The Lake" in the late 1990s. Putin later embroiled himself in illegal transactions with oil companies. This alliance, in the opinion of several experts, was the origin of his considerable wealth.[41]

Corruption as a Basis of Putin's Regime

With a weak but efficient state machine, and with a yearning for "eternal" power and well-protected wealth, Putin could only build his society on feudal principles, with him as a "feudal monarch." In this role, he would be well shielded from his rivals by his own military power, by his people assigned to rule various chunks of society with full autonomy, and by promising them immunity against any attempts made to punish them for their corruption.

In fact, Yeltsin and Putin superimposed the feudal model of government on society. Yeltsin and Putin arrived at the feudal model organically, in the same way French kings did after the collapse of the empire of Charlemagne. They were forced to feudalize society (i.e., to give great autonomy to their officials) in order to keep their power. Yeltsin's famous slogan "Take as much sovereignty as you can" was indicative of this, as it simply reformulated the words French kings had used in their *missi*, which they sent to their vassals, encouraging them to rule their regions as they wished.

The first beneficiaries of feudalization were those who held governmental offices, which they turned into their own fiefdoms; this, in turn, allowed them to sell their services to people in exchange for money and stocks, as well numerous other benefits including free travel, vacations, and, of course, money for election campaigns. In addition, those who paid the officeholder and received services could be relied upon to coerce their employees to vote in a particular way. In terms of the economic concept of "rent-seeking activity," this was the rent, that is, additional income, received by the officeholders (Russians use the term *kormlenie*, or "feeding," referring to the fact that each position "feeds" its holder with illegal revenues). This first "feudal" layer of "rent seekers" was composed of the top leaders and administrators at all levels – down to the chief of a small village. This layer also included the generals and high officers in the army, police, and federal security agency.[42] In fact, the system of corruption was organized on the hierarchical principle that assumes the vassal has to share part of his or her rent with superiors.[43]

[41] See the articles of Yulia Latynina. For example, "Prezident vseia nefti," September 30, 2011, http://www.gazeta.ru/column/latynina/3785962.shtml, accessed May 1, 2012.

[42] Regarding the cooperation of government and business in illegal activities for gaining additional income or rent in contemporary society, see Shlapentokh and Woods, *Feudal America*.

[43] The sociologists Caroline Humphrey and David Sneath preferred to talk about "the pyramidal extraction chain" (Caroline Humphrey and David Sneath, *Culture and Environment in Inner Asia: The Pastoral Economy and the Environment* [Cambridge: White Horse Press, 1996]).

The other major "rent seekers" were the people who, in their turn, enjoyed additional income because of the privileges they received from the power holders: business people looking for governmental subsidies, tax privileges, price supports, tariffs, farm or import quotas, and licenses, as well as the elimination of competitors during the sale of state property. Banks were able to gain a great advantage over competitors when government officials selected them as the agents for the distribution of budget money. Corporations and people who held big fortunes also received control over their employees from the officeholders. The government, for instance, allowed corporations practically to eliminate free trade unions and to prevent workers from taking the risk of confronting their bosses (see Chapter 6, "Treatment of Strikers in Soviet and Post-Soviet Times: Novocherkassk and Mezhdurechensk").

At the same time, officeholders often had to pay "rent" to a higher level of hierarchy to secure their fiefs. The holders of key positions – the presidential or regional administrations, the members of the national and local governments, and the leaders of the political parties – sold, both directly and indirectly, offices in the government, national and local, all the way up to membership on the security council or the position of deputy premier minister, as well as membership in any of the legislative bodies.[44] The officeholders also wanted to be loyal to their superiors, guaranteeing, for instance, the desired outcome of an election. As a result, Putin's times saw prosperity in the bureaucracy, and a commensurate immunity of bureaucrats, that was unprecedented in Russian history.

This first stratum whose members – whether as officials or as businesspeople – enjoyed the benefits of corruption was about five or six million people strong in the second decade of the 21st century (but if their relatives were added to this number, it would grow to tens of millions of people).[45]

The second stratum of beneficiaries of corruption was composed of those who held offices at the middle and low levels of bureaucracy, those who dealt with ordinary citizens who were seeking implementation of their legal rights – in court, in the offices that register new apartments or issue motor licenses, and in tax bodies, among other places. This sphere also included those who held military offices and who could release young men from military service.

The third sphere of corruption embraced administrators of colleges and hospitals, as well as doctors, nurses, and teachers, that is, everybody who could deliver services to ordinary people. Satarov refers to the third sphere as "corruption at the bottom," as opposed to an aggregation of the first two spheres, which is "corruption at the top."[46]

[44] The flood of big money into the Russian Duma is well documented. Between 2000 and 2005, the number of the deputies who were billionaires increased from seven to twenty-one (about 5 percent of the all deputies).

[45] Surinov (ed.), *Rossiiskii statisticheskii ezhegodnik*.

[46] Satarov (ed.), *Diagnostika: Rossiiskaia korruptsia*.

Of course, corruption entails more than just blackmailing citizens – for instance, by falsely accusing them of a violation of the law (e.g., in observing traffic, sanitation, or fire rules). Of no less importance is the use of this practice by citizens to avoid punishment for a violation of the law, such as by buying diplomas or higher grades or driver's licenses without the necessary certifications.

Relatives of Officials as Another Bulwark of the Regime: Omsk's Case

Innumerable data have shown how almost every member of the bureaucracy extends various privileges to close and remote relatives, including second and third cousins. See, for instance, what happened in the early 2010s, in the Omsk region, where Governor Leonid Polezhayev's "clan" was composed of all his relatives, a typical phenomenon in most Russian regions, including small administrative units such as small cities and villages. In 2011, one of his sons, Konstantin, then a hospital director, was caught buying medical equipment fraudulently but did not suffer any consequences for his actions.[47] In the same year, the governor's daughter-in-law, Natela, privatized a hospital and health resorts for herself, violating various laws. Another of the governor's sons, Alexei, became a billionaire, using his father's connections in the oil and gas business. Alexei's wealth was equal to the two-year budget for the entire Omsk region. What is more, this businessman founded a company in Cyprus, which controls the water supply in Omsk. The company regularly raised the tariff for water in the region, though prohibited by national law. This same son bought real estate in Florida, a fact that was hidden from the Omsk citizens. Polezhayev also protected his distant relatives, such as his niece and several of his spouse's remote relatives. Some of them were members of the Omsk legislature and the owners of companies located in Omsk; these individuals greatly exploited their connections with the governor. The governor did not forget about his friends either. As the local media found out, his old friend Valery Kokorin embezzled budget money the governor had given to him to build a club for business people.[48]

Little Beneficiaries of Corruption

The great "invention" of Putin's regime was involving not only officeholders in corruption but also millions of people with only modest positions in society.[49]

In the 1950–70s, the concept of "people's capitalism" was quite popular in the United States. It was invented by G. Keith Funston, president of the

47 Georgy Borodiansky, "Mozhno zaiavit's uverennost'iu: Sem'ia gubernatora Polezhayeva ne voruet vozdukh," *Novaya Gazeta*, April 8, 2011.

48 Georgy Borodiansky, "Postradal na tu zhe summu," *Novaya Gazeta*, September 14, 2011.

49 The Soviet system resorted to a similar strategy, although less successfully, when it made one-third of the adult population "little bosses" (see Shlapentokh, *Normal Totalitarian Society*.

New York Stock Exchange in 1951 as a challenge to socialist ideas. The major idea of "people's capitalism" lay in the dispersal of stockholding opportunities among the population, which was supposed to change the nature of the American economy and American society in general. This idea had many important defenders in the business community, as well as among American politicians and intellectuals. The idea of "people's capitalism," however, practically vanished from American economic debates after the 1980s.

Ironically, it was Putin who implemented the idea of "people's capitalism," albeit in a new form. He opened the door to an illegal stream of income to a considerable part of the Russian population. To grant everybody shares as promised, he gave the most ambitious people access to a powerful source of corruption.

The members of the stratum of "little bribers" were much more limited in the ways they could abuse their small powers, when compared to the members of the "feudal layer," because they did not have their own offices and were under strong control of their own bosses. Still, in a lawless society, these "little bribers" – teachers and professors, medical doctors and nurses, clerks who issued various official papers for people (e.g., foreign passports or the documents necessary for buying or selling apartments), sanitation and fire inspectors, who could, at will, certify your shop as meeting standards (or not), and traffic officers, along with a host of others – could extricate additional income from the ordinary people who depended on them; they could easily spoil these people's lives if the bribes were not paid. While the illegal income of these little bribers was quite small compared to what officeholders received, it still constituted a substantial part of the "little bribers'" budgets. Of course, the participants in horizontal corruption, with their modest illegal income from the bribes they received, minus the amount they had to pay out to bribe others, were not as loyal to the regime as the officeholders. Still, having adjusted well to the existing order, they were far from being active protesters.

A large, special group of participants in the corrupt activities were the hundreds of thousands of employees in private companies who received an official salary and a "gray salary" (a "salary in an envelope," in Russian vernacular), which helped the company significantly reduce their tax burden. These employees were well aware of their participation in illegal activities and did not shun it.[50]

Corruption as a Means in the Political Struggle

In every society, corruption is also used as a powerful weapon in political struggles. This circumstance makes the discovery of corruption a difficult business because political enemies not only find real corruption in each

[50] "Zarplata v konvertakh," February 3, 2011, http://moycent.ru/zarplata-chinovnikov/zarplata-v-konvertax, accessed May 1, 2012.

other's activities but also ascribe other nonexistent abuses of power to their counterparts.

The role of corruption in the various political struggles throughout Soviet and post-Soviet history has varied greatly. It was a powerful factor in the political struggle that occurred in the aftermath of the civil war, with the beginning of Lenin's NEP. The spread of corruption in the party and state apparatus was a main argument of those opposing Lenin. Dissenting voices – first within the Bolshevik ranks,[51] and then within the Trotskyists, with their ideas about the Thermidorian degeneration of the Bolsheviks – proclaimed the imminent fall of the Soviet system because of spreading corruption in the party and state apparatus, adding another view to the Soviet society of the 1920s.

With the emergence of Stalin's totalitarian society, corruption completely disappeared as a factor in political struggles. The lack of private business and big fortunes made corruption – though not embezzlement and nepotism – almost impossible. The Kremlin ascribed dozens of absurd crimes to "the enemies of the people," Grigory Zinovyev, Nikolai Bukharin, and Mikhail Tukhachevsky, but almost never accused them of corruption. During two prominent cases of the public removal of leading politicians – Lavrenty Beria in 1953 and Nikita Khrushchev in 1964 – corruption was not added to the list of offenses. Mikhail Gorbachev, whose numerous enemies proclaimed him guilty of hundreds of sins, was never accused of corrupt acts. Only on the eve of Perestroika did corruption become a factor in the political struggle, which somewhat augured the corruption wars that followed 1991. The KGB and the minister of internal affairs were in a hidden conflict during Brezhnev's times. The major weapon used by Yury Andropov, the KGB's chairman, against Nikolai Shchelokov, minister of internal affairs, was the corruption that reigned among people from his institution (mostly the police), including Brezhnev's son-in-law, a deputy minister of internal affairs. However, it was only after Brezhnev's death in 1982 that Andropov, who became the country's leader, began a real offensive against those he considered the bulwarks of corruption. At the center of Andropov's anticorruption campaign happened to be the director of Moscow's Yeliseyev supermarket, Yury Sokolov, who bribed a host of Moscow apparatchiks, including First Party Secretary Victor Grishin, nearly ending his political career.[52] Among the other investigations performed in the early 1980s at Andropov's request was one that studied corruption in the firm Ocean. Public attention to "the case of the city of Sochi" was even greater. This case implicated the first secretary of

[51] The members of so-called Workers' Opposition such as Gavri'il Miasnikov, Vladimir Antonov-Ovseenko, and Alexandra Kollontai were particularly active in assailing corruption among party apparatchiks.

[52] Much higher than in the Slavic republics was the corruption in Central Asia and in the Caucasian republics, where it flourished in the 1970s and 1980s. The so-called cotton case in Uzbekistan was at the center of media coverage during Perestroika. See Yuri Feofanov and Donald D. Barry, *Politics and Justice in Russia: Major Trials of the Post-Stalin Era* (New York: M. E. Sharpe, 1996).

Krasnodar, Sergei Medunov, in corruption activities. In the end, many people were fired from their positions and arrested, while Sokolov was executed and Shchelokov committed suicide.

However, with Andropov's death in 1984, the corruption battles were stalled and resumed only in 1986–7, even if there were attempts during Perestroika to discredit Gorbachev for his tolerance of corruption, particularly in Central Asia (a famous Uzbek cotton case).[53]

The situation changed radically after 1991. The fight against corruption came to a halt almost immediately with the implementation of economic reforms and privatization. It could hardly have been otherwise, since most of the ruling Russian politicians started to enrich themselves almost immediately, using the wild privatizations begun by the Kremlin. The members of Yeltsin's close circle, including Anatoly Chubais, Yegor Gaidar, Viktor Chernomyrdin, and many others, were denounced by the media as being totally corrupt.[54] The position of Yeltsin, still the charismatic leader of the country, who encouraged corruption and openly helped the members of his "family" amass wealth through various illegal methods, influenced the moral climate in the country, as well as attitudes toward corruption of the state apparatus, for many years. Putin's regime, with its mass corruption, maintained the practices created by Yeltsin's leadership.

In both Yeltsin's and Putin's times, the mutual accusation of corruption among businesspeople and politicians ("the war of *kompromat*," or "compromising materials" [smearing a person]) became a part of life. First, the former KGB agents and then the officials of the FSB – the heirs of the KGB – were broadly used by rival oligarchs to destroy their foes. The mutual accusations of corruption made it practically impossible for the public to separate the real facts of corruption from the invented ones. At the same time, the protection of an individual official involved in corruption became the highest service one official could render to another. Most analysts who discussed Yeltsin's selection of Putin as his heir explained that it was because Yeltsin believed that Putin, a former KGB agent, would fulfill a promise not to prosecute Yeltsin and his family for corruption after his retirement. Indeed, the first edict Putin issued as the new president was regarding the total immunity granted to his predecessor and his family against any accusations of violations of the law.[55]

In any case, corruption became the main theme of the political struggle in the country under Putin. Communists and nationalists joined liberals like Boris Nemtsov and Vladimir Milov in charging the new regime of being deeply

[53] Feofanov and Barry, *Politics and Justice in Russia*.

[54] Here is an example. By the end of the 1990s, it was admitted in Moscow that Gasprom was under the special protection of Premier Minister Chernomyrdin, who was a former boss of this corporation, and who, by all accounts, had a great deal of valuable stock in this company (*Izvestiia*, January 5, 1997). Furthermore, Chernomyrdin's two sons openly worked for Gasprom.

[55] Colton, *Yeltsin: A Life*.

corrupt.[56] Alexei Navalny emerged as a new leading figure in opposition to the governing regime in 2010–13, most powerfully as a crusader against corruption. His slogan calling the ruling party, United Russia, a "party of crooks and thieves," became extremely popular throughout the country.[57]

From 1991 forward, Yeltsin's and Putin's governments, as active promoters of corruption themselves, did almost nothing in the fight against corruption. The Kremlin even protected officials who were arrested in the West on corruption charges. Pavel Borodin, the manager of the Kremlin's properties in 2001, was typical in this respect. The attempt of the American and Swiss judicial systems to put him on trial for embezzlement failed because the Moscow attorney general would not cooperate with foreign agencies.[58]

Many actions against corruption undertaken by the Kremlin only *imitated* a real fight against it, doing nothing to stop the systematic rise of corruption in all spheres of Russian life. President Medvedev, unlike his mentor, spoke regularly about corruption during his tenure in 2008–12 and advanced many initiatives and bills intended to fight corruption. However, these actions were only a cover for the unwillingness of the ruling elite to change the rules of the game because they believed that corruption was an important, necessary mechanism in sustaining Putin's regime.

Still, when it was necessary to remove Yury Luzhkov, who was Moscow's mayor for almost two decades, Putin's regime resorted to accusing him of corruption – mostly for helping his wife build a "big business" by allowing her company a monopoly over the various building projects in the capital. In order to discredit Luzhkov, who was quite popular in Moscow, the regime ordered official TV to make a special documentary movie about the mayor, which, probably correctly, confirmed (as did Boris Nemtsov and Vladimir Milov in their book on Luzhkov's corruption) how Luzhkov's wife became a billionaire.[59] Yet, as soon as Luzhkov was removed from his position, the Kremlin forgot about the case and did not make any moves toward investigating this major corruption.

The big role of private business and universal corruption provided the authorities with a means of fighting political opposition that was practically unheard-of in the Soviet past. Indeed, none of those who challenged the Soviet system in the 1960–80s (the Stalin regime with its mass terror is irrelevant in this context) was involved in any sort of private business. It would have been simply ridiculous for figures like Andrei Sakharov or Solzhenitsyn, or even minor figures in the oppositional movement in the 1960–70s, to be involved

56 See the report of Boris Nemtsov and Vladimir Milov, *Putin. Itogi. 10 let* (2012), available at http://www.putin-itogi.ru/doklad/, accessed May 1, 2012.

57 Regarding Navalny, see http://navalny.livejournal.com/, accessed May 1, 2012.

58 Aleksandr Koliandr, "MID vstupilsia za Borodina," *BBC Russkaia Sluzhba*, January 18, 2001, http://news.bbc.co.uk/hi/russian/news/newsid_1123000/1123381.stm, accessed May 1, 2012.

59 Boris Nemtsov and Vladimir Milov, *Luzhkov. Itogi* (Moscow: Eksmo, 2010).

in commercial activity of any sort. The Kremlin firmly believes, and not without grounds, that it is impossible to conduct any business honestly in Russia, and that it is always possible to find breaches of the law in everybody's professional activities, at the very least in the payment of taxes. In this way the regime focused all of their efforts – and not without success, judging by public opinion in the country – on showing that oppositional leaders were no better than the corrupt officials they wanted to remove from power. The Kremlin did not miss any opportunity to sow suspicions about the legality of the income of those who became protest leaders in 2012. In the aftermath of the mass protests in the first half of 2012, Gennady Gudkov and his son, along with Ilya Ponomarev and Ksenia Sobchak, were described in the progovernmental media as people who enriched themselves by illegal means.[60]

Another example of how money entered political life in Putin's regime in a way that would have been unbelievable in Soviet times: in June 2012, Putin signed a law that those who participate in protests where public order is violated could face fines of 300,000 roubles ($9,100) – more than the average annual salary of that time. The previous fine for similar acts was 1,000 roubles. The organizers of such rallies could be fined up to 1 million roubles. "Can you imagine authorities in Stalin's times fining people for their participation in demonstrations?" exclaimed a prominent liberal, Yulia Latynina.[61]

The Tolerance of Corruption among Ordinary Russians

The specific character of Putin's regime lay not only in its support by "office-holders," and the mild support of the "little bribers," but also in the Russian population's perception of corruption. In fact, Russian minds combine a belief in the omnipresence of corruption in their society with a belief in its inescapability and the necessity to adjust to it. In other words, in their way, Russians accept the concept of simplistic functionalism of corruption in the country – as discussed earlier – and are not concerned with fighting corruption, since they think this fight is hopeless. They are concerned with having stability in the rules of corruption and with having access to the information regarding to whom they must give bribes and how much.

Indeed, the absolute majority of Russians, no less than 70–80 percent, assume that corruption embraces all spheres of social life, and the same number also believe that corruption is "a normal phenomenon"; they see it as being the way it was under Yeltsin, as well as under Putin, and expect that corruption will only be greater in the future.[62] At the same time, many Russians are sure that

[60] See, for instance, Alexander Grishin "U Sobchak proveraiut vse iee firmy" *Komsomol'skaia Pravda*, June 18, 2012.

[61] Yulia Latynina, "Pervaya popravka," *Novaya Gazeta*, June 8, 2012.

[62] Fund of Public Opinion, September 2011, http://bd.fom.ru/pdf/d35ukvr11.pdf, accessed May 2012.

corruption, when laws do not work, helps to solve many problems in everyday life and that the struggle against corruption is hopeless.[63] Navalny and other corruption fighters discovered mass corruption among members of the State Duma in the spring of 2013. It was found that many of them had real estate property worth millions of dollars. This discovery could only strengthen the conviction in the country of the venality of the regime. However, the majority of Russians "are not upset with corruption," as Russian sociologists found,[64] and they are indifferent to the movies and other materials that denounce it. It is remarkable that while critics of the regime, liberal or Communist, label corruption as a leading problem in society, the population relegates it to the bottom of their list of problems. Indeed, in a March 2011 survey with open-ended questions about the major problems of Russian society, only 8 percent named corruption, compared with 30 percent who mentioned a low standard of living and 22 percent who mentioned unemployment.[65] It was not only ordinary people who dismissed corruption as the highest problem of the country; even liberals did.[66]

The case of Pavel Borodin – the corrupt official mentioned earlier, who worked as the head of Kremlin property and was very close to both Yeltsin and Putin – clearly demonstrates the attitudes of Russian liberals toward corruption. Borodin was arrested in New York in late 2000, at the request of the Swiss judiciary, for stealing money from the Russian state and laundering it in Switzerland. He was kept for a few months in a New York jail and then fined by the Swiss court. The lack of cooperation from the Moscow office of the attorney general did not permit the Swiss court to mete out a harsher sentence. Prominent cultural figures and famous liberals – such as the poet Andrei Voznesensky, the theater directors Oleg Tabakov and Galina Volchek, and the famous TV journalist Alexander Lyubimov, not to mention businesspeople and officials – almost unanimously supported Borodin and refused to recognize his complicity.[67]

[63] Stenogramma otkrytogo seminara "Podotchetnost' vlasti i korruptsiia," May 12, 2011, http://www.levada.ru/stenogramma-otkrytogo-seminara-podotchetnost-vlasti-i-korruptsiya-vozmozhna-li-borba-s-korruptsiei-v, accessed May 1, 2012.

[64] Public Opinion Foundation, September 2011, http://bd.fom.ru/pdf/d35ukvr11.pdf, accessed May 2012.

[65] Public Opinion Foundation, March 2011, http://bd.fom.ru/pdf/d13apro11.pdf, accessed May 2012.

[66] In 2001, one of these authors, Vladimir, as an American sociologist, tried to raise the subject of corruption at a prestigious and very liberal institute of sociology in St. Petersburg. One participant politely explained to him – apparently speaking for the entire group – that the issue was of no great interest to them. "Corruption is impossible to measure," she began. "And it is useless to study because both the people and the government are indifferent toward it. Moreover, we are all participants in corrupt activity."

[67] *Gazeta.ru*, February 1, 2001; *NTV*, January 24, 2001; *NTV*, January 25, 2001; *Komsomolskaya Pravda*, January 25, 2001; *ORT*, January 21, 2001; *Moskovskie Novosti*, January 29, 2001.

Russians in a Parallel Society

Russians have been aware for a long time that they do not live in a society regulated by official laws but by rules created by corrupt officials for their own benefit. It is a parallel system that coexists with the official system. Feudal barons did exactly the same thing in the remote Middle Ages, in Russia as well as in Europe (as a matter of fact, a system based on corruption, or on the personal relations between people, is not a single parallel system that coexists with the official system; we can point to other parallel systems such as those based on religious rules or the criminal system).

Russians expect a bureaucracy to make the rules of corruption clear and, in some way, "transparent." For this reason, they considered the transition from the wild, anarchist corruption of 1990s to the more or less orderly corruption of the 2000s as progress. Indeed, since emerging from near-anarchy in the early 1990s, the rules of corruption among bureaucrats, businesspeople, and ordinary Russians have become more explicit and better orchestrated. During Putin's regime, unlike the unpredictable conditions of the past, most people (61 percent) knew how much, or how little, to pay in bribes to officials. Very approximately, the average bribe, according to official police estimates in 2011, was over $8,333 – over ten times the average monthly salary. Businesses know the cost of protection (known as *krysha,* the Russian word for "roof," to use the criminal jargon that has long been accepted in the Russian vernacular).[68] Only 2 percent of Russians who admitted to bribing someone were disappointed with the outcome.[69] This balance between expectation and results has soothed the anxiety associated with corruption.

Of course, Putin's regime could not guarantee complete stability in the rules of corruption. The weak central administration, despite the commendation of its "vertical of power" as the basis of order, could not preclude the permanent conflicts between different power clans, like that between the Prosecutor General's Office and the Investigative Committees, or between the FSB and the Federal Drug Control Agency, not to mention the regular conflicts between local clans. The temporary victors in these conflicts could change the rate of their services to their clients. For this reason, many Russians, particularly businesspeople, became irritated that they often did not know how to solve their

[68] A veteran police officer in Moscow, who had served as an investigator within the force, explained: "It's much easier to solve whatever issue you need using a cop. They all but have a price list for this type of service. In the past, it was done more through relatives or friends of friends. Now I think it's enough to just show up and ask for whatever it is you need. Say a cop checked you for something. You resolved the issue (presumably through a bribe). And after that you can come back to the cop because he knows you and you've given him money. You just go up to him and say, 'Hey, you want to earn some more money?'" (interviewed by Anna Arutunyan in January 2010. The interviewee identified himself as Andrei).

[69] Satarov (ed.), *Diagn`ostika: Rossiiskaia korruptsia.*

problems with bribes.[70] Moreover, the tepid attitudes of most Russians toward the protest actions in 2011–12 could easily be ascribed to the fear that the new regime that could have replaced the current one would introduce new masters and new rules of corruption, and that it would take a lot of time to adjust to them.

Failed Attempts to Fight Corruption under Medvedev and Putin

Vocal attempts by President Dmitry Medvedev to fight corruption and, as part of that campaign, to reform Russia's police force, were met with skepticism from the start – but that seems to have been the result of a general attitude that Medvedev's powers as president were substantially limited by Vladimir Putin. Indeed, little remained of Medvedev's anticorruption reforms, aside from increased salaries and the renaming of the police force from the Soviet era *militsia*, or militia, to the more Western-sounding *politsia*, or police.

More interesting are Vladimir Putin's attempts to fight corruption since returning to the presidential post in May 2012. These attempts have raised a multitude of questions about whether they are serious or mere token gestures to the opposition – since corruption was one of the chief complaints voiced during the mass protests in the winter of 2011–12. The failure of these recent attempts – and the scandals that they have sparked – underline the integral role that corruption (and feudal relations in particular) occupy in Putin's administration.

Putin previously downplayed corruption even while paying lip service to the need for fighting it in his previous terms. However, he began raising the issue more frequently since returning to the presidential seat in spring 2012.

But his most striking coup in the apparent attempt to fight corruption was the ouster of Defense Minister Anatoly Serdyukov over fraud allegations at a firm linked to the Defense Ministry.

The case of Serdyukov's ouster provides us with a compelling example of how corruption cases in the upper echelons of power are actually attempts to settle political scores and resolve clan struggles rather than genuine moves to fight graft.

Serdyukov's ouster in November 2012 was over a criminal investigation into allegations that Defense Ministry officials embezzled some $100 million through the Oboronservis commercial firm. On the surface, it appeared much like the start of a massive campaign by the Investigative Committee to rein

[70] One of the authors of this book, Anna Arutunyan, conducted several interviews with Russian businesspeople in 2009–11. Several of them complained about the lack of a clear "price list," which makes businessmen very vulnerable to prosecution by those officials who were not bribed. One businessman specifically told her that everyone knows that a *krysha* wouldn't help you when someone with a more powerful *krysha* came after you.

in rampant corruption in the defense sector, which cost the state some $232 million in 2012 alone, according to Investigative Committee figures.[71]

But a closer look at the circumstances of Serdyukov's ouster – and the fact that six months later he remained merely a witness despite evidence cited by investigators that he knew about the fraud – suggests that the true motivating factors involved something other than fighting corruption.

The Investigative Committee's probe into the selling off of state assets through Oboronservis culminated in a raid of the apartment of Yevgeniya Vasilyeva, a director at Oboronservis and a former head of the Defense Ministry's department of property relations. But the raid proved fateful for Serdyukov, who was discovered in a bathrobe in Vasilyeva's apartment.

This suggested that family loyalty could have been a major motivating factor behind Putin's decision to oust Serdyukov. Serdyukov was married to the daughter of one of Putin's key allies, Viktor Zubkov, and his affair with Vasilyeva, revealed during the raid on her apartment, was seen by some sources close to the government as an unforgivable betrayal.

Another motivating factor behind Serdyukov's ouster was political rather than personal. Serdyukov, who has been a deeply unpopular defense minister, was increasingly under fire from lobbyists for Russia's military industrial complex, which Serdyukov had allegedly neglected in favor of more efficient imports in his effort to rearm the military. There was also evidence that one of the key lobbyists for the military industrial complex, First Deputy Prime Minister Dmitry Rogozin, had become a prime contender for Serdyukov's post. In the end, Putin decided to replace Serdyukov with the less ambitious, but more popular former Emergencies Minister Sergei Shoigu.[72]

While several Defense Ministry officials were taken into custody, Serdyukov appeared to be all but immune to genuine persecution, remaining as a witness. Putin, confronted on the issue by journalists after his press conference in December 2012, said that there was "nothing" to charge Serdyukov with but vowed that there would be no leniency in the investigation as a whole.[73] Still, Putin appeared very agitated as he answered the journalists' questions.[74]

This suggests that even if investigative probes into corruption cases are genuine, they are severely restricted by interests of loyalty and property, especially in the high-stakes military sector, where some $750 billion were set aside for

[71] *Rapsi News*, "$232 mln lost from corruption in Russian armed forces in 2012," February 21 2013, http://rapsinews.com/anticorruption_news/20130221/266492601.html, accessed March 28, 2013.

[72] Anna Arutunyan, "Shady dealing, sex scandals and Russia's defense crisis," *The Moscow News*, November 12, 2012, http://www.themoscownews.com/politics/20121112/190846846.html, accessed March 28, 2013.

[73] Irina Gruzinova, "Putin o korruptsii: Skoshchukhi ne budet! Slyshite? Ya vam govoryu!," *Slon.ru*, December 20, 2012, http://slon.ru/russia/vopros_slon_putinu_posle_press_konferentsii_o_serdyukove-867349.xhtml, accessed March 28, 2013.

[74] Putin's off-camera reaction during this question was observed by Anna Arutunyan.

reform, and where corruption has been known to eat away some 20 percent of the military budget.

This process was most aptly summarized by Pavel Zaitsev, a former Investigative Committee official, in a comment to one of the authors: "This is normal, at least in Russia, that the interests of certain groups are used by the government to fight corruption. If these [rivalries] weren't happening, we wouldn't even know about these [crimes]."[75]

In other words, a corruption campaign existed in the news and on paper to create a semblance of striving for law and order, but it was subjugated to the interest of politics and staying in power.

More importantly, this campaign, if it existed, appeared doomed from the start because it countered a key understanding shared by officials in Putin's administration about the possibility of private gain through holding public office. An even more public example of this process was the scandal that erupted around the State Duma deputy Vladimir Pekhtin, who gave up his mandate when the oppositionist blogger Alexei Navalny revealed that Pekhtin had $2 million worth of undeclared luxury condos, a house, and a plot of land in Florida.[76]

This was far from the first time that Navalny had made similar revelations about Russian state officials with undeclared property – his allegations against the Investigative Committee chief Alexander Bastrykin were believed to be the reason that the Investigative Committee, in an apparent retaliation, would go on to launch an embezzlement investigation against Navalny. But the evidence against Pekhtin became a turning point precisely because Pekhtin was the head of the Duma's Ethics Committee, and Pekhtin himself was behind a bill that would criminalize state officials' owning property abroad. Pekhtin was one of the key legislators behind a deoffshorization campaign that Putin announced in December 2012 in a bid to curb capital flight from Russia.[77]

Pekhtin, who resigned on his own initiative, would not go on to be prosecuted. But his case showed the inherent contradiction in Putin's Kremlin's launching a genuine anticorruption campaign, because the same officials behind it would be forced to start with themselves. At the same time, Pekhtin's case while again discrediting the State Duma and the pro-Kremlin United Russia party was used by the Kremlin administration to enhance Putin's status in the mind of ordinary people by ascribing to him a new role as the fighter of corruption and diminishing at least partially Navalny's aura as the main knight in the battle against the monster of corruption. Besides, by introducing a law

[75] Anna Arutunyan, "Politics and rivalries hinder Investigative Committee," *The Moscow News*, January 21, 2013, http://www.themoscownews.com/politics/20130121/191156603/Politics-and-rivalries-hinder-Investigative-Committee.html, accessed march 28, 2013.

[76] See Navalny's Livejournal post from February 12, 2013, http://navalny.livejournal.com/771665.html, accessed March 28, 2013.

[77] Michael Weiss, "Tropical hypocrisy: One Russian lawmaker's Florida real estate problem," *Atlantic*, February 27, 2013.

in the wake of the Pekhtin affair prohibiting officials to have property abroad and advancing the slogan about "the nationalizing elites," Putin wanted a guarantee once again from the middle and low levels of his administration of their full loyalty to him, which he did not want to share with officials who had villas and other properties. Of course, all these measures had practically no relevance to the top echelon of the political elite. As it was, the Kremlin did not allow even one public trial in 2012–13 against any high official, whether national or local.

Conclusion

The comparison of corruption in the different Russian regimes clearly shows that the scope of corruption depends on the power of the state and the degree of its repressions against the people. Corruption grew systematically, from a minimal size in Stalin's regime to a relatively large share in Khrushchev's and, particularly, in Brezhnev's times. It reached astronomic proportions in the post-Soviet regimes. The growth of corruption after 1991 was probably unavoidable. The privatization of the state economy created favorable conditions for corruption, which did not exist before. The feudalization of a society, with its weakening of the state and the high autonomy of its officeholders, was another major factor behind the outburst of corruption. However, while these "objective" factors account for a great part of corruption's growth, the transformation of the leaders of the country to people who encouraged corruption for their own benefit – one of the major elements of feudalization – also played an extremely large role in spreading corruption inside the country. For this reason, the pluses of privatization can only partially justify corruption in the eyes of most Russian experts.

Corruption poses greater concerns to society in the long term. Russian corruption undermines labor ethics, particularly among younger generations. Russian youths firmly believe that bribes and connections are the best, and perhaps the only, way to become successful.[78] Widespread corruption creates a parallel, semifeudal chain of command that competes with the official hierarchy. The weakness of law enforcement agencies, as well as the army – now almost totally demoralized – is, to a great extent, the product of corruption. The same weakness of the state apparatus was revealed by the failure of the

[78] In a survey, Russians attributed "success in life" more to "dishonesty" (76 percent) and "connections" (88 percent) than to "hard work" (39 percent). Only 14 percent mentioned "education" as a factor in becoming successful. Even more indicative are the data from the survey of Moscow students – the elite of the Russian youth – that was conducted by the Moscow High School of Economics in 2002. When asked what the conditions for success in life are, 64 percent of students pointed to "connections" and 49 percent to "resourcefulness." Significantly fewer students thought that "the quality of education" (35 percent) and "hard work" (27 percent) would yield success in contemporary Russia. (See Azer Efendiev, "S nadezhdoi na znakomstva," *Izvestiia*, August 23, 2002.)

FSB and local police forces to prevent the numerous murders of prominent people in the country. The continuing spate of murders can be attributed to a feeling of immunity among the hired guns. In the first decade of this century, law enforcement agencies failed to find the perpetrators of several dozen murders of some of the most prominent people in Russia.

Corruption eats away at the state apparatus, turning state employees into people who are indifferent to the national interests of the country. They know that their current positions and prospects for promotion do not depend so much on their honesty and the professional fulfillment of their duties as on their informal relationships, based on corruption, with their superiors and with oligarchs.

At the same time, with the continuing corruption, a state may lose its chance to earnestly combat corruption and not replace the real fight against it with actions that are just for show. In Putin's Russia, it would have been difficult to find several thousand honest officials who were ready for an ascetic life and the struggle for their country's prosperity rather than their own interests. It would also have been difficult to find the judges, police officers, and investigators needed to accomplish this mission.

The real danger of corruption was/is linked even less to the economy than to Russia's overall efficiency and preparedness. Corruption jeopardizes the country's ability to battle serious problems, including the threat of terrorism. An economically challenged country may react efficiently to military threats, natural and technological disasters, or the outburst of ethnic conflicts, as long as the strength of the state and the integrity of public values are intact. But in Russia's case, the state has been infested by corruption and an atomized population remains indifferent to public values.

4

Enemies and the Issue of Legitimization in the Soviet and Post-Soviet Regimes

The images of enemies – those entities who have hostile intentions toward a particular society, whether originating within its borders or beyond them – play an important role in the life of nations, social groups, and institutions.[1] Of course, these images are especially important for societies with strong authoritarian structures: hierarchical organizations with strong leaders who pursue their own goals, using repression and ideology as a means to these ends. If the authoritarian structure is dominant, it is a "normal" or "pure" authoritarian society, as was the case in the Stalin and post-Stalin eras.

However, the authoritarian structure can also function in a society with various centers of economic and political power. This type of predominantly feudal society was present in post-Soviet Russia. The strength of an authoritarian government varies as a feudal society evolves from one stage to the next.[2] The history of post-Soviet Russia illustrates this thesis. Indeed, the central administration was very weak in Yeltsin's time, and then became relatively strong in Putin's time, although Putin's Russia did not reach the same level of authoritative might as the Soviet government.[3] (Authoritarian structures can

[1] Martha L. Cottam, Beth Dietz-Uhler and Elena Mastors, *Introduction to Political Psychology*, 2nd ed. (New York: Psychology Press, 2010); David O. Sears, Leonie Huddy and Robert Jervis (eds.), *Oxford Handbook of Political Psychology* (Oxford: Oxford University Press, 2003); Kenneth Boulding, *The Image: Knowledge in Life and Society* (Ann Arbor: University of Michigan Press, 1956), p. 175. Ole Hoisti, "Cognitive Dynamics and Images of the Enemy," in J. C. Farrell and A. P. Smith (eds.), *Image and Reality in World Politics* (New York: Columbia University Press, 1967); *Ben Shalit, The Psychology of Conflict and Combat* (New York: Praeger, 1988).

[2] As happened, for instance, in medieval France.

[3] In this book we operate with three types of societies in Russian postrevolutionary history. However, it is possible to separate this history into seven different periods: the civil war and War Communism versions of the totalitarian society (1917–20); the softening of the totalitarian society during the NEP (1921–6); the reconstruction of the totalitarian society under Stalin (1927–9); the harsh totalitarian society headed by Stalin (1929–53); the soft society led by Khrushchev (1954–64); the hardened totalitarian society of Brezhnev and his two heirs (1964–84); and

certainly also be part of predominately democratic societies; this point will not be discussed in this book, however.)[4]

The ultimate cause of the differences in attitudes toward enemies among the different Soviet regimes, as well as between Soviet and post-Soviet regimes, lies in the degree of their self-confidence, in their belief in their right to govern, or in their legitimacy, which assumes that the ruled also accept the role of their rulers as the masters of society. The early Communist regime, having come to power through violent revolution, could not rely on a functional legal-rational state to legitimize its rule; it leaned instead on ideology. Stalin's rule occurred during a phase when that ideology had not been fully entrenched, and the regime was still in its revolutionary and aggressive-defensive phase; therefore Stalin was always concerned about its legitimacy.[5] Stalin's personality exacerbated the usual fear that regimes possess about the intentions of those who, whether based domestically or abroad, want to destroy the relatively new regime and its leaders. Many authoritarian regimes – the product of revolution – behaved in the same way during their initial stages – even if the number of the victims varied. Robespierre, Tito, Mao, and Castro are just a few examples.[6] Up to the last minutes of his life, Stalin looked for both his personal enemies and those of the regime with which he completely identified himself. [7]

Contrary to Stalin's regime, the post-Stalin regimes were already confident of their own legitimacy and stability, fully leaning on an ideology that had been successfully entrenched and widely accepted by the population (see Chapter 2). Within that legitimizing ideology arose the first sprouts of the legal-rational state: all post-Stalin leaders were, indeed, elected by party bodies (the Politburo and the Central Committee), whose legitimacy was indubitable to Soviet society and abroad.[8]

the erosion of the totalitarian society under Gorbachev (1985–91) (see Shlapentokh, *Normal Totalitarian Society*).

4 See Vladimir Shlapentokh, *Contemporary Russia as a Feudal Society: A New Perspective on the Post-Soviet Era* (New York: Palgrave Macmillan, 2007); Shlapentokh and Woods, *Feudal America*.

5 As Vasily Grossman noted in his *Life and Destiny* (s.l.: s.n., 1960), only after the Stalingrad victory in 1943 could Stalin be confident that his state had a future, and that nobody would have the capacity to destroy it.

6 Stalin's concerns about the legitimization of the regime went so far as to suggest he formally adopt a very democratic constitution and carry out the election of the parliament with a Western flavor – the participation of all citizens (before this, those people with bad social origins had no right to vote) in elections, the direct election of the national Soviet parliament (in the past, the political system operated with multistage elections: local Soviets elected Soviets of a higher order), and secret voting, even if there was only one candidate on the ballot. Stalin deemed it necessary to introduce a new Western-like election, despite the fact that this act undermined the major tenet of the Soviet ideology about the "dictatorship of the proletariat," with a full rejection of bourgeois democracy.

7 See Edvard Radzinsky, *Stalin: Zhizn' i smert'* (Moscow: AST, 2007).

8 The case of Leonid Brezhnev was particularly remarkable. His legitimacy as the supreme leader of the country was absolute, even when he was dying. When Brezhnev's physician, Dr. Chasov,

Somewhat paradoxically, the legitimacy of Yeltsin's and Putin's "hybrid" democracy was far more vulnerable than the legitimacy of the totalitarian Soviet Union. The reason for this is that both Yeltsin's and Putin's administrations rested on the motions of democracy in a situation where actual legal democratic procedure had never been entrenched. The official source of Yeltsin's and Putin's legitimacy were democratic elections, not ideology. And yet all of the elections, starting from 1996, were, to various extents, rigged.[9] These electoral irregularities might not have been such a problem had Putin's regime officially sought to derive its legitimacy elsewhere, but instead Putin has repeatedly insisted on the democratic nature of the Russian government, and on full conformity with democratic procedure, often accusing Western democracies of failing to live up to their own democratic standards. The growing gap between what was practiced and what was preached consistently undermined the state's legitimacy. Granted, the Soviet ideology of communism was also far removed from reality, perhaps even more so than post-Soviet official ideology with its praise of democracy, but the difference was that the Soviet population largely accepted the ideology itself, even it did not believe that state officials always conformed with it. Putin, however, has found himself almost as vulnerable as Stalin in terms of his legitimacy. And yet he has continued to insist that democratic elections are the source of his legitimacy; only in 2012, when popular protests pushed him toward repressions, did he start considering other, more authoritarian sources of legitimacy, such as the Russian Orthodox Church. But even amid these implicit overtures to deriving legitimacy for state power from itself, explicitly Putin continued to insist on democracy

The reason for this insistence – and the reason that enemies of the regime would also be treated much differently in post-Soviet Russia, and Putin's regime in particular – is to be found in another realm: property relations and the influence of big money on politics, and on the behavior of the leader and on his narrow circle.

In fact, the role of money in post-Soviet society is deeply correlated with the degree of feudalization in society; the weakness of the central administration is mostly the result of the involvement of the leader and his friends in actions meant to enhance personal enrichment.

The priority of personal enrichment and market relations (or, more accurately, personal enrichment through market relations) made insistence on democracy a necessity, even if democracy often failed as an adequate source of

had some concerns about the state of his country, he told Yury Andropov that a medical sister had acquired a magical power over the dying general secretary, who was already in a state of intellectual disorientation, and that she was able to persuade him to make any decision. The chief of the KGB, with his legendary steel will and real devotion to the Soviet system, replied to the doctor, like a child who does not dare to question the authority of a ferocious father, "I can do nothing. He is general secretary."

[9] While the absolute majority of the party apparatus were against Gorbachev by 1990, no one attempted to remove him from his position as general secretary.

legitimacy. Putin, thus, was focusing on ensuring his legitimacy in the eyes of the West as well as in eyes of his own people – even as he made anti-Americanism an important part of his rhetoric for domestic audience.

This precarious balancing act made it necessary to blunt the aggressive use of enemies in Russian politics considerably.

The Functions of Enemies' Images

The functions of enemy images in an authoritarian society, as well as in any other, are multifaceted. Pragmatically, this is a salient image of an enemy that warns the regime and society against those who want to undermine or even destroy it and helps to mobilize the nation against the ensuing danger. The image of Hitler's Germany as an enemy of the USSR in the 1930s helped to enhance Stalin's efforts to strengthen the country's preparations for the imminent war. (However, several factors in Stalin's politics acted in the opposite direction).[10] At the same time, the opposition to the regime inside the country often views the enemies of the regime as its allies, such as Russian liberals who treated the United States in a manner that was the opposite of the official propaganda, heartily supporting American foreign policy, including the war in Vietnam.[11]

But the image of the enemy also has to perform a very important ideological function for domestic consumption. Maintaining society's hatred of the enemy is necessary to justify repressions (and the fear of them) as the major instruments of an authoritarian regime. Hatred of the enemy is necessary for strengthening the cohesiveness of a society, and is vitally important to the ruling class and its leaders, as it helps them maintain legitimacy in the eyes of others and quiets internal opposition to their use of power.

Images of the enemy were an essential part of the Soviet ideology, in which the "negative" elements always seemed to surpass the "positive" elements in importance.[12] Negative emotions and values like fear have a stronger impact on human behavior than positive emotional rewards like the anticipation of pleasure. "The radiant future," as a part of Soviet ideology, had a serious impact on the minds, and even the behavior, of the Soviet people, especially the

[10] At the same time, in contrast to the danger emanating from Hitler's Germany in the 1930s, the danger of war in the 1920s, after the end the civil war, was minimal, though the Kremlin artificially enhanced the threat for domestic purposes. The Kremlin targeted France and England as the country's two major enemies without serious evidence.

[11] While the Soviet regime promoted the ugly image of the United States, Soviet liberals nurtured a romantic image of America. For the image of America in the Soviet Union, see Vladimir Shlapentokh, "The Changeable Soviet Image of America," *Annals of the American Academy of Political and Social Science* **497** (1988), 157–71.

[12] Vladimir Shlapentokh, *Fear in Contemporary Society: Its Negative and Positive Effects* (New York: Palgrave Macmillan, 2006).

young; however, the image of the enemy who endangers the Soviet system and sows war appealed much more forcibly to the Soviet mentality.

Ideology of Hatred: Stalin's Time

From the very beginning, Soviet rulers chose a security strategy that banned any compromise with domestic enemies and adopted a practice of stringent repressions to quell any dangers to the regime. The ideological basis that facilitated this hatred of the enemy in Stalin's time was the cult of state and the thesis about the "dictatorship of the proletariat" as a single condition upon which to build a socialist society.

Soviet leaders began to develop the cult of the state almost immediately after they seized power in 1917. The leadership quickly abandoned all of the democratic elements of their program of the transformation of society that Lenin and other Bolshevik leaders had described in their prerevolutionary declarations. Lenin extolled the active role of the masses in governing society in his famous book *State and Revolution* only a few months before the seizure of power in October 1917. The inclusion of a nationalist component in Soviet ideology in the early 1930s only magnified the cult of the state in society. Russian Marxists and Russian nationalists both needed the powerful and repressive state to achieve their goals.

The concept of a "dictatorship of the proletariat" was an important pillar of the Bolshevik ideology, which served to justify the rejection of compromise with those who were regarded as enemies of the regime. In fact, the dictatorship of the proletariat was a commandment to all Soviet people to be unflinching and cruel with enemies and to use only the language of violence with them. Indeed, this slogan, which has often been treated as cheap ideological posturing, was actually one of the most important Bolshevik "declarations of intention" because it was not about the leadership of the working class, and it never had been. Instead, it was about the need for the use of dictatorial, cruel, and merciless methods in order to destroy enemies of the new regime without any hesitation.

The dictatorship of the proletariat implied that spreading the fear of physical repressions was the most effective way to prevent a rally of any sort from being carried out by enemies against the regime. The concept of the dictatorship of the proletariat, which instilled cruelty toward, and the denial of, any compromises with the enemy, was accompanied by another concept – "the irreconcilable class struggle," which identified people who did not share the regime's Communist views and/or those who belonged to a hostile milieu, whether from the prerevolutionary dominant classes or foreign societies, as enemies. Domestic and foreign enemies of all sorts were depicted in speeches by the leaders, in official documents, in propaganda, and in movies and novels as bloodthirsty people who dreamed only about ways to damage and destroy the socialist motherland and Russia.

Maxim Gorky, the famous Russian writer who was known as a humanist before the revolution, proclaimed that "if the enemy does not surrender … he shall be killed." This formula became a motto for Stalin's regime during the mass terror of the 1930s.[13] Orwell portrayed the role of the enemy in a totalitarian society brilliantly when he described the two minutes hate of Emmanuel Goldstein (Goldstein was the perennial adversary of the ruling party) – which all residents of Oceania were obliged to watch on screen.[14]

Soviet society's hostility toward compromise was successfully inculcated in the public mind of the Soviet people to such a degree that some authors suggested that a focus on conflict, rather than compromise, was an organic feature of the Russian mentality, as it was shaped many centuries ago. Some of them, like Vladimir Lefebvre, contrasted the Soviet and Western attitudes toward compromise, suggesting that a Western ethical system based on individualism saw compromise as the normal solution for the conflict between "good" and "bad," while the Soviet system, based on collectivism, saw compromise as the betrayal of the "good."[15]

Remarkably, the majority of urban citizens supported Stalin's mass terror in the late 1920s and 1930s. In several cases, people were dissatisfied with the "lenient verdicts" that sentenced offenders to mere imprisonment rather than execution.[16]

Hatred in Post-Stalin and Post-Soviet Russia

The level of hatred pumped into the public mind decreased significantly in the post-Stalin era. The focus then was not so much on the dictatorship of the proletariat as on the pivotal role of the state and the party (its alter ego). The accusation that intellectuals – or, God forbid, party apparatchiks – were even inclined toward compromise, political or ideological, with those who were not in the Soviet camp was one of the most damaging reprimands apportioned by the authorities to their cadres.

[13] The importance of educating people in the hatred of enemies and in the necessity to exterminate them without any compassion inspired a cohort of young Soviet writers like Alexander Fadeyev, with his novel *Razgrom* (Moscow: s.n., 1927), or Dmitry Furmanov, with his novel *Chapaev* (s.l.: s.n., 1923), and poets like Eduard Bagritzky and Iosif Utkin. All of them were inspired by the idea of the world proletarian revolution (at least until 1941), which demanded mercilessness toward its enemies.

[14] Vladimir Shlapentokh, "George Orwell: Russia's Tocqueville," in Thomas Cushman and John Rodden (eds.), *George Orwell into the Twentieth Century* (Boulder, CO: Paradigm, 2004).

[15] Vladimir Lefebvre, *Algebra of Conscience* (Dordrecht: Kluwer Academic, 2001).

[16] Sarah Davies, *Popular Opinion in Stalin's Russia: Terror, Propaganda and Dissent, 1934–1941* (Cambridge: Cambridge University Press, 1997), pp. 119–32.

It was only in the 1960s that the Soviet intellectuals, who in the beginning were very shy, became more outspoken in challenging the ideology of the destruction of the enemy by all means. In fact, the advancement of the idea of "humanistic values" or "universal human values" was spearheaded against the "class ideology," which had promoted the extermination of everything different from the official position.[17] In fact, the intellectuals' campaign for universal values such as altruism, kindness, friendship, and respect for tradition was directed against the class approach and its cult of hatred of enemies.

The movie *Forty One* by Grigory Chukhrai (1956) was almost revolutionary for Russians. In this movie, a young female sniper from the Red Army, performing her duty mercilessly, shoots a White officer with whom she had previously fallen in love. The movie, and the candid portrayal of the sniper's betrayal, was an unheard-of challenge to "class morale," and was one of the most colorful signs that Soviet society had moved from a cult of hatred to a more civilized mode of thinking during Khrushchev's "thaw." The intelligentsia's strong interest in classical Russian literature was also an indicator of the retreat from "class morale" and the associated disdain for those who are "not with us." The survey of *Literaturnaia Gazeta* readers conducted by one of the authors of this book in 1968 found that the intelligentsia was becoming attracted to the older Russian writers who had appealed to kindness toward "others."[18] Perestroika played a special role in the softening of attitudes toward enemies.

While hatred disappeared from official texts during Yeltsin's years (although there was a growing hatred among ordinary people, directed against the oligarchs and the ruling elites), it again became an important part of official media with Putin's arrival in power.

The role played by hatred in official propaganda of Putin's regime, with its intense concerns for its legitimacy, turned out much closer to Stalin's regime than to the time of Brezhnev. Putin's regime has not, however, used enemies in its propaganda to the same degree that Stalin's regime did. He did not wish to antagonize the West unduly with an excessive, Stalin-like hatred of enemies, and, in this way, endanger the big fortunes of the ruling elites – who mostly resided in the West, who used the West for education of their children and for medical treatment, and who ultimately looked to the West as a place for refuge.

[17] See Vladimir Shlapentokh, *Soviet Intellectuals and Political Power* (Princeton, NJ: Princeton University Press, 1990).

[18] When asked about their preferred Russian authors, the respondents gave 36 percent of their votes to Tolstoy, 32 percent to Chekhov, 21 percent to Dostoevsky, 18 percent to Kuprin, and 17 percent to Bunin (the figures do not total 100 percent since some respondents endorsed several authors). Vladimir Shlapentokh (ed.), *Chitatel i Gazeta: Itogi Izucheniia Chitatelskoi Auditorii Tsentralnykh Gazet. Vyp.2, Chitateli "Literaturnoi Gazety"* (Moscow: Institut Konkretnykh Sotsial'nykh Issledovanii, 1969).

Domestic and Foreign Enemies

The analysis of the place of enemies within an ideology requires distinguishing between foreign and domestic enemies. The relative role of the two categories of enemies is one of the most important characteristics of the regime's propaganda. In the 1920s, Stalin's regime, with its ideology of the "besieged fortress" and its belief that the West intended to destroy the USSR, clearly focused on foreign enemies (including practically all Russian emigrants), making domestic enemies, as a rule, out to be people who were in the service of foreign enemies.

Practically all of the defendants in the show trials in Moscow in the middle 1930s, such as Zinovyev or Bukharin, were accused of being foreign agents, as were all of the military generals, such as Mikhail Tukhachevsky or Iona Yakir, who were declared traitors and killed at that time. The authorities connected the defendants in the "doctors' plot" in 1952, who supposedly planned to kill the Soviet leadership, with American Zionist organizations. Even in the aftermath of Stalin's death, Beria was accused by his former colleagues in the Politburo of being a former British agent.

It is also true that foreign enemies were widely present in Stalin's propaganda for their own sake, and not only as the masters of domestic enemies. They were depicted as bloodthirsty warmongers and nasty human beings. Stalin's propaganda did not hesitate to attack Western leaders personally. The notorious article by Boris Gorbatov on the American president Harry Truman in *Literaturnaia Gazeta* in 1947 was one example of the defamations of foreign politicians. This piece prompted the furious protest of the American ambassador, Walter Bedell Smith.[19] Following Stalin's example, in 2011, Putin went so far as personally accusing U.S. Secretary of State Hillary Clinton of fomenting an Orange Revolution in Russia,[20] while Russian official media verbally assailed the new American ambassador in Russia, Michael McFaul; it was impossible to imagine this happening in the USSR after 1953.

A special group of writers were known in the country as the masters of denouncing and derogating Western businesspeople and politicians. Konstantin Simonov's play *Russian Question* (1947) was commissioned by the Kremlin to create a gallery of unpleasant depictions of American politicians. Samuil Marshak, a famous poet, presented an ugly image of the American tycoon in his comical poem "Mister Twister." A talented collective of painters, like Kurkryniksy and Boris Efimov, created hundreds of lampoons of Western politicians. Putin also developed his own cohort of journalists and experts, such as Mikhail Leontiev, Vyacheslav Nikonov, Maxim Shevchenko, and Sergey Kurginian, who could accuse the United States of all possible vices. Specialists in anti-American

[19] B. Gorbatov, "Garry Truman," *Literaturnaia Gazeta,* September 20, 1947.

[20] "Vladimir Putin obviniaet Hillari Klinton v razzhiganii protestov," December 8, 2011, http://newsstreet.ru/blog/456.html, accessed April 30, 2012.

propaganda in Soviet Russia, like Valentin Zorin or even Yury Zhukov, were merely looked upon as moderate critics of the United States' real problems.

Back in the post-Stalin regime, the role of foreign enemies did not change radically. Khrushchev continued to operate with the concept of foreign enemies as the central feature of his propaganda. The United States continued, although in a much milder form, to be the leading enemy and was joined by West Germany (especially during the Hungarian revolutions in 1956) in playing the role of the salient foe. Additionally, Tito's Yugoslavia and later, by the end of Khrushchev's rule, Maoist China joined America on the podium of enemies.

After Khrushchev, though, the role of foreign enemies in propaganda declined dramatically. In the 1960s and 1970s, Soviet authorities relented somewhat in their declarations that all their opponents were in the direct service of the West. While Sakharov and Solzhenitsyn were pronounced enemies of Soviet society, they were not also denounced as agents working for the CIA or U.S. State Department. "Anti-imperialist propaganda" continued to make up an important part of the Soviet ideology – it increased somewhat during the Czech events in 1968 – but the personal attacks against Western leaders practically disappeared from Soviet media. What is more, Soviet outlets rejected opportunities to use the Watergate affair of the early 1970s for disparaging Western democracy and simply did not mention it in order to "save face" for Nixon, a collaborator with Brezhnev in the implementation of the policy of détente. Ronald Reagan, after declaring the USSR an "empire of evil" in 1981, only earned a relatively moderate rebuff from Moscow, and no one proffered personal attacks on the new president.[21] In the short period of Andropov's tenure (1982–4), personal attacks against Western leaders were renewed – especially on President Reagan – but with Gorbachev in power, all attacks against Western leaders totally disappeared.

The Soviet leaders were very concerned about Mao's foreign policy and his internal ideological propaganda, with its strong egalitarian and antibureaucratic overtones, but they were still very restrained in their critique of the Mao regime. Even personal attacks on Chinese leaders were spared in Soviet media during the apex of the tensions in Soviet-Chinese relations around 1969–75. The Soviet media never attacked the personality of Mao and mainly denounced "the group of Mao" for its expansionist inclinations, even when the Maoist Red Guard attacked the Soviet embassy in Beijing.[22]

Putin's regime, however, returned to a practice that almost mirrored Stalin's times in its advancement of foreign enemies to the levels of highest concern. The repertoire of foreign enemies in Putin's Russia became much larger than that of the post-Stalin period. It is curious that in the aftermath of the Afghan invasion, on the eve of Perestroika, when the USSR was almost fully isolated from the international community, the dose of foreign enemies in propaganda

[21] See the newspaper *Pravda*, February 8 and 17, 1981.

[22] See, for instance, the article in the newspaper *Pravda*, January 10, 1969 or February 7, 1967.

was very moderate. The 2008 issue of *Izvestia*, which contained forty articles, did not include one article on economic or scholarly success. Six articles talked about various problems in the economy; fourteen articles talked about various foreign enemies; the rest were about cultural and sporting events. The 1980 issue of the same newspaper included forty-nine articles: nineteen talked about economic achievements; six articles were about foreign enemies; eleven articles discussed friends abroad (such materials were totally absent twenty-eight years later); and the remaining articles were about cultural and sporting events. In fact, foreign enemies play a much greater role in Putin's propaganda than do domestic ones.

Of course, after the Orange Revolutions in 2004–5, America became the most popular foreign enemy. The Kremlin, with its propaganda machine, was able to persuade two-thirds of Russians to hold negative attitudes toward America. A clear sign of anti-American hysteria was the showing of the pseudodocumentary movie *9/11* on the main Russian TV channel on September 12, 2008. This movie ascribes responsibility for the terrorist acts on September 11, 2001, to American security services. America was also declared responsible for the mass protest actions in Moscow of December 2011–February 2012. Putin made several statements about the involvement of the United States in fomenting the protests against his regime. The quasi-documentary movie *Anatomy of Protest* was shown by the official channel NTV in March 2012; it directly portrayed the protesters as having been paid by the American government.

Several Western countries, such as England, Poland, and Estonia, have been found at the center of xenophobic propaganda at varying times. Satellites like Poland and, in particular, the former Soviet republics hold special places in the rosters of enemies. Among these are the Ukraine, Belorussia, and, especially, Georgia. The president of Georgia, Michail Saakashvili, was attacked by Putin and Medvedev in the most heinous ways, including the use of many vulgar expressions. The personality of Mikhail Saakashvili became the object of Putin's almost physiological aversion.[23] His hatred for Victor Yushchenko, who became the Ukrainian president in 2004, was somewhat less passionate.[24]

The Typology of Domestic Enemies

All Russian regimes differ from each other in the characteristics of their respective repertoires of domestic enemies. The most important typology of these enemies is based on their "reality" (this typology is also relevant to foreign enemies).

[23] By the way, Putin made a new record in his list of vulgarities, promising the Georgian president "to hang him by the balls."

[24] Only Senator McCain, guilty of the same sin (being doubtful of Putin's legitimacy; promising the Russian leader the fate of Colonel Qaddafi), is the object of Putin's scorn as intensely as Saakashvili is. (See, for instance, Vladimir Putin's speech in the stadium Luzhniki, available at http://echo.msk.ru/blog/echomsk/861828-echo, accessed April 20, 2012.)

All of the regimes (as well as other authoritarian regimes) operated with four types of domestic enemies: real, invented, potential, and "reformed."

Real and Invented Enemies: Stalin's Case

The Soviet regimes had real enemies, who directly challenged the order in the country. They were strikers, participants in public demonstrations, active nationalists – Russian and non-Russian – enemy collaborators, and the authors and disseminators of anti-Soviet leaflets. Additionally, people who talked publicly against "the system" were placed in the realm of real enemies: the people who declared sympathy for the West (since the middle of the 1920s); Zionists; people who read books and journals published in the West (aside from those of foreign Communist Parties), like Orwell, Koestler, or samizdat; people who listened to foreign radio and disseminated information from it; people who met foreigners in the USSR without official permission; dissidents; the Soviet authors of books labeled anti-Soviet (like Evgeny Zamyatin, Boris Pasternak, or Andrei Sinyavsky); or even the authors of articles endorsed by the Soviet censors for publication but later denounced as being anti-Soviet. The categories of enemies included authors of letters to Soviet institutions and newspapers, if the letters contained anti-Soviet statements. Among the domestic enemies were also the members of the nonofficial political groups, including those who studied Marx or Lenin.

Stalin's "Invented" Enemies

The invented enemies are those who were repressed by the regime but who did not commit any of the crimes included in the catalog of anti-Soviet actions and who, at the same time, did not fit any category of potential enemies. Stalin's regime (like Mao's regime and some other authoritarian regimes in their initial stages, though not the Nazi regime) needed more enemies than the political police could have arrested if they only took real anti-Soviet crimes into account. As a result, Stalin's regime invented enemies. Stalin's machine for inventing enemies functioned at maximal capacity in the middle 1930s. Its productivity declined after 1938, when the system was satisfied with the great assortment of potential enemies," people who could perpetrate anti-Soviet crimes.

There were several sources for the supply of invented enemies. Among the most effective were the depositions of the arrested, which were largely manufactured by the torture the NKVD inflicted on its victims. The memoirs of former Gulag prisoners are full of narrations about forced confessions containing the names of people who were supposedly involved in anti-Soviet actions. Those who refused to provide the interrogators, whose work was appreciated by their superiors, with the harvest of new names could indeed consider themselves heroes.[25] The political police informants were also obliged to deliver the names

[25] See Lev Kopelev, *Ease My Sorrows: A Memoir* (New York: Random House, 1983); Raisa Orlova, *Memoirs* (New York: Random House, 1983); Pyotr Grigorenko, *Memoirs*; Aleksandr

of the people to whom they attributed, often falsely, nonexistent violations of Soviet rules. The third category of the producers of invented enemies was the army of voluntary informers – people who took revenge on others, whatever their motives, or who hoped to get the positions or apartments left vacant by the departure of the arrestee. Of course, among the voluntary informers were also people motivated only by purely ideological considerations, rather than being motivated, even partially, by personal greed. In any case, the number of invented enemies in the 1930s was enormous. And some authors have suggested that this long laundry list of "invented enemies" made up close to the majority of the Gulag inmates.

Potential Enemies

In addition to those enemies whose actions reveal their animosity toward the regime or to whom these actions are ascribed, authoritarian rulers always operate in opposition to potential enemies.

For the Soviet authorities, the potential enemies were all people who, in the "objective" opinion of the leaders, had the propensity to hate the Soviet system or be in collusion with its adversaries. In Stalin's time, the list of potentially dangerous people included many types: members of the former dominant class and their children (including members of the bureaucracy and officers); White emigrants, even if they did not participate in the struggle against the Soviet regime; priests; kulaks; the members of non-Bolshevik socialist parties; people expelled from the Communist Party; members of the large and diverse groups of so-called special migrants (people who were transferred against their will to the eastern region of the country); people from territories annexed in the 1930s (Western Ukraine, Belorussia, Bessarabia, and the Baltic republics); people who visited the West after 1917; several ethnic minorities in the 1930s and 1950s (Germans, Poles, Koreans, Crimean Tartars, Chechens, Kalmyks); prisoners of war; those who simply lived in the occupied territories (1940–60); and Jews (late 1930–80). Most of these categories of potential enemies were rescinded from the list kept by the KGB after 1953.

The Real Domestic Enemies after Stalin

With Khrushchev, the role of domestic enemies declined even more sharply than that of foreign enemies. Most important was the disappearance of invented enemies (nobody was accused by the KGB of nonexistent actions), but even the category of potential enemies was drastically reduced. Under Khrushchev, and then under Brezhnev, besides Zionists and Jews, the list of

Gorbatov, *Years of My Life: The Memoirs of General of the Soviet Army, A. V. Gorbatov* (London: Constable, 1964).

potential enemies included friends of dissidents, people who sympathized with the West, non-Russian nationalists, and, of course, people who declared their desire to emigrate (1970–80).

As a matter of fact, in Brezhnev's eighteen-year tenure, he rarely even used the term "enemy," not even during the developments related to the Prague Spring.[26] For the sake of stability, the Kremlin did not permit criticism of either a chairman of a collective farm or, all the more, the party secretary of the district, in order to prevent alienating ordinary people from the bureaucracy. As a result, the number of negative domestic materials in the media was reduced almost to zero.[27] The concept of potential enemies (not to mention invented enemies) almost completely disappeared in Brezhnev's time. There was an exception made for the intelligentsia, which, since 1968, had mildly been declared to be a population group infected by the "virus of Western liberalism," as opposed to the working class. The Jews, Jewish professionals in particular, were also considered by the party, and particularly by the KGB, as people with a higher propensity than any others to evolve into the camp of real enemies. With the birth of emigration in the early 1970s, the concept of the potential enemy regenerated fully; in this iteration, the concept of the enemy (which was mostly related to Jews) was equated with the desire to emigrate.

Still, it seems that the role of domestic enemies was never lower in twentieth-century Russian history than it was in the official propaganda under Brezhnev. It is also true, in comparison with prerevolutionary Russia, when the assortment of domestic enemies such as anarchists and social revolutionaries – terrorists, Bolsheviks, Jews, and even liberals like Cadets – were always presented in governmental media as the committed enemies of the monarchy and order in society. Meanwhile, even such obvious enemies of Brezhnev's regime as the dissidents were ignored by the media. For example, even such an open and steadfast enemy of the regime as Alexander Solzhenitsyn had relatively little hostile publicity during the period he was proclaimed a foe of the regime, in 1970. Only in January and February 1974, when *The Gulag Archipelago* was published in the West and the writer was deported, was there a stream of articles in *Pravda* denouncing the author – these were mostly republished materials commissioned by the Kremlin from foreign presses.[28] However, after that, the anti-Solzhenitsyn articles almost disappeared from *Pravda* and the Soviet media in general, until the beginning of Perestroika.

[26] See Brezhnev's speeches at the Twenty-Third, Twenty-Fourth, and Twenty-Fifth Party Congresses.

[27] I noted this interesting tendency in Brezhnev's time, during my surveys of *Pravda* readers in 1968 and 1976. Many of my respondents, full of hatred for the local authorities, were furious over the lack of critical materials in the leading newspaper of the country.

[28] See, for instance, the newspaper *Pravda*, January 7–19, 1974.

Enemies after 1999

Continuing the new traditions of Perestroika, Yeltsin's regime allowed criticism of the regime without turning the opposition into enemies of society. The revolutionary development in Yeltsin's regime (which continued in Putin's time) was the recognition that "the enemy of the regime" had the right to live freely in society. This represented unbelievable progress for Russia. Only militant separatists, particularly in Chechnya, like General Dzhokhar Dudayev, were declared enemies of Russia, though not immediately and only with the beginning of the first Russian-Chechen war in 1996. But with a brusque turn toward authoritarianism and the commensurate strict control over media, the role of domestic enemies in Putin's Russia increased immensely, along with a dramatic increase of foreign adversaries.

The Treatment of Enemies by the Authoritarians: Repressions

In the treatment of enemies, authoritarian regimes choose two strategies: 1) reactive, which supposes the elimination or neutralization of enemies without compromise; and 2) proactive, which supposes the prevention of enemy activity and offers special rewards to those who help the regime exterminate enemies.

Indeed, the history of the Soviet Union is laced with the merciless destruction, mostly physical, of enemies (real, potential, or imaginary). It started with the civil war, which usually – and this is true not only for Russian history – takes "no prisoners." The cruelty of the Russian civil war, where, indeed, "brother killed brother," left an indelible impact on the Russian mind. It was not until seventy years after the end of the civil war that Russian society realized how much the fratricidal hatred in the country that emerged during the civil war and was then cultivated by the Soviet regime influenced the mentality of the people. After the civil war, Lenin delivered a lesson to the country on the rejection of compromise, sending the best minds of the country to the West in 1922. The "philosophers ship" (the ship used by Lenin to send Russian intellectuals considered as counterrevolutionaries abroad) entered history textbooks. Then the country went through stages that were differentiated from each other by the name of the most important enemies for the given period.

By various conservative computations, such as data from the KGB from the 1930s to the early 1950s, roughly 3.8 million people were arrested and sentenced to death, internal exile, or the Gulag by "nonjudicial bodies" (the notorious troika). From this group, 786,000 were executed. These figures, as the KGB data in 1990 asserted, "do not include the victims of dekulakization, starvation and deportation."

Reformed Enemies

With their Manichean vision, the Soviet leaders were mostly inflexible in their policies toward their opponents. They rarely retreated from their previous positions. However, even with this rigidity, they had a concept of reformed enemies.

It was Leon Trotsky who created this category for Soviet society. During the civil war, Trotsky offered the former officers of the tsarist army a chance to serve in the Red Army (later, however, most of them wound up in the Gulag). Stalin did the same with the few outstanding Russian cultural figures who fled Russia during the civil war, inviting them to return to the USSR. Among them were the writers Alexei Tolstoy, Alexander Kuprin, and Marina Tsvetayeva; the composer Sergei Prokofiev; and the singer Alexander Vertinsky. Some of them, like Tolstoy, were able to adjust to the Soviet reality and were even treated as privileged people in exchange for their ideological subservience, while others perished, including Tsvetayeva, who refused to accept the system.

At the same time, in the early 1930s, the Kremlin, having included Russian nationalism in its ideology, "forgave" several intellectuals who were incarcerated or exiled in the 1920s and early 1930 as members of the so-called academic affairs group in a sort of proactive action. Among them were the historians Robert Vipper, Yuri Gotie (Gautier), Evgeny Tarle, Sergei Platonov, and Nikolay Likhachev, all of whom, after their release, arduously served the regime, as if trying to show Stalin that their past ordeals could not influence their total loyalty to the regime. Generals Konstantin Rokosovsky and Alexander Gorbatov, who were arrested in the late 1930s, followed suit, and after being released from the Gulag in 1940, they faithfully served Stalin, their tormentor, both during and after the war. Some exceptions were even made for former members of the non-Bolshevik socialist parties, who, being forgiven, worked for Stalin with particular ardor. Among them were Andrei Vyshynsky, former Menshevik, who was the attorney general at the show trials in Moscow, and Ivan Maysky, also a Menshevik, who was Stalin's faithful diplomat. However, all these cases were exceptions to the generally vindictive and uncompromising Soviet policies toward enemies.

The Impact of Stalin's Repressions on the Next Generations of Russians

After Stalin's death, the scale of the repressions was drastically curtailed. With the mass rehabilitation of many hundreds of thousands of people from the Gulag in 1953–7, repressions of Stalin's scale were no longer a part of the arsenal of the Soviet state. The new Soviet regimes understood that Stalin, in order to keep power, resorted to "overkill" and that the same goals could be reached while repressing many fewer people. Of course, the mass terror brought forth by Stalin made such a deep impression on the minds of the Russian people – the stories of the terrible past were transferred from one generation to the next – that post-Stalin regimes could benefit from the fear instilled by Stalin without applying his methods. Khrushchev allowed the media to talk about Stalin's repressions (he permitted the publication of Solzhenitsyn's *One Day in the*

Life of Ivan Denisovich in 1962), but Brezhnev ordered silence about the mass terror.[29] However, Khrushchev and Brezhnev clearly assumed that the memory of Stalin's repressions was enough to protect their order with fewer arrests.

Fifty years after Stalin's death, in post-Communist society, Putin could also exploit the deep-rooted dread of mass repressions in the Russian psyche. His ideological policy was quite cunning on this issue. Putin's administration allowed, for instance, movies about the Soviet past, with vivid pictures of Stalin's terror (see the semidocumentary movies that were shown on TV in 2011, about Yekaterina Furtseva, a leading party apparatchik in Stalin's time, or about Marshal Georgy Zhukov) without directly condemning Stalin. In this way, Putin's regime, even with his authoritarian elements and some casual repressions, offered itself as a good alternative to Stalin, while still alluding to the possibility of mass repressions, carried out either by Putin's regime out of necessity or by those extremist political forces that could replace it.

Repressions in the Post-Stalin Era

After 1953, the repressions were drastically curtailed. In fact, the number of people sentenced for anti-Soviet acts had systematically declined from 935 a year in 1956–60 to 108 in 1981–5.[30] The state's repressive machine had only targeted people who were involved in outright anti-Soviet acts. The individual critiques of the regime that had served as the basis for an arrest in the past were still documented by the KGB, but without major reprisals. The private life of the citizenry was respected by the authorities and nobody was persecuted for ideas expressed inside the family.

At the same time, the post-Stalin regime continued to persecute harshly all those who openly challenged the regime. No demonstration against the government was permitted, and eight (some authors allege eight participants) daring people who went to Red Square to protest the Soviet invasion in Czechoslovakia on August 25, 1968, were arrested the moment they unfurled their banners. All of them were sentenced to long years of prison (compare this with the anti-Putin rallies that consisted of many thousands of participants in 2011–12!). The authorities mercilessly persecuted the members of the new nonofficial organizations created in 1969–70 for the defense of human rights. Among those persecuted were the Moscow Helsinki group, as well those

[29] A remarkable case: Having allowed the restoration of the names of politicians and intellectuals who had been murdered by Stalin's firing squads, Brezhnev's regime did not permit any discussion of the circumstances of their deaths. Their biographies in the official *Encyclopedic Dictionary* ended in a Kafkaesque manner. For example, the article on Mikhail Tukhachevsky, a leading military strategist, said only that he died in 1937; there was not one word about his execution at Stalin's order. The articles about certain murdered writers, such as Osip Mandelshtam, and scientists such as Nikolai Vavilov, ended in the same way. (See Vladimir Shlapentokh, "Name dropping, Russian style," *International Herald Tribune*, July 10, 2007.)

[30] *Istoriia Rossii 1945–2008*, www.prosv.ru/Attachment.aspx?Id=6459, accessed April 20, 2012.

engaged in samizdat activity, particularly the publication of the *Chronicle of Current Events*, as well as those who published *Pamiat'* (Memory), a collection of articles on historical issues that had been silenced by official propaganda; the magazine *Poiski* (Search); and other publications.

The trial of the writers Andrey Sinyavsky and Yuli Daniel in 1966; the trial of the organizers of samizdat Yurii Galanskov, Alexander Ginzburg, and Vera Lashkova in 1968; and the exiles of Solzhenitsyn in 1974 and Andrey Sakharov in 1979 were signals to enemies of the regime of the Kremlin's determination to apply harsh measures to everybody involved in antistate activity, even if these measures looked quite mild in comparison with those of Stalin's times, with respect to Solzhenitsyn and Sakharov.[31] Many people who signed protest letters against the restoration of Stalinism, the invasion of Czechoslovakia, and the trials of the dissidents in 1967–78 were punished in various ways. However, these punishments did not include arrests, and, in most cases, the protesters were not even fired from their jobs. Unlike Stalin's time, when all of them would have been treated "equally," this time the authorities not only limited the number of arrests but also meted out punishments according to the signatories' importance to the military machine. Scholars in mathematics or physics, for instance, were not as severely punished as those in the fields of the humanities.[32]

The Brezhnev regime, in order to diminish the number of arrests and trials related to dissidents (note that it also denied the existence of political prisoners in the USSR, just as Putin would later do), created an innovative repressive mechanism: sending critics of the regime to psychiatric hospitals. This method was used against General Pyotr Grigorenko, writer Vladimir Bukovsky, the poet Alexander Yesenin-Volpin, and several others.[33] Of the seventy-one persons arrested for political actions, twenty-four were sent to psychiatric facilities. Of course, these actions were terrible for the victims, but still, comparatively, their fate was much better than that of those who were destroyed by Stalin's juggernaut.[34]

At the same time, Brezhnev's regime wanted to decrease the number of arrests of its real foes, using "preventive medicine" for this purpose. The KGB

[31] It was a crucial moment in 1974, when the Politburo was making a decision about the repression of Solzhenitsyn – whether to send him to the West or the East (Siberia). The decision to send the writer to Western Europe was a victory of the trend of softening repressions.

[32] Such was the practice in the Academgorodok, where, in 1968, thirty scholars signed protest letters against the trial of Alexander Ginzburg and his comrades. The mathematicians and physicists were reprimanded but not fired, whereas the humanitarians lost their jobs.

[33] Regarding the use of psychiatric hospitals for political repression see Sidney Bloch and Peter Reddaway, *Psychiatric Terror* (New York: Basic Books 1977); Yevgenia Albats, *KGB: State within a State* (London: IB Taurus, 1995); Paul Wanke, *Russian/Soviet Military Psychiatry, 1904–1945* (New York: Rutledge, 2005).

[34] V. Bredikhin (ed.) *Lubianka – Staraia ploschad, Sekretnye dokumenty TsK KPSS i KGB o repressiakh 1937–1990 gg. v SSR* (Posev, 2005), available at http://www.sps.ru/?id=213821, accessed April 20, 2012.

called people who were involved in some anti-Soviet activity into its offices and warned them about the consequences of continuing their activities. In many cases, this measure was enough to stop the undesirable behavior. In pursuing the course of softening repressions, the regime committed an unprecedented act; it released Pyotr Yakir and Viktor Krasin from prison in 1973, after they recanted their anti-Soviet behavior.

Repressions in Putin's Era

With his reduced power as the head of a quasi-feudal monarchy, Putin was obliged to curb repressions against his enemies from the very beginning of his rule, even as he turned to a more authoritarian style in comparison to that of Yeltsin. The necessity of keeping the country open to the world, demanded by big corporations and by Putin's ruling elite (who kept their fortunes in the West), also played an important role in restraining the use of coercive methods in dealing with enemies. And, of course, Putin's regime, which claimed to share Western democratic values (the Soviet regimes never made such a claim), had to recognize the existence of the opposition in society. But at the same time, with big money at his disposal and corporations under his direct control, Putin had a more diversified arsenal for dealing with his enemies. Putin's numerous means of carrying out coercive actions against those whom he did not like were possible because of a lack of respect for law in the country and in the law enforcement agencies. The same lack of respect for their own laws and the availability of many means provided by private business allowed Putin's regime to rig elections, local and national.[35]

Just as the post-Stalin leaders realized that they could achieve the same goal as Stalin did through his mass repressions while radically reducing their scope, so Putin's administration reached the conclusion that big money allowed them to co-opt and absorb dissent without jeopardizing the survival of the regime. Another radical change in Putin's dealing with enemies, the readiness to compromise, had been anathema to other post-Stalin regimes.

Repressions of the Old Style

Even with all these changes, Putin's regime did not completely abandon the Soviet techniques for fighting its enemies. It incarcerated Mikhail Khodorkovsky, a businessman who, because of his wealth, was a threat to the regime. It forced two other oligarchs who were also involved in political activity, Boris Berezovsky and Vladimir Gusinky, to leave the country. Several other politicians, among them Eduard Limonov, spent several years in prison.

[35] Regarding the rigging of the parliamentary election in 2011 and the presidential election in 2012 see Olga Matiukhina, "Glava Izbirkoma: Kak byli sfal'sifitsirovany dumskie vybory," *Moskovskii Komsomolets*, February 9, 2012.

As in the past, the regime used police to prevent demonstrations and meetings, regularly arresting participants, quite often brutally. During the presidential campaign of 2011–12, the number of arrests initially reached several hundred people, even if the authorities showed a level of tolerance that would have been unbelievable in Soviet and post-Soviet/pre-Putin times. The harassment of protesters was incomparably milder and the sentences were much softer. Putin's regime also showed restraint in dealing with protests with ethnic overtones, as during the Manezh Square (Moscow) demonstration of Russian nationalists in December 2010, or the Kondopoga ethnic conflict between Russians and Chechens in 2006. The treatment of political prisoners like Khodorkovsky was also unusual from the Soviet perspective. In Soviet prisons, even in least restrictive, relatively liberal times of the Brezhnev regime, the prisoner was extremely limited in his communications, even with relatives, as Bukovsky scrupulously described in his famous book about his life in the Soviet prison.[36] Meanwhile, Mikhail Khodorkovsky, the most well-known political prisoner in Russia, could regularly publish his articles not only in Russian newspapers but also in the foreign press.[37] Of course, in no way should this fact lead us to forget that he had already spent eight years in prison (by 2012) and had been exposed to all the harshness of life there, including the risk of being killed or mutilated.[38]

Decentralization of Repressions, the Role of Proxies, and the Role of Fear

The repressive techniques of Putin's regime were much more flexible than those used by his predecessors. This is a direct result of the feudal character of society. In all Soviet regimes, for instance, each act of incarceration of political figures was strongly centralized, directly or indirectly. Even recruiting an informer was a process strongly controlled by several levels of the KGB hierarchy. The execution of a political enemy outside the judicial system was incomprehensible, even during Stalin's reign. During Khrushchev's and Brezhnev's times, the KGB was almost perfect in its observation of laws.[39]

But a new element of violence and repression began to emerge as early as the 1990s – the extrajudicial removal of journalists and political and business foes, usually with the involvement of local and regional – rather than federal – law enforcement elements. In other words, the murders and attacks

[36] See Vladimir Bukovsky, *I vozvraschaetsia veter* (Moscow: Novoe Izdatelstvo, 2007).

[37] See, for instance, Mikhail Khodorkovsky, "Notes from behind the fence," *New York Times*, March 30, 2012.

[38] "V krasnokamenskoi kolonii soversheno napadenie na Khodorkovskogo," *Grani.ru*, April 15, 2006, http://grani.ru/Society/Law/m.104524.html, accessed April 20, 2012.

[39] For an expert on these matters, such as the famous dissident and prisoner Vladimir Bukovsky, see Bukovsky, *I vozvraschaetsia veter.*

on journalists, which began under the Yeltsin administration, were caused as much by corruption and business interests as they were by politics. In Yeltsin's and Putin's feudal times, local authorities and oligarchs had the power to use repression, including murder, against their opponents. The case of the murder of a journalist, Larisa Yudina, in Kalmykia in 1998, which was widely discussed in the media, is only one of the numerous examples of the participation of the local authorities in crimes of this sort.[40] The murder of journalists and businessmen in the region would go on to become a fixture under Putin.

The effect of these extrajudicial retributions in the Putin era is in itself an interesting phenomenon: crimes, often motivated by politics as well as by corruption and business interests, turned into a form of repression through the fear that they evoked in society. Given the feudal and fragmented nature of Putin's regime, the attacks were not always direct political orders handed down from the top. No doubt many repressive actions were perpetrated by subordinates who knew well what would be pleasing to the leadership of the country and who knew how they could earn points for promotion without demanding even an oral writ of the superior, a normal practice in any hierarchical organization.

However, given that investigative bodies failed in almost all cases of murder to discover the sponsors, the Russian leadership became implicitly responsible for the crimes.

By several accounts, Pavel Grachev, as minister of defense, prompted the murder of a Moscow journalist, Dmitry Kholodov, a critic of corruption in the army, in 1994 by his subordinates when he had publicly called Kholodov an "inside enemy" and put him on a blacklist of journalists. The murder of the opposition journalist Anna Politkovskaya in 2006 is widely believed to have originated within the security structures around the Chechen leader Ramzan Kadyrov, an ostensible protégé of Putin's himself, who has been linked to other murders. While Politkovskaya's attackers have been tried, the organizers have not been found. The attack on the journalist Oleg Kashin (which he survived) and the brutal attack on the lesser known local journalist Mikhail Beketov (which left him disabled and, indirectly, led to his death in April 2013) in 2010 are thought to be the work of local structures, with the involvement, in Kashin's case, of activists in pro-Kremlin youth groups. Regardless of their origin, the effect is the same: not having been adequately investigated, these murders and attacks on critics of local and federal government are perceived as repressions of the state against its critics.

Even if the number of people murdered during Putin's time was small by Soviet standards, it was still enough to instill fear among the intellectual community. Whereas the fear of arrest was not so pervasive as in Soviet times, the

[40] "Ubiistvo Larisy Yudinoi do sikh por ne rassledovano," November 22, 2010, http://www.yabloko.ru/news/2010/10/22, accessed May 5, 2012.

fear of mutilation, or even being murdered in the streets or in the entryway of your house – a fear unknown in Soviet times, even Stalin's – was quite potent for Russian activists in Putin's time. In any case, each challenge to the regime by an outstanding journalist or politician not only generated great respect from the general public for his or her courage, but also produced apprehension about his or her security. When people such as Alexei Navalny or Sergei Udaltsov became visible in the protest actions of 2011–12, the liberal media were full of concerns about their physical safety.[41]

Precision Repressions as a Response to the Protests of 2011–2012

As we have already noted, the fact that Putin's government allowed and authorized the protest rallies that broke out in December 2011 against the rigging of parliamentary elections was virtually unprecedented in Russian history.

Yet these protests would be met with a form of repression. After the May 6 protest rally on Moscow's Bolotnaya Square turned violent (with some evidence suggesting the police themselves provoked the violence), the government unleashed a crackdown. In June, dozens of raids against opposition activists would take place. That summer, state television aired a documentary that uncovered a plot to stage an uprising with foreign funds, implicating the leader of the left-wing Left Front movement Sergei Udaltsov and several other activists. While the most popular protest leader, Alexei Navalny, would not be implicated in political accusations, he would be charged instead with embezzlement. His case went to trial in the spring of 2013, and he faced up to ten years in prison. By spring 2013, a total of twenty-seven people had been arrested for their involvement in that rally.

These were far from the mass protests of Soviet times. Their sporadic and haphazard nature led many observers to call them "precision" repressions, which, through fear, largely achieved a better effect than mass repressions in quelling protest sentiment. One protest leader, the State Duma deputy Ilya Ponomarev, denied that these were even repressions in a conversation with one of the authors, calling them instead "petty harassment."

In a climate conducive to creating and maintaining contempt for the law among officials, Putin and his administration had dozens of ways of eliminating opponents, most of which were inconceivable in Soviet times. A targeted person could be murdered by hired thugs, or inmates in prison, or criminals released from prison for this purpose, and so on.[42] Ramzan Kadyrov, the president of Chechnya, played a special role in this decentralized system of murder. By being linked to murders in places as far away as Austria, Dubai and Qatar,

[41] "Udaltsovu, Navalnomu i Nemtsovu vmeniat nepovinovenie politsii," *Gazeta.ru*, May 6, 2012, http://www.gazeta.ru/politics/news/2012/05/06/n_2330389.shtml, accessed May 6, 2012.

[42] See Andrey Illarionov, "Dekabr'skie tezisy dlia grazhdan Rossii," *Grani.ru*, December 27, 2011, http://grani.ru/blogs/free/entries/194518.html, accessed May 5, 2012.

Kadyrov was able to spread the fear of himself not only to Moscow and other areas in Russia[43] but also abroad.[44]

Buying the Masses

The use of money and compromise in dealing with the discounted masses was definitely Putin's innovation. The Russian leaders always brutally crushed dissenting subjects. It is enough to remember the shooting of the crowd in front of the Winter Palace on January 9, 1905 (the notorious "Bloody Sunday"), and the lethal crackdown on the protests of Novocherkassk workers in 1962 by Khrushchev's regime. Putin changed this standard in a radical way.

The first tests of his new policy were the disturbances that emerged when Putin's government declared its intention to replace benefits-in-kind with money as compensation in 2005. This idea sparked protest demonstrations of pensioners in several cities. No arrests were made and the government retreated from its initial plans almost immediately, undertaking several measures to restore the previous benefits in one form or another.[45]

The second test occurred during the developments in Pikalevo (a town located two hundred kilometers from St. Petersburg) and Mezhdurechensk (the center of Kuzbass, the coal mine basin in Siberia), where the workers went on strike, staged mass protests, and even cut off traffic on the major highways. Instead of a confrontation, Putin again chose the tactics of accommodation and retreated before the demands of the protesters, in high contrast to Soviet reactions to similar events. (The developments in Pikalevo and Mezhdurechensk are discussed in a separate chapter.)

Buying Intellectuals

Corrupting the intellectuals who were either already engaged in some sort of oppositional activity or had the potential to be was not, of course, Putin's invention. While Stalin did not use these tactics – he only lavished benefits on those who already served him, like the writers Konstantin Simonov and Alexei Tolstoy – leaders after Stalin started to do it, although in a very limited way.[46] Putin caused a sort of revolution in the regime for dealing with intellectuals. He hired intellectuals, who could be in the camp of his critics and ready to support

[43] During a radio program on October 31, 2010, the journalist Leonid Radzikhovsky refused to discuss the politics of Ramzan Kadyrov, the Chechen leader of Putin's vassals, openly, explicitly saying that he could lose his life if he chose to discuss the matter. See the radio program *Osoboe mnenie,* October 31, 2010.

[44] "Avstriisky sud: Verdict za ubiistvo byvshego okhrannika Kadyrova," *Golos Ameriki,* June 2, 2011, http://www.voanews.com/russian/news/Austria-Chechnya-2011-06-02-123004053.html, accessed May 5, 2012.

[45] About the protest actions see "Rossiiane protiv zameny l'got," *Gazeta.ru,* July 2, 2004, http://www.gazeta.ru/2004/07/02/box_4136.shtml, accessed May 1, 2012.

[46] It is discussed in Evgenii Evtushenko, *Volchii passport* (Moscow: Vagrius, 1998).

the regime, with access to the most lucrative positions on television and in the movie industry. Lilia Shevtsova, a prominent political scientist, described how the fear of losing their comfortable lives turned intellectuals into obedient myrmidons of the regime and explained the various theories they used to rationalize their behavior.[47]

Big money made it possible for Putin's regime to avert, if only partially and temporarily, the danger of opposition from the creative intelligentsia. In early 2008, among the 142 people whom Russians identified in a survey as members of the elite, the creative intelligentsia was represented by 76 individuals. Practically all of them are materially successful people. However, only 7 of them refused to take part in actions that favored their current regime, and only the actor Oleg Basilashvili participated in opposition activities.

The efficacy of corrupting intellectuals turned out to be quite successful, even if it was unable to reach everybody in the intelligenstia. On one side, among the five hundred people whom Putin chose as his representatives in his presidential campaign were many dozens of prominent intellectuals who did not hide: orchestra directors like Valery Gergiev, theater directors like Oleg Tabakov, actresses like Chulpan Khamatova, and others. Despite contempt from the intelligentsia, they joined Putin's propaganda machine largely because the presidential administration supported their activity with big money. On another side, following the oppositional traditions of the Russian intelligentsia, several of its members, such as the writers Boris Akunin and Dmitry Bykov, the TV journalist Parfenov, and a few others, headed the protest movement against the rigged parliamentary and presidential elections. Putin was able to split the intelligentsia; with his money and power, he prevented the flight of most of the intellectuals into the camp of the opposition.

Conclusion

All of the authoritarian regimes discussed in this book, Soviet and post-Soviet, have common features in the treatment of their enemies, real or imaginary, in addition to their many differences. While the Soviet regimes functioned in predominately pure authoritarian societies – which changed from Stalin to post-Stalin times – the authoritarian regime in post-Soviet Russia was under the strong impact of the feudal elements of a new society and, in particular, of big money.

Repressive techniques were used very differently by each of the regimes. There was an evolution from harshness and blind terror, to repressions only against the opponents of the regimes, to the relatively rare use of repressions perpetrated against select enemies. The regimes also differed very much in their attitudes toward several elements in their policies toward enemies. During Putin's regime, the invented enemies, who were so important in Stalin's time

47 Lilia Shevtsova, "Pro sloiki," *Novaya Gazeta*, January 12, 2011.

but disappeared afterward, and the potential enemies, who continued to play an important role in Brezhnev's time, almost faded away. We also observed the softening of repressions, together with a dramatic jump from the rejection of compromise with enemies to the acceptance of this idea after 1991. Putin's regime resorted to money as a way to solve conflicts with workers and to neutralize the intelligentsia as no regime had in the past. Without a doubt, feudal elements in society, the large role of big fortunes, and, especially, the strong material interests that the ruling elite had in keeping the façade of democracy and maintaining tolerable relations with the West accounted for the dramatic decline of enemies in the official ideology of Putin's regime.

5

Political Police Before and After

For many, Russians and foreigners alike, Russia's KGB was the major symbol of totalitarianism, so it is not surprising that the 1991 destruction of the monument to Felix Dzerzhinsky, the founder of the Soviet political police, was interpreted as a sign of the end of the Communist regime for Russians and for the whole world.

The KGB's major goal in society was to inspire fear, and to prevent and fight any form of resistance to the existing regime. The people's fear of the KGB reached its peak during Stalin's reign, then declined significantly after 1953, although it remained a powerful building block of Soviet society even in post-Stalin times. Until 1991, there were KGB departments in every office, factory, college, and theater, in addition to their place in every army and police unit. Furthermore, the vast network of KGB informers guaranteed that every adult was under the watch of the political police, directly or indirectly.[1]

The KGB and related agencies (the Ministry of Internal Affairs, among others) prevented the creation of any organization outside their system. This pervasive presence, together with the aforementioned network of informers, enabled the agencies to blanket every unit of society. Among their recruited informers were several outstanding members of the intellectual community. The KGB and its predecessors supervised all areas of the Soviet population, but particularly the intelligentsia.

The status of the KGB in post-Stalin Soviet society was quite ambivalent. On one hand, it was hated by most of the intelligentsia, and as soon as Perestroika permitted it, a torrent of books was unleashed, like Anatoly Rybakov's novel *Children of the Arbat,* and movies like Tengis Abuladze's *Repentance*, which denounced the KGB, characterizing it as an almost criminal organization. On

[1] See Shlapentokh and Shiraev, *Fears in Post-Communist Society*. For the role of informers in Soviet society, see Yuri Shchekochikhin, *Raby KGB: Religia predatelstva* (1999).

the other hand, among ordinary people whose patriotic feelings were nurtured by official ideology, the KGB carried great prestige as an organization that defended the country against its internal and external enemies. A cult of secrecy, which the KGB cultivated, together with a fear of spies and foreigners, helped the KGB sustain its image as the defender of the motherland.

The phenomenal success of detective movies about Soviet KGB agents in Nazi Germany is only one piece of evidence of the respect the Soviet masses held for this institution. That Vladimir Putin, the son of ordinary workers, applied to serve in the KGB when he was in the ninth grade is further evidence of the KGB's prestige.[2]

There was also a general consensus in society (including among dissidents) that the KGB was the least corrupt institution.[3] One rarely heard rumors about KGB officers taking bribes. The high prestige of the KGB as a noncorrupt organization was enhanced by the integrity of its longest acting chief, Yury Andropov. In the early 1980s, many experts both inside and outside Russia were skeptical of whether or not a former KGB chief could ascend to the position of general secretary, suspecting it could produce severe discontent among the people. However, his appointment actually had the opposite effect. Andropov's arrival in the Kremlin was greeted positively by the masses, who were very critical of bureaucracy.[4] After his death, and following the events of 1991, Andropov's reputation as an uncorrupt leader flourished.[5]

The collapse of the Soviet system looked as if it had delivered a mortal blow to the KGB. In 1991, the new chairman of the KGB, Vadim Bakatin (1991–2), behaved as if he indeed wanted to destroy the institution.[6] Vladimir Bukovsky, a famous dissident and known hater of the KGB, gained Bakatin's permission to access the archives of the KGB – unheard-of at any time since the creation of the Cheka.

The KGB in Transition

The 1990s were quite a painful period for the officers of the KGB, who went from being the most feared and prestigious government officials to being almost despised in the country. The nadir in the life of the KGB was the aforementioned

[2] Richard Sakwa, *Putin: Russia's Choice*.

[3] See, for instance, the memoirs of General Petro Grigorenko, *Grigorenko: Memoirs*; Lev Kopelev, *Ease My Sorrows: A Memoir*; or Vladimir Bykovsky, *I vozvraschaetsia veter*.

[4] Zhores Medvedev, *Andropov* (Oxford: Basil Blackwell, 1983).

[5] According to various surveys conducted after the fall of the USSR, Andropov turned out to be one of the most popular Russian leaders in Soviet history. In 1996, sixteen hundred Russians were asked to name leaders of the past or present who ensured the most order in society. Nineteen percent of the respondents chose Andropov; 12 percent, Stalin; 11 percent, Brezhnev; 6 percent, both Lenin and Yeltsin; 3 percent, Khrushchev; and 2 percent, Gorbachev (*Moskovskie Novosti*, April 27, 1997).

[6] Vadim Bakatin, *Izbavlenie ot KGB* (Moscow: Novosti, 1992).

event in August 22, 1991, when the crowd destroyed the monument honoring Dzerzhinsky, located in the front of the major KGB building on the square with the same name. When this occurred, people in the vicinity saw the faces of KGB officers glued to their windows, watching, with horror and disbelief, as people who had trembled at the mere mention of the word "KGB" the day before were demolishing the holy place dedicated to their god. The people inside the building were not sure whether the same crowd that leveled the sacred statue would then storm the KGB headquarters.

It seemed that the fate of the KGB officials would be the same as that of the army officers in 1958, when Khrushchev decided to reduce the army; this created a climate in which former officers, without any skills for civic life, were glad to find any job.[7] However, the fate of the entire KGB community – which encompassed many agencies – was to be different (in this text, the term "FSB," which was the agency officially created in 1995, will usually refer to the security community in general; we will also, as Russian authors and as FSB officers do, use the term "Chekists," derived from the word *Cheka*, the first organization of the Soviet political police, as a denomination for people who work in the security community).

The FSB in the New Feudal-Authoritarian Society

There were two major factors that ultimately created a different future for KGB officers than the one that was experienced by army officers in 1958.

First, the new Yeltsin-led leadership began working to perpetuate its power by nondemocratic means almost immediately, using old KGB techniques and coercive methods against political opponents. Second, the emergence of a feudal society with a weak central administration and powerful big businesses created a new demand for people with experience in the KGB who could protect the security and wealth of the new feudal actors. The emergence of great fortunes waiting to be amassed changed the mentality of the people in the political police, who suddenly had unprecedented opportunities for enriching themselves and living a good life; corruption became "normal" business for the FSB's generals and officers.

The Russian leadership only appeared to be hostile to the KGB for a few years (1989–91). By 1992, the attitude of the new Russian president, Boris Yeltsin (who rose to power as the champion of democracy), began to change toward the FSB. By that time, Yeltsin had evidently chosen a path designed to

[7] Kirill Kabanov, a former KGB officer who served in the organization's anticontraband department between 1991 and 1994, vividly recalls the sense of dejection that officers around him were feeling: "The special services were in the most dire position. Earning $50 a month they were pushed into business. They were provoked into certain hidden relations. Ideologically, a majority of the people who came over from the KGB felt disadvantaged, felt a sense of betrayal. First their colleagues abroad were betrayed. Then this humiliation of Lubyanka under siege – all this forms complexes" (from interview with Anna Arutunyan).

keep him in power as long as possible; he was prepared to ignore all democratic procedures, if necessary. He was ready to dismantle the parliament as early as 1992. In March 1993, when the Russian parliament was only inches away from impeaching him as president, Yeltsin ordered his retinue to prepare for the arrest of all deputies in the event of impeachment. Furthermore, he had plans to use chemical gas in order to "smoke" the deputies from the building. In the fall of 1993, he used violent means to eliminate the State Duma and its members from political life.[8]

Almost immediately upon his gaining the presidency, Yeltsin surrounded himself not only with liberals like Yegor Gaidar and Anatoly Chubais, but also with such people as the former KGB officer Alexander Korzhakov, who became Yeltsin's confidant and whom Yeltsin elevated to the rank of general. In his biography, Korzhakov contended that he, along with the FSB director Mikhail Barsukov, "governed the country for three years" (1993–6). This notion has been strongly supported by several other sources.[9]

After Yeltsin's resignation, the differences between the FSB and the KGB continued to diminish. The seemingly casual event when Yeltsin chose a KGB agent as his heir (he also considered selecting a person with a non-KGB or military background like Boris Nemtsov, Evgeny Primakov, Sergei Stepashin, or Viktor Chernomyrdin) had an enormous effect on the role of the FSB in society.

The role of the FSB is anything but well documented in the origin and maintenance of Putin's rule. There are suspicions, strongly denied by the Kremlin, that the FSB was behind the deadly explosions of several residential buildings in Moscow in 1999. These theories argue that the FSB blew up the buildings in order to blame the acts on the Chechens and justify a new war against Chechnya, which, on the eve of the presidential election, would make it easier for Putin to appear as the country's savior. Many people in Russia believed that the political police were also behind the murder of various oppositionist politicians and journalists in the first decade of the twenty-first century, as well as in the 1990s.[10] Many Russians consider the publications in the media of the transcripts of the conversations between oppositionist political figures, as well as the videos of the intimate life of oppositional figures, to have been facilitated by the FSB. Hacker attacks on the Web sites of media outlets that were critical of Putin, such as *Ekho Moskvy* and *Novaya Gazeta*, are also attributed to the FSB.

Many people even believe that the FSB currently plays an even greater role in Russia than the KGB did in the Soviet Union. However, this conclusion is

[8] Sergei Khrushshev, *Khrushchev on Khrushchev: An Inside Account of the Man and His Era* (Boston: Little, Brown, 1990); Victor Grishin, *Ot Khruscheva do Gorbacheva* (Moscow: Aspol, 1996), p. 28.

[9] Alexander Korzhakov, *Boris Yeltsin: Ot rasveta do zakata* (Moscow: Interbuk, 1997).

[10] Gessen, *Man without a Face.*

wrong, even if its advocates point, with reason, to the expansion of the FSB under Putin's watch.

When Were the Political Police More Influential, Now or in the Past?

Indeed, the appointment of Vladimir Putin, a KGB agent, as the president of the country was a sign for Russians that Putin would increase the power of his KGB colleagues. It is a regular occurrence in society, particularly in authoritarian societies, that a new leader takes those whom he can trust to the highest echelons of power. These are usually people he has worked with in the past. The crueler the regime is and the more victims the regime has produced, the more important for the leader to stay in power in order to avoid revenge by his rivals or being tried (if a democratic regime were to be installed); the more important it is for the leader to trust in the people who run the political police, army, and main regions of the country. (This phenomenon is well known to researchers of criminal structures, where the bosses' trust in members of their gangs is of pivotal importance.)

Stalin installed several people from Georgia in the security service, such as Beria, Kobulov, Dekanosov, and Tsanava (he spoke in Georgian with them). Khrushchev took many people from the Ukraine, where he had worked in the past, to the highest positions in the country; Brezhnev added people from Moldova and Dnepropetrovsk; and Yeltsin had his people from Sverdlovsk. However, not even the gloomiest predictions of the liberal analysts in 1999 could foretell what actually happened when Putin found himself in the Kremlin.

In fact, Putin filled many of the leading positions in the country with KGB people, or at least army generals. By 2006, according to the prominent sociologist Olga Kryshtanovskaya, some 26 percent of state officials had a military background (of those, 46 percent were from the FSB). Other authors contended that by 2010, 77 percent of those who held the highest state positions had a KGB background (26 percent spoke of their background openly in their official biographies; 51 percent preferred not to publicize their past).[11]

Former KGB fellows permeate all echelons of power.[12] Nikolai Patrushov, the FSB director under Putin, and Sergei Ivanov, the deputy premier minister and head of Putin's presidential administration, were both KGB generals. Sergei Naryshkin, who served as both the head of the presidential administration and the speaker of the State Duma, also has deep roots in the KGB. The Interior Ministry was headed from 2003 to 2011 by the former KGB general Rashid Nurgaliyev. Sergei Chemezov, who was appointed as the head of Rostechnologies (an umbrella agency that also oversees arms trading), and Igor

[11] Olga Kryshtanovskaya, *Interview*, radio program *Ekho Moskvy*, February 4, 2007, http://echo.msk.ru/programs/albac/49320, accessed March 20, 2012.

[12] Yury Fel'shtinsky and Vladimir Pribylovsky, *Korporatsiia. Rossiia I KGB vo vremena prezidenta Putina* (Moscow: TERRA, 2010).

Sechin, Putin's right-hand man, are widely believed to have been in the KGB. Several more of Putin's dignitaries, such as Mikhail Fradkov and Viktor Ivanov, were also KGB people.

Some authors suggest – not without reason, considering the data cited previously – that the spread of political police among the commanding structures of society was never as extensive in Russian history as under Putin.[13]

Indeed, if we are speaking about the expanse of the political police cadres (but not about the role of the political police), we can say that never in Soviet history, even in the darkest years of terror, were there as many former KGB people at the highest levels of bureaucracy as there have come to be under Putin. In Soviet times, none of the KGB people (except for the chairman of the KGB, who could be a member of the Politburo) could hope to have a higher position than being a member of the bureau of the party regional committee or a member of the Central Committee. None of them was ever appointed as minister or as the first party secretary of a region (although the opposite movement was known: Semyon Ignatyev, for instance, was the Bashkir party secretary before being appointed as the minister of the KGB in 1951 by Stalin). But even more important is the fact that the KGB people were never able to make independent political decisions in the country,[14] contrary to the contentions of various authors who have strongly overestimated the political role of the political police in Soviet society.[15]

[13] See Andrei Soldatov and Irina Borogan, *Novoe dvorianstvo: Ocherki istorii FSB* (Moscow: United Press, 2011).

[14] The published data (1990–3) showed that in the midst of mass terror in 1937, the NKVD required the Kremlin's approval for any action. For more on this issue, see Natalia Gevorkian, "Vstrechnye plany po unichtozheniu sobstvennogo naroda," *Moskovskie Novosti,* June 21, 1992. Forty years later, when Andropov was the chairman of the KGB, he was as obedient to Leonid Brezhnev as Yezhov had been to Stalin. Even in his last years, when Brezhnev was practically on his deathbed, Andropov did not act on his own initiative. Brezhnev, for instance, forbade Andropov to report the corrupt activities of the Ministry of Internal Affairs and its head, Nikolai Shchelokov, who was Brezhnev's pet (see *Komsomolskaya Pravda* November 29, 1991).

[15] Vladimir Bukovsky, a famous dissident, was one of them. He saw the KGB as a crucial, independent institution that set the course of domestic and foreign policy. In his opinion, Yury Andropov (its director from 1967 to 1982) was the sinister political genius of the Soviet establishment, who was responsible for all major developments in the country and many political events outside it (including the attempt to murder the pope). Bukovsky's theory about the origins of Perestroika showed how he exaggerated the position of the KGB in Soviet society. According to the author, the whole project of Perestroika was contrived by Andropov in the late 1970s, and Gorbachev was chosen as the best candidate for its realization; see Bukovsky, *Judgment a Moscou*, pp. 484, 487. In his eyes, Perestroika was designed by the KGB in order to prevent Soviet Communism from crumbling under the growing pressure of the discontented population, and to save the regime and superficially embellish the "Soviet concentration camp" à la Potemkin (Bukovsky, *Judgment a Moscou*, pp. 213, 262, 283, 489). Only a few authors presented a well-balanced view of this organization's place in society (see Anatoly Sudoplatov and Vladimir Malevanny, "Proschanie s epokhoi perevorotov," *Nezavisimaia Gazeta*, August 28, 1998).

Regardless of the level or degree of KGB activity, the general secretary and regional party secretaries maintained tight supervision over the organization and restricted its fellows from playing political roles. Felix Dzerzhisnky, Rudolf Menzhinsky, Genrich Yagoda, Nikolay Yezhov, and Lavrenty Beria, as well as Stalin's last heads of the KGB (Vsevolod Merkulov, Viktor Abakumov, and Semen Ignatiev), never made even the slightest attempt to show their independence by making public political decisions. Stalin regularly dealt death sentences to KGB agents.[16] As a result, Chekists secured a place in the Soviet list of Stalin's victims. In 1951, in connection with "the doctors' plot," Stalin accused the entire KGB of having lost its "vigilance" in fighting enemies. After 1953, the activity of the KGB declined significantly. The agency was supervised not only by the party leader and his aides, but by regional party leaders as well. The KGB's right to monitor high party apparatchiks was prohibited, unless the general secretary gave direct orders to investigate a specific official. Even Yury Andropov, the most powerful post-Stalin head of the KGB (1967–81), was under the full control of the ailing Brezhnev, or those to whom he had delegated his power.[17] Even more important for understanding the KGB's place in Soviet society is another fundamental fact. Only a few of the KGB's high officials, and specifically its chairman, Vladimir Kryuchkov, rather timidly tried to save the USSR while the absolute majority of generals and officers did not go to the defense of the "system," and its patriotic and nationalist ideology, when the KGB accepted its defeat in August 1991. It was indeed a moment of truth.

And if it is wrong to overestimate the role of the KGB in the Soviet times as an independent political actor, it would also be wrong to do the same with respect to the FSB. Whatever data exist showing the degree to which the KGB and FSB officers have penetrated the highest echelons of power under Putin, it would be ludicrous to take seriously the conspiracy theories that suggest that the country is now controlled by "the FSB corporation" which allegedly appointed Putin, directs his behavior, and can replace him at any moment when he ceases to obey.[18] The major evidence offered by the advocates of this theory is Putin's 2000 joke, as he toasted his FSB colleagues on National Chekist Day: "The mission to take power has been successfully accomplished."[19]

In fact, the Russian leadership changed the head of the FSB eight times between 1996 and 2008, without any fuss. Putin replaced everybody in the

[16] Anatoly Sudoplatov, the son of the notorious KGB general Pavel Sudoplatov, wrote an article with Vladimir Malevanny about the decimation of KGB personnel in 1936–7. They wrote: "Stalin delivered a blow against the second pillar of power of the regime (the first being the army) in order to demonstrate that this institution was ultimately only in his hands" (Sudoplatov and Malevanny, "Proschanie s epokhoi perevorotov").

[17] Roi Medvedev, "Vo glave KGB," *Sovetskaia Rossiia*, December 5, 1991; see also the article by Brezhnev's personal doctor, Evgenii Chasov, "Na ego rukakh skonchalas' tselaia epokha," *Komsomol'skaia Pravda*, September 27, 1991.

[18] Felshtinsky and Pribylovsky, *Korporatsiia. Rossiia i KGB*.

[19] See Soldatov and Borogan, *Novoe dvorianstvo*.

highest echelon of power with the swiftness of a juggler. J. Edgar Hoover, as the head of the FBI, seemed to be more entrenched in official power than any chairman of the KGB and the FSB in all their history. Just as the KGB was in the Soviet Union, the FSB is under the control of the Russian political leadership.

Furthermore, despite the presence of the political police in every corner of Russian society, the influence of the FSB on the behavior of the population, as well as its ability to fight foreign agents and its intelligence services in foreign countries, is much weaker than that of the KGB was on the eve of the collapse of the Soviet Union. The main reason for this is the impact of the feudalization of Russia and of big money on FSB activities.

Big Money and Big Property as the Cause of Changes in the FSB

As mentioned previously, the behavior of the officers of the FSB has been strongly influenced by the emergence of possibilities to enrich themselves using all the opportunities provided by the feudalization of society and the weakening of the central administration. Of course, KGB officers received a very decent salary by Soviet standards (close to those of scholars with degrees), and yet, their lifestyle was still very modest. They could only dream of having luxury goods or their own country house. There was only a short period, immediately after the victory in the war and during the occupation of Germany, when Soviet generals, such as Ivan Serov of the KGB or Marshal Georgy Zhukov of the army, took the risk of sending freight trains with seized wealth from occupied Germany to the Soviet Union. While these two gentlemen avoided Stalin's punishment, several generals who followed their example were not so lucky. Currently, the birth of large private property ownership and big fortunes has opened up unbelievable opportunities for the enrichment of FSB people.

The possibility of enriching themselves, and of owning "big property" in Russia or abroad, radically changed the mentality of all of the people in the political police, but first and foremost it changed that of the senior staff.[20] Almost overnight, many former KGB and current FSB generals became the owners of big estates. Some of them acquired residences in Rublevka, a famous enclave for wealthy people that is close to Moscow. Because Putin appointed KGB/FSB people as his representatives on the boards of directors of major companies, they became stockholders, which turned them into members of Russia's wealthy class. Interior Minister Nurgaliev blurted out in 2011 that most of his officers own property abroad.[21] From this statement it can be extrapolated that FSB officers, who hold more advantageous positions than policemen, also grabbed property. A scandal in the "Chekist family" brought the enormous wealth of FSB General Alexander Bulbov to light in 2007. He

[20] See Soldatov and Borogan, *Novoe dvorianstvo.*

[21] Rashid Nurgaliyev, "Chego ya tolko ne nasmotrelasia na pereattestatsii," *Komsomolskaya Pravda*, July 21, 2011.

controlled several large businesses and a great deal of real estate in Moscow and Kaliningrad.[22]

KGB and FSB People at the Service of Big Companies

The big fortunes and big business that emerged in the lawless post-Soviet society changed the nature of the country's political police in the most radical way. First, there was a new demand for security experts almost immediately after the collapse of the Soviet system. Big property was born in Russia when society entered a period of intensive feudalization wherein the state was unable to protect the physical safety of either rich people or their property. This circumstance was immediately used by KGB people, both those who were leaving the institution and those who decided to stay in it. Many of them offered their services to the fledging corporations, whose leaders very much appreciated the professionalism of people from the KGB. Philip Bobkov, the former head of the KGB department responsible for the persecution of dissidents, became the head of security in Media-Most, the company of a new magnate, Vladimir Gusinsky. Bobkov also took with him several other people (some data state up to seventy) who had also participated in fighting dissidents in the 1970–80s.

Mikhail Khodorkovsky invited Major General Alexei Kondaurov to hold the same position at his bank Menatep. When he founded the National Exchange Bank (VTB), Alexander Konyakhin invited Leonid Shebarshin, the former chairman of the KGB, to work in the bank. Another KGB agent, of low rank, Vladimir Putin, was invited by Anatoly Sobchak, mayor of Leningrad, to take responsibility for security and other matters in his office.

The KGB people could offer not only their security expertise (the private security agencies could also have recruited former policemen and army officers) to big business but something even more unique: access to information both damaging to rivals and about governmental headquarters – where these magnates were fighting for privileges from the state. It was the KGB officers who opened the "war of *kompromat*" (the war of damaging information), which started to rage in the early 1990s and continues today. Those with experience in the political police could also offer corporations several other invaluable services, such as the illegal tapping of conversations of people in rival companies or even in government offices, and participation in black raiding, the illegal expropriation of competing firms.[23]

The former FSB captain and anti-corruption advocate Kirill Kabanov told one of the authors about this in an interview. This is the way he described how compromising materials were created and used:

[22] Anatoly Shvedov, "Zheleznyi kriuk raz'est vnutrenniaia rzhavchina," *Izvestiia*, October 11, 2007.

[23] Felshtinsky and Pribylovsky, *Korporatsiia. Rossiia i KGB*.

I invite an agent over and say, Agent Loyal, please write me something about Ivan Ivanovich Ivanov. What do you want me to write? Well, you told me once that he is a traitor; that he is corrupt and a bribe taker. Write that. So he sits down and writes just that: Ivan Ivanovich Ivanov is a bribe taker and has accepted bribes from so and so and so. The material is registered; I go to my boss, get it stamped, and the paper is filed, as either highly classified, classified or whatever.

In the meantime, Ivanov is about to take a government post. And I happen to learn about this before meeting with the agent. Then there is a query about the existence of compromising materials on this man. Is there any information that could form the basis of a denial to work for this man?

There are three variants. The first is that my boss calls me in and says, Ivanov is our guy. Now give me that compromising material on him, and I'll deal with it [meaning that it is hidden or destroyed].The second is that I go to Ivanov and say, here's the deal, now if you want a solution please give me some money. The third variant is that Ivanov is a very decent guy. There's just nothing on him except that he can't hold his tongue. In that case, I sit down and write, "Yes, there is information that could form the basis of a denial."

In the late 1990s the oligarchs, with Yeltsin's tacit permission, practically controlled the FSB. It is well known that some oligarchs, particularly Boris Berezovsky and Roman Abramovich, with the support of other newly rich people concerned about retaining their wealth under the new regime, were instrumental in appointing Putin as the chairman of the KGB and, later, as president of the country.[24] Soon after the death of Berezovsky in March 2013, a leading Russian journalist who had followed Berezovsky closely throughout the 1990s insisted that it was not just money interests that Putin was selected to protect, but chiefly the government's entire domestic and foreign policy.[25] Big money transformed the FSB into a new type of institution, one that was deeply engaged in business and corruption – an unprecedented development in the whole of Russian history.

Big Corporations as Surrogates of the FSB

Not only does the FSB serve the big corporations in various capacities, big business also does useful work for the FSB. Businesses are, of course, the source of fabulous personal income for the FSB's officers and generals, but are also an instrument that can fulfill functions that, in the past, were performed by the KGB or related organizations.

Gazprom, the producer and distributor of gas, is a semistate and semiprivate company; it is under the total control of the Kremlin and was used to destroy

24 "Istoria konflikta Berezovskogo s Putinym," *Gazeta.ru*, August 28, 2001, http://kompromat.flb.ru/material1.phtml?id=262, accessed March 20, 2012.

25 "Alexei Venediktov o Borise Berezovskom." *Ekho Moskvy radio*. March 24, 2013. Transcript available here: http://www.echo.msk.ru/programs/svoi-glaza/1038068-echo/, accessed March 25, 2013.

independent media outlets. In 2001, Gazprom became the owner of the NTV television station, which had previously belonged to Vladimir Gusinsky, who, under the threat of long incarceration, "sold" the station to Gasprom. As soon as the station fell under the control of Gazprom, it became pro-government and its best journalists left. Their attempts to create a new independent TV company, TV-6, failed in 2002, this time because of the intervention of another corporation (Lukoil-Garant). At the same time, various governors actively used local businesses to destroy the independent media in their regions.[26]

Corruption

The Russian political police, that former symbol of incorruptibility, had opened its gates to full-scale corrupt activity by its fellows.

The case of the Three Whale (Tri Kita) furniture company was typical in this respect. In 2000, an investigator from the Attorney General's Office discovered an elaborate scheme for the illegal enrichment of businesspeople and officials from the Customs Service. The customs service reduced the tariff payment for imported foreign furniture to a minimum, while leaving the prices paid by Russian consumers at the old level. With this trick, the furniture sellers received extra profit, which they shared with the highest officials of the FSB and the Customs Service. At the beginning of the investigation, however, the case was closed by the Prosecutor General, the major witness was murdered, and the investigator was sentenced for an abuse of power. In 2007, Putin ordered the investigation reopened. Yet, even though the owners of the firm were sent to jail, no one from the FSB or the Attorney General's Office was implicated in the case.[27]

The most amazing, even if quite explicable, actions of the FSB leadership were that it not only failed to condemn the voluntary cooperation of its people with companies, but actively encouraged it by creating the special institute whereby FSB officers on reserve were attached to individual corporations, a direct push by the FSB people to abuse their status for personal enrichment.[28] During the period of the New Economic Policy (NEP, 1921–1928), the Kremlin, with good reason, was terribly afraid of contact between Cheka people and party apparatchiks on the one side and "NEPmen," the people who became

[26] "Gazprom potreboval raspustit' sovet direktorov," *Lenta.ru*, February 14, 2012, http://lenta.ru/news/2012/02/14/sovet, accessed March 20, 2012.

[27] See Ivan Goriaev, "Delo ne v trekh kitakh, a glubzhe," *Grani.ru*, January 3, 2002, http://grani.ru/Politics/Russia/Cabinet/m.936.html, accessed February 21, 2008. According to Gennady Yevstafiyev, a KGB general interviewed for this book, this twilight zone between legal obligations and personal gain was just one step short of betrayal. Those who remained just did their old job – defending national interests of the state – but some started taking advantage of their positions. "The most dangerous thing for an agent is becoming cynical," he said. "That is the first step toward betrayal."

[28] See Soldatov and Borogan, *Novoe dvorianstvo*.

rich during the few years of capitalist renewal in Russia, on the other. Now the heirs of these Chekists were sending their subordinates to magnates whose financial resources are many times higher than those of the "NEPmen." Of course, it became almost nonsensical to send an FSB officer to spy on a company from which he or she could received revenue surpassing his or her official salary several times over, and expect him to remain loyal.[29]

Ordinary Criminal Activity

The involvement of KGB officers in criminal actions was simply unknown in Soviet times. But the situation changed radically in the post-Soviet era. Several officers of the FSB – not to mention officers of the Ministry of Internal Affairs – have turned out to be deeply involved in the activities of the mafia. In 2007, Viktor Cherkesov contended that a counterintelligence officer's behavior was difficult to separate from that of an ordinary criminal. Cherkesov noted, with melancholy, that "the criminal element exerts the pressure on all social strata and groups," including the Chekist community. He talked about "the criminalization of 'war' officers."[30]

Showing only the tip of the iceberg, in recent years the Russian media have published a great deal of data about the participation of FSB officers – again, putting aside the officers of the Ministry of Internal Affairs – in criminal activity. In February 2012, for instance, according to media reports, a senior officer of the Moscow directorate of the FSB, Andrei Lepetko, was arrested for organizing the murder of a businessman.[31]

The Political Police as a Corporation and the Loyalty of Its Members

The change in the mentality of the security police has had an immense impact on the FSB as a "corporation," making it much weaker than the KGB. Throughout Soviet times, the latter institution was a cohesive organization of loyal members. Indeed, while we can still name several defectors from the foreign service of the KGB, we can mention only one from the internal services who betrayed the organization and acted as a STASI agent, helping dissidents, as seen in the

[29] This duality – involving anachronistic written rules and the opportunity to make money from budding private enterprises – created a powerful incentive to use one's FSB connections for private gain rather than solely serving the FSB. One FSB officer described his own dilemma: "The main question is the old point about two salaries. (Active reserve agents were, by law, supposed to give up the difference in salary if a private job paid more.) I was sent with elements of disguise, so I was forced to do my official job and then the job for the FSB, having meetings with agents at night, so why am I refused a second salary?" See Soldatov and Borogan, *Novoe dvorianstvo*, p. 454.

[30] Viktor Cherkesov, "Nel'zia dopustit', chtoby voiny prevratilis' v torgovtsev," *Kommersant*, October 10, 2007.

[31] Sergei Mashkin, "Konstruktora pogubili vekselia," *Kommersant*, February 9, 2012.

German movie The *Lives of Others* (2006). Viktor Orekhov, as an agent of the KGB, warned Soviet dissidents (such as Yury Orlov, Alexander Podrabinek, and Natan Shcharansky) of their imminent arrests.[32]

The KGB officers greatly appreciated their jobs and were proud of them. But it is hardly the same now, even if Putin has managed to restore some of the status of the FSB officers, having raised their salary and, in particular, opened a way for them to find a semilegal or illegal source of income.

Since 1991, officers have been quitting their "sacred" place of work in droves, although this process has decelerated a bit over time. Many of them have even left the motherland for work abroad. Describing this process, the FSB general Viktor Cherkesov recognized that "only a part of the community survived," while the majority left: "Some simply quit," "some betrayed it," and "some turned out to be criminals."[33] This open talk cost the general his career.[34]

The talk about the "corporate" cohesiveness of the FSB looks preposterous now, as does the vow that "there are no former KGB people" – an invocation repeated regularly by Putin and his colleagues; in the new context, this only means they have agreed to help each other in dubious activity, similar to the tendency of ethnic criminal groups to recruit people whom they can trust over others.

In the past, the strict authoritarian model was the best tool for understanding how the KGB functioned. So, to many Russians – including a young Putin – the mysterious KGB looked as if it were a league of noble knights bound to each other by a devotion to the motherland. But the feudal model, which assumes internal conflicts inside the organization, currently describes the FSB more accurately.

In 2007, a sensational article by the seasoned KGB man Viktor Cherkesov revealed information about life inside the Chekist community to an astounded Russian public. Such a disclosure of information was unheard-of in Soviet society, which was able to conceal potential scandals inside the KGB.[35]

[32] Yevgenia Albats and Zoia Setova, "Dissident iz KGB," *New Times*, December 27, 2010, http://newtimes.ru/articles/detail/32636, accessed March 20, 2012.

[33] Viktor Cherkesov, "Nel'zia dopustit', chtoby voiny prevratilis' v torgovtsev," *Kommersant*, October 10, 2007.

[34] Cherkesov, "Nel'zia dopustit'."

[35] Only now, decades later, has the Russian public finally learned, for instance, about the conflict between Viktor Abakumov and Ivan Serov, both high figures in the KGB kingdom in the 1940–50s, which was very closely regulated by Stalin. Neither did the Russian public know about the confrontation between Andropov, chairman of the KGB, and Minister of Internal Affairs Nikolay Shchelokov, who was also supervised by Brezhnev; he protected both bosses against each other. The confrontation only culminated when Andropov took power in 1982. He instantly liquidated even the appearance of independence for the Ministry of Internal Affairs, as the rival to the KGB, and sent his officers to take most of the important positions there, including that of minister, which was taken by Vitaly Fedorchuk, former minister of the KGB in the Ukraine. Shchelokov was fired from all his positions, and he committed suicide 1984.

Cherkesov described how the fight that raged in the 1990s and beginning of the 2000s was not between some high officials but between different clans of the Chekists, particularly between those who worked directly in the FSB and those who worked in the Federal Drug Control Agency and Customs Service – a contest that took place with the participation of dozens of officers.[36] In fact, the struggle around the company Three Whales, which was mentioned earlier, was a fight between two clans: one headed by the deputy head of the Customs Service, Boris Gutin, and the other by the head of the FSB's economic department, Yuri Zaostrovtsev. Several institutions and their representatives joined in this struggle, siding with one or the other of the factions – the Ministry of Internal Affairs, the Prosecutor General's Office, and the Federal Drug Control Agency.

The fragmented structure of the FSB has also generated another phenomenon that is well described by the feudal model. Kirill Kabanov, a former FSB officer and current anticorruption activist who was interviewed for this book, described the relations between a KGB officer and his boss – who provides him with opportunities to make money – as a type of lord-vassal relationship.

The cohesiveness of the FSB has turned into a myth because of the climate defined by the slogan "Enrichissez vous" (enrich yourself), which created a culture of envy in the FSB. In the past, neither the salaries of KGB generals nor their perks were debated among the rank and file. Now the revenues of FSB dignitaries and their ties to big business, often illegal or semilegal, became sources of envy for less successful officers.[37]

The KGB Ideology: The Focus on Russian Nationalism

The cult of enrichment and tolerance for corruption undermined the morals of the FSB directly, of course, but they also obliterated the KGB ideology, a version of the nomenclature ideology, which officers espoused.

The Soviet ideological structure was quite complex, consisting of two subideologies, which differed from each other, although they overlapped. One was addressed to the public (open), while another was addressed to the nomenclature (closed) at the highest levels of the party apparatus, the KGB and the army.

Both ideologies – the public/open and the nomenclature/closed – also had complex structures. From the 1930s forward, the public, or open, ideology consisted of two components: socialist ideas and Russian nationalism. The nomenclature had these same elements, but, unlike the public ideology, it did not recognize such socialist dogmas as social equality or internationalism and fervently rejected the ludicrous thesis about the leading role of the working

36 Viktor Cherkesov, "Nel'zia dopustit'"; Aleksandr Privalov, "O kriuke, na kotorom visit Rossiia," *Ekspert*, October 15, 2007.

37 Soldatov and Borogan, *Novoe dvorianstvo*.

class in Soviet society. All of these socialist dogmas were mocked by high-level party apparatchiks, as well as by the KGB officers. This was particularly true of the people who worked in the foreign departments of the KGB and the Central Committee, all of whom traveled or even worked in the West, and could not escape the impact of Western life on their minds. The consensus among all of Putin's biographers is that his several years in the Communist GDR as a KGB agent had a tremendous influence on him, making him a hidden admirer of the Western style of life (the difference between the foreign and domestic departments of the FSB seemed to have totally disappeared in the post-Soviet period; it is now almost impossible to find an FSB officer who has not regularly traveled to the West).[38]

However, it is dangerous to simplify the attitudes of the KGB's people toward the socialist component of the official ideology. The socialist elements were dear to the KGB people as well as to party apparatchiks for two reasons. First, the Soviet version of socialism praised the submission of the individual to a collective, which was a surrogate term for a draconian state. Obviously the idea that the interests of the state are supreme has also been an organic part of Russian nationalism, which demanded that Russians make sacrifices for the motherland by serving, for instance, as secret informers. The marriage of the two supposedly antagonistic constructs, socialism and nationalism, as we have been observing in Russia since the early 1930s, has also occurred in practically every country that has proclaimed itself socialist.

Second, in the view of the KGB (and the party), socialist slogans, even the most simplistic and unrealistic (like social equality or the special role of the working class in governing the society), had to be respected by the population as an important part of Soviet propaganda. Therefore, while treating these and other socialist dogmas with contempt, the KGB nonetheless spent a lot of its resources persecuting those who were critical of the socialist ideal; first and foremost were those dissidents who denounced the official dogmas. The fight against the liberal intelligentsia, which was critical of some socialist postulates, received a lion's share of the budget and labor efforts of the KGB after 1953. While the KGB people themselves had ambivalent attitudes toward socialist ideas, they had no reservations in their praise of Russian nationalism, with its belief in the superiority of the Russians over other ethnic groups living in the Soviet Union and, of course, over the rest of the world.

Of special importance were other ingredients of the KGB ideology such as xenophobia and anti-Americanism. The belief that the West, the United States in particular, was the committed enemy of the USSR and of Russia was, in general, an indisputable viewpoint in the KGB milieu. It is not surprising that KGB leaders like Vladimir Kryuchkov and many others ascribed the collapse

[38] Anatoly Chernyaev, *Dnevnik pomochnika presidenta SSSR* (Moscow, 1997); also his *Sovmestnyi iskhod. Dnevnik dvukh epoch* (Moscow, 2008).

of the Soviet Union to the CIA.[39] Anti-Semitism was among those xenophobic ingredients of the ideology that were also crucially important for KGB officers In fact, any who did not share the view among their colleagues of Jews as potential traitors would not have survived in the KGB until the collapse of the Soviet Union.[40]

It is true that when he gained power, Andropov tried to instill some respect for socialist ideals, focusing on social justice as a leading value. He evidently assumed that the discontent with injustice in society could undermine the might, and even the security, of the state, which was his main concern. He also tried to restrain the aggressiveness of Russian nationalism somewhat by making his focus not so much on Russia as on the Soviet empire, with Russia positioned as its leading nation. However, during the short period of his rule (1982–4) he was not able to change the ideological climate inside the KGB.

The FSB Ideology and the Impact of Wealth

Whatever complexities existed within the attitudes of the KGB toward the Soviet public ideology, officers of the KGB nonetheless considered the Soviet Union's collapse to be a tragedy for both the country and its personnel. The lack of a strong official ideology diminished the authority of the political police; it was no longer seen as legitimate, as it had been since the formation of the Soviet system. This development deeply undermined the motivational structure of KGB agents. The generals and officers were unable to understand what the "national interests" that were now being spoken of by the new leaders of the state and the political police meant.

A KGB/FSB official who worked as an investigator in the crucial transition period between 1990 and 1994 described the confusion of the time in an interview with one of the authors of this book:

> When I started working in the FSB, the difference was that we didn't mix [personal gain with legal responsibility]. People went there – and I know this about myself and my colleagues – for the sake of an idea. The ideas of the government, of government interests, of law and order – all of them disappeared. But now, there is no idea in Russia. However bad the idea that Russia used to have, it was still there. Now there is nothing. What is it that we are trying to attain? Personal profit? But then where are the boundaries? In America you are supposed to have a house, a television set and a car. Nothing has been

[39] Vladimir Kriuchkov, *Bez sroka davnosti* (Moscow: Prosveschenie, 2006).

[40] For more on anti-Semitism in the KGB see Gennadii Kostyrchenko, *Gossudarstvennyi antisemtism v SSSR Moscow, 2005*. It is remarkable that even the harshest critics of the KGB prefer to ignore the role of anti-Semitism in it. Only a few authors, like Leonid Zorin, a famous writer, in his novel, *Sober Man* (s.l.: s.n., 2001), have vividly described how no one entertaining party with the participation of the KGB people before 1985 could avoid diatribes against Jews and numerous rude anti-Semitic jokes. Alexander Proshkin also belongs to this tiny category of Russian cultural figures. He raises the same issue in his film *To See Paris and Die*.

formulated for us. Are we all supposed to be like Berezovsky? What is our idea? Is it to hold the 2014 Winter Olympics?

In any case, Putin accepted the FSB as an institution in the total ideological disarray and moral vacuum of post-Soviet Russia. Putin could not include many socialist elements in a new ideology. His praise of big private property ownership, which was important to him and his personal circle, made it impossible for him to talk very much about social inequality or social justice. He has only casually mentioned these issues when addressing the public, as he did when talking to those who gathered to support his candidacy at the Luzhniki sports stadium on February 23, 2012. As far as we know, he has never raised them in a public speech to FSB personnel.[41]

The exclusion of most elements of socialist phraseology from this ideology was necessary because of the ostensible wealth of the ruling class and the gigantic growth of social inequality in comparison with the Soviet past. Of course, social inequality was quite high in Soviet times too (even if not as high as in Putin's Russia), but Soviet officials – including KGB generals and officers – had to hide evidence of their relative prosperity, as well as their special stores, hospitals, and sanatoria, from public eyes. The accusation of lacking modesty – in this case, publicly showing wealth and living the high life – was one of the most dangerous reprimands possible for a KGB man or party apparatchik.[42]

Putin decided to create a new ideology for the FSB and for the whole country, almost solely from the idea of patriotism based on the existence of "national interests." The patriot card was particularly important for substantiating the special role played by the political police in saving the country from chaos and disintegration. Past Soviet leaders never attributed such a crucial role to the KGB and its predecessors as Putin has.

Nikolai Patrushev, the head of the FSB, named his colleagues the "new nobility."[43] Another leading FSB general, Viktor Cherkesov, did not mince words in 2007 when he declared that only the Chekist people had saved the country from "falling [in]to the abyss" with "the KGB hook" on which the whole country hung. He had also developed the same ideas earlier, regarding the political police as the saviors of Russia, and tried to console himself with

[41] "Vystuplenie Putina na mitinge v Luzhnikakh 23 fevralia 2012," *RIA Novosti*, February 23, 2012, http://vecheinfo.ru/index.php?option=com_content&view=article&id=509:-23-2012&catid=1:latest-news&Itemid=1, accessed March 20, 2012.

[42] The attitudes of Soviet leadership toward conspicuous consumption were in stark contrast to the positions of the current masters of Russia, who have never rebuked anybody for a lack of social tact. To illustrate this, it is enough to mention the sirens on the cars of high officials that allow them to ignore traffic rules and humiliate ordinary drivers who are forced to stop in order to give way to the limousines of bureaucrats. Putin himself, unlike all other Soviet leaders, has made a habit of showing off his extravagant lifestyle. For example, the public has been made aware of his diving trip in search of old amphorae in the Azov Sea and of his many exotic hunting trips.

[43] See Soldatov and Borogan, *Novoe dvorianstvo*.

the beliefs that KGB people always remained faithful to their institution and that there was no such thing as former KGB officers in society.[44]

In the past, the patriotic component of Soviet public ideology had aggressive Russian nationalism, anti-Semitism, and anti-Americanism as its motor. More recently, however, Putin has decided to use only one of these notions, anti-Americanism, which he still uses only in a limited sense.

Putin did not want to instigate Russian chauvinism, being afraid of the emergence of a strong Russian nationalist movement that could endanger his position because of his wealth and his close ties with the West and with Russian oligarchs. Most surprising was Putin's positive attitude toward Jews. In fact, Putin eliminated state anti-Semitism, breaking an official tradition in Russia of almost a thousand years.

In rejecting Russian chauvinism and anti-Semitism as the basis for the ideology of the country and the FSB, Putin promoted Orthodox religion and anti-Americanism. The Orthodox Church blesses FSB activity and its leaders and officers at all levels. The FSB reciprocates the church's support by aggressively fighting against all denominations and sects that assail the dominance of Orthodoxy in Russia.

In Soviet times, the Orthodox Church was totally controlled by the party and the KGB, which endorsed all dignitaries, from ordinary priests to the patriarch. The patriarch Alexy II (1990–2008) was a KGB agent,[45] as was the new patriarch, Kirill (since 2009), and thousands of other priests.[46]

Now, the Kremlin arranges the relations between the FSB and the church, as they are seen as equally important institutions. The leaders of the FSB occasionally show respect for the church dignitaries, and even attend church services, as do Putin and Medvedev. The FSB even participates in the building of churches. A new one, close to the Academy of the FSB in Moscow, is scheduled to be built in 2013.[47] In fact, however, the subordinate position of the church to the political police, perhaps in a less conspicuous way, is essentially the same as it was in the past, with the last two patriarchs reputed to come from a KGB background.

The FSB and the Orthodox Church found common ground in post-Soviet Russia: the yearning for big property and commercial activity. The church, like the KGB, had nothing to do with business in any form in Soviet times.

44 Viktor Cherkesov, "Nel'zia dopustit'."

45 "Confirmed: Russian patriarch worked with KGB," *CatholicCulture.org*, September 20, 2000, http://www.catholicculture.org/news/features/index.cfm?recnum=13868, accessed March 20, 2012.

46 Leonid Velikhov, "Kontakty s KGB byvali vo imia pol'zy tserkovnoj, a byvali – vo imia lichnoj," *Sovershenno Sekretno*, http://www.sovsekretno.ru/magazines/article/1041, accessed March 20, 2012.

47 Alisa Po, "Okolo Akademii FSB postroiat modul'nyi khram," *Village*, November 7, 2011, http://www.the-village.ru/village/situation/situation/109951-modulnye-hramy, accessed March 20, 2012.

The church, because of its relations with the FSB, has now become involved in a variety of businesses and enjoys the privileges of an important economic actor. The legal selling of tobacco imported without custom by the church, a gift of the Kremlin in the 1990s, is only one of the numerous examples of the church's commercial activity. Patriarch Kirill, under his secular name as Vladimir Gundiayev, when he was still serving at the lower levels of the church hierarchy, was at the helm of tobacco imports and engaged in the oil and food businesses as well.[48] The FSB and the church face a similar struggle in warding off their detractors, who accuse both institutions of greed and corruption at levels that prevent them from performing their duty to society. At one point in winter of 2012 the backlash and accusations grew so strong that the patriarch appealed to Russians not to identify the church with ordinary corporations, as did the FSB leaders. Seeking protection against public anger, the church called the accusations part of a smear campaign to discredit it.[49]

This cooperation does not seem to perplex the FSB, despite the fact that all of its predecessors were not only aggressive atheists but also brutal persecutors of the church: some 141,000 priests were killed after the Bolsheviks came to power. The Orthodox Church, in its turn, fails to see anything extraordinary in its friendship with the descendants of its executioners.

While refusing to use rude chauvinism as the basis of his ideology and being aware of the limited potential of the Orthodox religion in the minds of the Russians and the FSB people, Putin made a focus on anti-Americanism the main pillar of his propaganda. The anti-Americanism had to be transmitted from the Soviet past, since Yeltsin's regime was rather friendly to the United States. Putin regulates the anti-Americanism propaganda on an almost daily basis. In his first years he kept it at a relatively low level but never allowed it to lose its important place in the state-controlled media. However, after the Orange Revolutions in the former Soviet republics in 2004, Putin began to see America not only as the image of the enemy for propaganda but also as a power behind the regime changes in the Ukraine and Georgia. Furthermore, Putin felt that the United States desired to see the same thing happen in Russia. He increasingly viewed the United States as a hostile entity, blaming the State Department for organizing mass protests in Moscow in December 2011 and February 2012 in order to destroy Putin's regime and the Russian Federation. This belief in the foreign roots of any resistance to the regime was also a core of the KGB's ideology, which suggested that all dissidents – including Sakharov and Solzhenitsyn – were created by the CIA. The same vision of the protest movements as a foreign resistance is now deeply embedded in the collective minds of the FSB.

[48] See Alexander Soldatov, "Za chto rabu Bozjiemu Kirillu," *Novaya Gazeta*, February 15, 2012.

[49] "Patriarkh prizval ne otozhdestviat' RPTs s biznes-korporatsiei," *Islamnews.ru*, August 25, 2011, http://www.islamnews.ru/news-80281.html, accessed March 20, 2012.

Fear of the Political Police Then and Now: A Nice Inefficiency

With the impact of big money and lack of strong Russian nationalism, the political police cannot scare the population to the same degree they did in the past. The fear of the political police and of the brutality of special police divisions like OMON has certainly not disappeared from post-Soviet society; it is particularly pronounced in Putin's Russia, but it is much lower than it was in the Soviet Union. Still, since the 2000s, many Russian intellectuals have once again started to feel the fear of the political police – much more so than in Yeltsin's time – to the point of even avoiding discussing sensitive matters on the phone. The possibility of being murdered by the political police, mostly indirectly through hired hands, and due to reasons having more to do with corruption than politics, has become a source of fear for many oppositional journalists and politicians. By 2012, the list of the victims of such murders had become quite long. In some ways it is paradoxical that the fear of such murders has increased significantly in comparison with that of the post-Stalin period, when the KGB could only arrest people and did not murder them on the streets.

Still, the overall amount of fear in post-Soviet Russia has declined enormously in comparison with the Soviet times. The number of possible targets of persecutions has been curtailed immensely, now being focused only on very active people, thereby excluding the majority of the population.

The Yuri Levada center made an attempt to measure the relative role of different types of fear in post-Soviet Russia. The center discovered that existential fears (fear of the death of close relatives or of one's self) are the leading fears on a 5-point scale (1 minimal, 5 maximal). Russians assessed them in 2003 at 4.17 and 3.57, respectively. Fears that have social origins were ranked somewhat lower: the fear of criminals (3.48), the fear of poverty (3.36), and the fear of the arbitrariness of the authorities (3.35).[50]

The major cause of this unmitigated softening of the political police in Russia lies in the big property that emerged in Russia after 1991, which radically changed the motivations of the Russian leaders, as well as of the people in the FSB. The pursuit of private material interests among the political police and other leaders was totally alien to Soviet rulers and, thus, did not influence their political decisions in either domestic or foreign policy. Now, the permanent worries about their property abroad, about the possibility of traveling abroad, and about the fear of being included in some black list prepared by the Western media or government has forced Russian leaders to be quite cautious in ordering the special services to harass undesirable people on a large scale.[51]

50 Levada, Yury, "Chelovek sovietkii: Chetvertaia volna," *Vestnik Obshchestvennogo Mnenia* 4 (2004).

51 Vladimir Shlapentokh, "Wealth versus political power: The Russian case," *Communist and Post-Communist Studies* 37 (2004), 135–60.

Still, despite many negative developments inside the FSB – and the public is mostly aware of them – the general population continues to trust this organization to a relatively high degree. In 2005, 25 percent of the people trusted the FSB, which was lower than the trust in the president (41 percent) and the church (41 percent) but higher than in the courts (15 percent) and the police (12 percent).[52]

However, the objective role of the political police in Putin's Russia – despite the indicators mentioned – is much smaller than it was in Soviet times. The FSB is not a genuine heir of the KGB. In the past, the NKVD was as sinister as the Cheka or the GPU, and the Ministry of the KGB was no worse than the NKVD. Nothing like this happened this time with the FSB. Because of greed and corruption, Putin's political police do not inspire the same omnipresent fear as the KGB and its predecessors.

Conclusion: The Efficiency of the KGB and the Inefficiency of the FSB

If one takes into account the goals that Soviet leadership set for this institution, the KGB in the post-Stalin period was quite an efficient organization.

It can be said that all Soviet leaders were satisfied with the Soviet political system (Gorbachev was a fateful exception for the USSR), even while all of them, including Stalin, wanted a more efficient economic system. Indeed, the KGB, since the late 1920s and as late as 1985, made a crucial contribution to maintaining the totalitarian order in society and to extirpating any serious resistance at the outset. Perestroika was in no way stimulated by public disturbances. The dissident movement had practically been eliminated by 1985. There were no serious strikes or protest meetings in the country, nor any serious nationalistic movements in the Soviet republics.[53]

The KGB and the GRU (the intelligence service of the army) were also successful in the international arena. The agency's international network of direct agents and "agents of influence" spanned the world. While a performance comparison between Soviet and Western espionage remains debatable, the ability of Soviet intelligence to plant spies around the globe is an admitted fact by practically all experts.[54] It would be difficult to overestimate KGB achievements in the realm of technological espionage.

With the new ideological and moral atmosphere, the FSB became a victim of the deprofessionalization that embraced all sectors of Russian life. As did many others, FSB officers understood that in a new society it was neither their professional skills nor their devotion to the interests of the country that would

[52] Levada-Tsentr, *Press-Vypusk*, September 2004.

[53] Ludmila Alexeyeva and Valerii Chalidze, *Mass Rioting in the USSR* (Silver Springs, MD: Foundation for Soviet Studies, 1985).

[54] Christopher Andrew and Vasilii Mitrokhin, *The Sword and the Shield: The Mitrokhin Archive and the Secret History of KGB* (New York: Basic Books, 1999).

lead to a stable career and material benefits, but rather it was their connections and ability to use various corruption schemes. The obvious deterioration of the network of informers – the KGB's crucial instrument for all its activities[55] – is a very important development for any special service: the ideological stimuli, together with fear, that were so important for recruiting informers in Soviet times do not work as well now as they had in the past. This partially explains the numerous failures of the FSB in the fight against terrorism and major crimes. The times when the KGB could easily recruit almost everybody in the country as a secret informant are long gone.

The same weakness of the state apparatus was revealed by the failure of the FSB and local police forces to prevent the numerous murders of prominent people in the country. The continuing spate of murders can be attributed to a feeling of immunity among hired guns. In the last ten years, law enforcement agencies have failed to find those who perpetrated the murders of several hundred businesspeople in Russia. The shameful failure of the FSB-GRU intelligence operation in the United States in 2010 was a clear sign that inefficiency and sloppiness had penetrated even the once-glorious Russian intelligence services.

No doubt FSB professionals, analysts in particular, in post-Soviet Russia are much freer in their actions than in the Soviet past. As is well known – the author knows from his own experiences – the KGB mostly shunned sociological studies and was afraid to ask the best experts for help in collecting data. Now the analytical departments of the FSB have no such constraints in their work.[56]

Still, despite all its weakness in comparison to the KGB, the FSB remains one of the pillars of the regime, along with the special units of the army and OMON of the Interior Ministry. The recent dramatic rise in the salaries of FSB and army officers, whose incomes now surpass the average salary in Russia by three to four times (with generals enjoying even higher salaries), shows how much the regime was concerned about the loyalty of the *siloviki* (the Russian term for security agencies, including the police, the military and the FSB). It is hardly likely that in the case of a big political crisis the FSB will be more enthusiastic in the defense of the regime than the KGB was in 1991. But still, the future of Putin's authoritarian regime depends extensively on the FSB, even if it looks inefficient now.

55 See Shchekochikhin, *Raby KGB*.

56 Andrei Soldatov and Irina Borogan, "V chem. FSB uzhe prevzoshla kGB," *Agentura.ru*, http://www.agentura.ru/press/about/jointprojects/ej/analisys, accessed March 20, 2012; see also Vladimir Shlapentokh, *Sociology and Politics: The Soviet Case* (Falls Church, VA: Delphi Associates, 1985).

6

Treatment of Strikers in Soviet and Post-Soviet Times: Novocherkassk and Mezhdurechensk

The radical differences between the Soviets and Putin in dealing with the real opposition were shown quite clearly in their dealings with workers' strikes. The Soviet regime almost immediately resorted to coercion and violence while Putin's regime has mostly used a tactic based on concessions and money to cope with resistance to the actual order.

The Novocherkassk Case

The Novocherkassk rebellion is a good case to show how the Soviet regime, even in Khrushchev's mild time, reacted against those who dared to resist the authorities. In fact, it was Khrushchev's thaw, and his denunciation of Stalin just six years earlier, that helped push local residents to a breaking point: the political thaw led to more openness and allowed more people to criticize the authorities, at least in conversation; dire poverty had the population in rural regions subsisting on potatoes and cabbage; malfunctioning economic reforms lead to a simultaneous increase in prices on core products like butter and meat, and decreasing wages at factories in single-industry towns.

On June 1, 1962, as the locals of Novocherkassk were discussing their dismay over a 25 percent hike in the prices on meat and butter (they were already living virtually without meat; now they could not afford butter either), a morning radio announcement at the factory told them that their salaries would be cut as well.

The combination of these two occurrences – increased critical openness and deepened poverty – caused a breaking point, and what started with a few dozen workers gathering together to complain soon swelled chaotically into a hundreds-strong strike, and then thousands took to the streets and blocked the railway.

According to a KGB analytical document prepared in early 1962 and filed in a "classified" folder until Perestroika, the authorities in Moscow knew about the incident from the start. KGB agents thoroughly monitored social responses to each newly-introduced economic measure and painstakingly documented what average workers were saying about meat and butter price hikes. Disguised KGB agents were also present at the strike and mass rally, reporting developments to their superiors. The workers had a simple request for the authorities – to explain what they were supposed to do when falling salaries and rising prices meant they were unable to feed themselves.

Still, no one except the local management at the plant and a local Communist Party official made any attempt to explain to the workers what was going on. When the director of the plant and the local party official finally addressed the crowd, the remarks were feeble attempts to persuade people to disperse; predictably, they did not work.

Instead, the government moved to brute force in a bid to demonstrate to the masses that thaw or no thaw, the Soviet state had zero tolerance for any mass action. Soldiers fired on the crowd, killing twenty-six and wounding up to a hundred more. When a rally was repeated the following day, dozens were arrested, fourteen were convicted, and seven were executed after a show trial. It was a brutal illustration of a government refusing to negotiate.

Putin's Treatment of Revolts

The handling of similar revolts during Vladimir Putin's tenure demonstrates a vivid contrast between the respective repression policies of two authoritarian regimes. As a relatively weak authoritarian leader, Putin could not afford to deal with enemies in the same harsh way as Stalin, Khrushchev, or even Brezhnev. With his vulnerable legitimacy, and with a personal interest in keeping an open society and protecting the wealth of the ruling elite in Russia and abroad, Putin has largely resorted to the kind of compromises that were so deeply alien to Soviet leaders during attempts to resolve conflicts between the population and the authorities.

Of no less importance is another element of Putin's rule – private capital as leverage. With a significant chunk of the economy belonging to private owners, many of them loyal oligarchs, Putin forced the capitalists, through the application of soft pressure and investment incentives, to make concessions to the workers and thus keep them at bay.

Against this backdrop, the events in Mezhdurechensk present us with a curious case of Soviet-era legacies of revolt on the part of the people and soft-repression tactics – including a careful balance of coercion, co-option, compassion, generous monetary concessions, and the occasional good tsar/bad boyar performance – on the part of the government. At the heart of the problem is an intertwined connection of private interests that, given the lack of legislation effectively governing private property, on the one hand, and the obligations of its owners to the workers, on the other, has to be mediated by the government through personal connections, very often through Putin's personal clout.[1]

Mezhdurechensk, 2010

The developments in Mezhdurechensk – a coal basin city in the Kemerovo region in south Siberia – started on May 9, 2010, with a methane blast that shook the town's Raspadskaya mine, killing ninety.

This mine had already seen its share of miner strikes and uprisings in 1989. Since the 1930s, miners have been represented in Russia as a somewhat separate category of workers, more influential and potentially threatening to the political regime. The 1989 strikes by miners, who were then the most politically active part of the working class, helped Yeltsin to overthrow the Soviet system.

In the 1990s and early 2000s, the transfer from a planned economy to market capitalism had a profound effect on the mining industry. The Raspadskaya mine was a private enterprise, controlled partially by Roman Abramovich's Yevraz Group and partially by the mine's general director, Gennady Kozovoi, and its chairman of the board, Alexander Vagin. But the ownership mechanisms involved a tangled net of half a dozen Cyprus-based offshore companies, most of which either controlled Yevraz or were controlled by Abramovich's Millhouse Group.[2] It is important to note that, with Putin's arrival in power, Abramovich belonged to the group of the oligarchs who were very close to the president and who enjoyed a great deal of protection from the authorities in exchange for the transfer of money and stocks to Putin and his people.

To be profitable, a private mine is normally forced to resort to a piecework rate, which replaces the previous, constant monthly salary. In an economy where the state struggled to combine market capitalism with Soviet era welfare, unless the state agrees to subsidize the mine (and this had not occurred in the case of Raspadskaya), miners often have to choose between piece-rate wages and no wages at all, which is what would happen if the mine were to close.

Let us look at what happened across the board in May 2010.

The People Revolt

Just before midnight on May 8, a powerful methane-sparked blast rocked through the collieries of Raspadskaya. Another explosion went off at about

[1] In February 2008, President Putin laid flowers at the memorial to the victims of the suppression of the Novocherkassk uprising. This indicates that Putin is well aware of the dangers of a collision course with one's own people. Suppressing marginalized members of the liberal opposition is one thing, but when the discontent concerns salaries and food, far softer methods must be applied in order to maintain political stability.

[2] D. Pylnova and D. Shkrylyov, "Kto vladeltsy shakhty Raspadskaya?" *Novaya Gazeta*, May 12, 2010, http://www.novayagazeta.ru/data/2010/049/12.html, accessed March 20, 2012.

4:00 a.m. At once, there was widespread speculation that the blast was the result of tampering with safety equipment. Indeed, previous blasts in the Kuzbass region in 2007 – including one that killed 39 people and another that killed 110 – were linked to workers blocking or removing methane checkers. There were strong motives to tamper with safety equipment – inactive methane checkers meant that miners could continue working, even in dangerous conditions, in order to secure more wages under the piece-rate pay. Workers at Raspadskaya, Russia's largest mine, had a salary that consisted of a 35 percent fixed rate, with the rest based on how much coal a worker would bring in.

For a grieving miner who lost comrades, or a grieving relative, all of this must have weighed heavily during the bitter week of mourning following the blast. Two articulated demands were formed: make managers accountable for accidents, forcing them to invest more money in safety; and raise the fixed part of the salary to 70 percent. Locals described the week after the twin blasts as a state of utter bleakness that surpassed the depths of typical mourning. Miners, widows, and other workers drank and cried, cried and drank. The landscape of the town can partially explain the despair: a late spring among the half-bare, rolling foothills surrounding the industrial buildings had yielded frost and snow in mid-May. That was in addition to the common problems perennially found in the Russian provinces – horrendous roads that could make a seasoned driver carsick, with potholes that were only hastily filled just in time for Putin's visit.

Though the government promised compensation and a way of bypassing bureaucratic red tape, as expected, things went wrong. That, coupled with the general despair and the growing demands for reforming miners' pay and safety standards, ultimately turned what was planned as a public memorial into a protest rally. On the evening of May 14, between four hundred (by official accounts) and three thousand (by unofficial accounts) people congregated in the square in front of the Palace of Culture, holding candles. About two hundred people broke off and decided to block the railways. They were demanding to speak to the governor, Aman Tuleyev, and the general director and owner of the mine, Gennady Kozovoi. Neither went out to talk to them, but the mayor, a modest-looking "man of the people" named Sergei Shcherbakov, addressed them, urging them to abandon the tracks and find a more civilized means of negotiation. Shcherbakov was no Basov – the party boss who curtly told the Novocherkass workers that there would be no reconsideration of the price hikes and ordered them to disperse. Instead, Shcherbakov, an administrator, was eager to take the workers' side – a big change in comparison with the Soviet times – sympathizing with them against Kozovoi, admitting that there was little he could do to a private corporation.

Meanwhile, into the game entered Yelena Pershina, the wife of a miner; she became a leading person in the initial stage of the mass protests. Pershina organized the "Mezhdurechensk Initiative," which almost immediately led to productive talks with the mayor and the governor. The participants of the protest were given pledges that the local authorities would do everything they could to improve the situation at the plant and to work out some sort of compromise with the owners.

It must be said here that, although the general grievances were with the owners of the mine and its management, the protesters were still under the spell of the Soviet system and were well aware of the continuing role of the state in post-Soviet Russia. Even if the mine was privately owned, their demands were still nominally addressed to the government – a scenario that is very similar to what happened at the Novocherkassk locomotive plant, where workers addressed their complaints directly to the state and the Communist Party.

If Russia had well-established labor institutions, the issues at the Raspadskaya mine could have been the object of an organized strike, and of follow-up negotiations with the management and the owners, with the labor union acting as a mediator. But labor unions have traditionally been weak in Russia (and the post-Soviet period changed nothing, another illustration of the role of authoritarianism in a new society), and they did not serve to establish crucial dialogue between the workers and management. Moreover, labor unions in post-Soviet Russia are still widely co-opted by the state, either directly or indirectly. This was once again the case in Raspadskaya. The official union, Rosugolprof – which was formed in 1989 as part of the initially independent, and now government co-opted, Sotsprof – lobbied the government on behalf of Raspadskaya, but it was far from clear whose interests they were representing. The key demands regarding management responsibility and an increase in fixed salary were clearly not on the agenda during their numerous meetings with Putin.[3]

Meanwhile, Raspadskaya was also an object of high strategic importance for the government, as the largest coking coal producer in the country. In 2008, its output amounted to 10 percent of the total output of the country.[4] It is no wonder, then, that Putin flew out to Kemerovo immediately after the blasts and remained there for days afterward. In the minds of the workers, it was clearly Putin who could change conditions at the mine, and change conditions he did.

[3] Sergei Zhelenin, the local Rosuglprof union leader in Mezhdurechensk, was noticeably ambivalent when he spoke about salary reforms. His union had proposed a new pay system to Putin in fall 2009, but Zhelenin did not seem to support it. "Let's say a miner is on fixed salary. Once he makes whatever it is he makes, he has no more incentive to get more coal," he told Anna Arutunyan in May 2010. As for making directors criminally responsible for accidents, that was out of the question. "Who's going to agree to be a director?" The other labor union, the Miners Independent Trade Union of Russia, also took a conciliatory tone, saying that the authorities were going in the right direction.

[4] A. Arutunyan, A. Potts, and E. Chaikovskaya, "Twin blasts rock Siberian mine," *The Moscow News*, May 11, 2010.

The Government Responds

In the case of Raspadskaya, the dialogue was once again between the workers and the state, not the workers and their employers. And if, in the case of Novocherkassk, the government responded with a blunt refusal to negotiate and the deployment of brute force, the state responded in the Raspadskaya case with a major concession in regard to an enterprise that was, for all purposes, private property.

After the first protest on May 14, Putin acted decisively but with behavior that was a hundred light-years away from Khrushchev's behavior in Novocherkassk. He ordered the state agency overseeing mining safety under direct control of his cabinet. He announced that the fixed rate for workers' salaries at Raspadskaya was to be raised to 70 percent. And he found a scapegoat – mentioning the mine director Igor Kozlov by name, and politely inquiring why he had never been fired. Unlike in Novocherkassk, all these statements and actions were underpinned by an apparently complex negotiation process between Putin and the owners of the mine.[5] By all accounts, Putin and Abramovich regularly interact on an informal basis. Coincidence or not, it is more than likely that Putin had discussed the Raspadskaya issue with Abramovich privately before reaching his decision to increase the fixed part of the salary to 70 percent.

During Putin's visit, one incident, accounts of which were circulated afterward by word of mouth among the local residents, served to bolster, at least locally, two important components of the Putin myth that have repeatedly been used as part of state propaganda: Putin as a patrimonial leader protecting the common people, and as a potential authoritarian threat to businesspeople who ignore the plight of the common people. According to the accounts, Putin, during a private meeting, reportedly went into a rage and slapped Kozovoi with a folder.[6]

[5] This trajectory was reinforced by two unconfirmed instances:The first is a rumored meeting between Putin and Abramovich around the time of the disaster, though this was never officially confirmed. It is true that Putin made a state visit to Austria in April, but that visit ended on April 24. Shortly after the explosions, the *Austrian Times* came out with a story about Abramovich's purchase of a $9.4 million villa in Austria and reported that Putin was spotted in it with Abramovich (the second instance). Numerous Russian media reported that Putin had stayed at the villa, but this was never officially confirmed, and the dates were not clear. If the visit had in fact taken place, it was likely merely a coincidence.

[6] According to accounts from different people who were present at Putin's meeting with relatives days after the disaster, he grew hysterical. It was reported that Kozovoi showed Putin a folder of pay stubs, indicating salaries of 70,000 roubles. But relatives had their own pay stubs, showing salaries of less than 20,000 roubles. When Putin was shown pay stubs by the relatives, he flew into a rage and slapped Kozovoi across the face with his folder. By other accounts, he threw the pay stubs in his face (one account has Putin actually hitting Aman Tuleyev). Then he told security, "Take the journalists out. They don't need to see this."

He then closed himself in a separate office with Kozovoi and Tuleyev, and outside, in the reception room, he was heard cursing so loudly that even the security people started to look uncomfortable.

If true, Putin's outburst – such public performances for the sake of ordinary people are fixtures of Putin's rule – seemed to accomplish several goals at once. For the public, it reinforced the typical good tsar/bad boyar stereotype, encouraging the people to seek Putin's aid. For the owners, it suggested that private property or not, it could be taken away if it were not handled property. Putin, after all, frequently threatens business owners with checks from the prosecutor's office, and the fate of Yukos is a constant reminder of that threat.

Whatever the case, in the absence of a clear, institutionalized system of corporate management and worker-employer relations, Putin thus reintroduced an element of patrimonialism into Russia's state capitalist system. Yes, the property belonged to Kozovoi and Abramovich, but ultimately there was nothing preventing the state from taking it back; after all, everyone clearly remembers when entrepreneurs were given their property by the state. As for the people, the tsar is eternally on their side, but his hands are tied. This behavior – the mythical outbursts, the concessions, and the decision to make a scapegoat of Igor Kozlov – clearly had the profound effect of ensuring that the threatened protests scheduled for May 22 did not take place.

The Kuzbass Initiative

Meanwhile, Pershina's "Kuzbass Initiative" was making headway. Her group of activists had productive talks with the mayor and the governor. They were given pledges that the local authorities would do everything they could to improve the situation at the plant and to work out some sort of compromise with the owners. Quite quickly, however, Pershina was co-opted by the local authorities, probably with her own assent. In exchange for Pershina's efforts to keep the peace, she and her comrades were allowed access to Kozovoi and given a facilitation of the negotiation process with local authorities. Immediately after the promises started pouring in, Pershina's tone seemed to change. She vehemently distanced herself and her activists from the group that blocked the railway. Her calls to keep conditions quiet after May 14 aroused suspicion among many journalists who were working out of Mezhdurechensk that her initiative had been infiltrated by local FSB officials.[7]

This development poses a striking contrast to the role of the KGB in the Novocherkassk uprising. In Mezhdurechensk, activists were identified and kept track of by security agents much as they were identified in Novocherkassk. But whereas the Soviet KGB either arrested the activists in Novocherkassk or made crude efforts to neutralize them, the local authorities

Others recalled that when Kozovoi walked out of the meeting, he was pale and his hands were shaking.

[7] When Anna Arutunyan met her on May 20, 2010 she insisted that her work only involved helping residents to get the benefits that they had been promised, and to traverse the complex paperwork trail.

in Mezhdurechensk – whether they were FSB or officials from city hall, jointly with representatives of Raspadskaya mine – moved to pacify them through negotiations and soft pressure. Essentially, the people won most of what they wanted. All this, however, does not negate the coercive element, which was fundamentally present in the government's handling of the aftermath of the Mezhdurechensk disaster.

After the first rally, and as the city prepared for the second one on May 22 that never occurred, some law enforcement reports claimed that as many as five hundred riot police troops were being deployed to the city from Novokuznetsk and the entire Kemerovo region. By May 20, dozens of armored riot police trucks were hidden in yards and alleyways, ready to be deployed if necessary.

Possibly the most desperate, and Soviet-looking, measure was the sudden announcement that the city would hold its Sports Day on May 22, right on the central square. That day, city hall called a press conference for the journalist pool that was in the city specifically for the protests, to tell them about the sporting events.

A provocative question from a journalist about why the government was holding a sporting event on a day when it was noticeably preparing for mass protests apparently enraged Mayor Sergei Shcherbakov. In any case, the wan-looking sporting events on the main square did manage to distract the attention of what appeared to be an exhausted population from what was about to transpire in front of city hall.

The element of coercion should not be underestimated in the Mezhdurechensk case. Miners were obviously afraid of speaking to outsiders, and many had indicated that there were indirect threats that the vocal activists among working miners would be fired. But while authorities were obviously wielding a big stick, it was ultimately the carrot – and the bread and circus – that did the trick.

At the heart of the contrast between neutralizing a revolt at a Soviet industry town and at a post-Soviet mining town is private property – the need for the state to negotiate with the owners made direct, centralized repression impossible. Coercion – or, rather, threat of coercion – was used in tandem with monetary concessions where possible. Putin was, in essence, paying the population to stay quiet.

7

Geopolitics, Private Capital, and Legitimacy as Foreign Policy Goals in Soviet and Post-Soviet Russia

Russian Foreign Policy and Legitimization of the Regime in Russian Recent History

Similarly to events in many other societies, the foreign activity of the Russian leaders after the 1917 revolution pursued two interconnected goals – one material and the other ideological. In the sphere of material politics, Russian leaders tried to expand Russian territory and Russian influence in the world, both politically and economically. The ideological manipulation – that foreign policy could be real or almost purely verbal – was necessary for solidifying the legitimacy of the regime. Indeed, a cherished ideology was necessary for increasing the prestige of the leader, both inside the country and, no less importantly, in the international community.

As we will show, the main goal of Putin's foreign activity was the defense of his legitimacy as the Russian leader, in the eyes of Russia and the world. Another factor influencing his foreign policy was the protection of his private interests. At the same time, he took very modest actions in the sphere of "material politics." In this respect, Putin's regime differed radically from those of all of the other post-Stalin leaders, who were almost completely unconcerned about their legitimacy and indifferent to their own private interests or those of their cronies.

The cause of this unique development in Russian history lies in the fact that Putin became leader in a deeply feudalized society. In such a society, the head of the relatively weak state apparatus (compare Putin's state with the Soviet totalitarian machine) has precarious legitimacy. Putin's main concerns were to deter rivals from his throne and to convince the Russian people and the world of the legality of his regime. The perceived legitimacy of the nation's leader had additional importance for Putin, as it had for Yeltsin, compared to previous rulers, because possessing a relatively high level of legitimacy served to protect him from the possible criminal persecutions that might find him if he were to lose his legitimacy.

In any case, no previous regime in Russian history had a foreign policy as influenced by concerns about the legitimacy of the head of state, by his private interests, by his greed, by his personal traits, and by his background.

Legitimacy throughout Russian History

For the ruler of any nation, at any time, obtaining and possessing legitimacy in their eyes and the eyes of others – "the right to govern" – are of utmost importance. Legitimacy is simultaneously a simple and a complicated concept, reflecting the belief (or disbelief) of people in the right of their bosses to hold a certain position – whether that of tsar, president, CEO, or chairman of a department – granting them the right of command over their citizens or subordinates. The history of almost every nation tells of dramatic episodes related to the legitimacy of its leaders.[1]

If the leader believes, to use a modified Weberian typology of authority, in his or her right to issue commands – either through a divine (hereditary), a revolutionary, or a democratic origin of this right – and if the subjects share his or her views on this issue, then society or any social unit within society is in a state of political stability. How the ruler achieves the consent of the people to recognize the legality of his or her government may be another story. From a Parsonian perspective, this occurs as a function of the internalizing of the ideology and values of the regime by the population; from a Hobbesian perspective, this is through, above all else, coercion. In the analysis of any society, including Russia, it is probable that the two perspectives have to be combined.

The Legitimacy of the Leader in Foreign Eyes

While the citizenry's recognition of the legitimacy of a ruler inside his own country is usually of primary importance to him, the position of foreign countries, especially those that are powerful and able to influence development inside countries other than their own, often has no less significance to the head of a regime.

The foreign threat to a regime usually takes one of four forms: (1) possible military intervention, (2) economic enslavement, (3) ideological offensives against the regime in order to delegitimize it in eyes of the domestic population

[1] See Max Weber, *Economy and Society* (Berkeley: University of California Press, 1978). Among the most recent works on legitimacy of government, see Darrow Schecter, *Beyond Hegemony: Towards a New Philosophy of Political Legitimacy* (Manchester: Manchester University Press, 2005), Jean-Marc Coicaud and David Ames Curtis, *Legitimacy and Politics: A Contribution to the Study of Political Right and Political Responsibility* (Cambridge: Cambridge University Press, 2002).

and international public opinion, and, finally, (4) material help to the domestic opposition.

The regime's attitudes toward foreign threats are usually quite complicated. A regime can hold sober perceptions of a foreign threat, strongly exaggerate this threat, or even concoct the danger of a foreign threat without a basis in reality, since a foreign danger is a universal way of justifying the existence and behavior of a regime.

Historians, and even contemporaries, are not always able to separate the perceptions of foreign threats that are based on real facts from those imaginary facts and intentional lies that are necessary for domestic politics. A major source of information about the views of leaders on foreign affairs are their public statements and, though only in rare cases, the materials from secret meetings, such as Stalin's speech at the meeting of the Politburo and the leadership of the Communist International on August 19, 1939.[2] Unlike official documents on domestic issues, the speeches and articles of the leaders should be, as a rule, treated as relatively authentic reflections of the position of the government. This is particularly true if we talk about hostile declarations. All hostile anti-Western statements of the Soviet leaders, from Lenin to Putin, conveyed their antagonism toward the Western governments. The notorious *History of the All-Union Communist Party* – written under Stalin's direct supervision in 1938 – is considered one of the most falsified texts in history. However, it conveys true information about Stalin's deep hostility toward the West and his real fear of military intervention and the destruction of his regime.[3] For this reason, the foreign speeches of the Russian leaders (as well as the leaders of any other country) should be taken, in many cases, literally at face value, as a source of information about their attitudes, positive or negative, even if these speeches do not reveal plans for how a regime will deal with foreign countries.[4]

Until the victory in the war with Germany, the Soviet regimes talked about three sources of threats from outside forces: military intervention, the ideological offensive, and material help to the domestic opposition (the economic threat was usually ignored).

[2] For the debates around the real character of this speech see V. Doroshenko, I. Pavlova and P. Paak, "Ne mif: Rech' Stalina 19 avgusta 1939 goda," *Vorposy Istrorii* 8 (2005) (these authors believed in its authenticity); S. Sluch, "Rech' Stalina, kotoroi ne bylo," *Otechestvennaya Istoriia* 1 (2004) (He denied it).

[3] TSK KPSS, *Istoriia Vsesoiuznoi Kommunisticheskoi Partii (bol'shevikov). Kratkii kurs* (Moscow: Politizdat, 1938), pp. 261–2.

[4] It is nearly impossible to pursue an aggressive policy toward foreign countries while hiding it from the population and the ruling class. Even a totalitarian regime wants the support of the masses when it is at odds with foreign countries. This is all the more true for regimes like Putin's, which are not completely confident in the future. Only in rare cases, when a country is preparing a surprise attack on a foreign nation, does the government hide its true intentions from the public. Between August 1939, when Germany and the USSR signed the nonaggression pact, to June 22, 1941, when the Nazis started the unexpected war against the Soviet Union, Berlin refrained from making any public declarations that seemed inimical toward Moscow.

Unlike the Soviet regimes from before 1945, Putin never mentioned the real danger of military interventions in Russia in his speeches, even if several Russian propagandists liked to talk about Western intentions to take physical control of Russia's natural resources and Siberia[5] (the threat of Chinese seizure of the Far East was usually avoided in official materials, and only rarely discussed in scholarly literature).[6] Putin also almost never talked about the economic control the West had over Russia; his personal support of and facilitation in the expansion of foreign companies into Russia made this practically impossible. But he profusely discussed two other threats stemming from the West: ideological delegitimization of his regime and help to the regime's opposition.

Legitimacy of the Rulers before 1917

Before 1917, the legitimacy of the Russian leaders lay in their monarchic origins, even if an election mechanism was also created when Mikhail Romanov was elected tsar by the Zemsky Sobor in 1612. With the monarchic principle as the basis for the government, the legitimacy of Russian tsars was never a serious political problem in the country.

Prior to the nineteenth century, only three tsars had worries reminiscent of those held by Putin: Boris Godunov, Peter the Great, and Catherine the Great. If we are to believe Alexander Pushkin's drama, Godunov was aware that many Russians believed him culpable in the murder of 10-year-old Dmitry, the single legitimate heir of Tsar Ivan the Terrible. According to several prominent Russian historians of the nineteenth century including Vladimir Solovyev and Vasily Kluchevsky, not even Godunov himself could overcome the doubt about his own legitimacy, with visions of "bloodied boys" even while on his death bed. Peter the Great was also worried when his son Alexei, with whom he had strained relations, fled to Vienna (and was given support by Peter's enemies), and supposedly negotiated ascending to power in Russia with the Austrians. In any case, the tsar spared no efforts to bring his son back to Russia, where he died the next year, probably executed on orders from his father, who suspected a plot against him. Catherine the Great, who participated in the murder of her husband, the legitimate tsar (via birth/family lineage) Peter III, was afraid of people who claimed to have a legal basis for taking the Russian throne. One of them – the self-styled Princess Elizabeth Tarakanova – was kidnapped in Italy in 1775, taken to Russia, and died in prison the same year. The absurd claims of Yemelyan Pugachev, the leader of a peasant insurrection, who was impersonating Peter III – whom Catherine had murdered in 1775 – could not have failed to preoccupy her. The news that this uneducated and boorish peasant was captured and executed filled the empress with joy.

[5] See Sergei Klyuchnikov, "Ne sdavai Sibir', Rossiia!," *Zavtra*, February 3, 2010.

[6] See Vladimir Shlapentokh, "China in the Russian mind today: Ambivalence and defeatism," *Europe-Asia Studies* 59.1 (2007).

Legitimacy for the Soviet Leaders

After seizing power in 1917, Bolshevik leaders were deeply preoccupied with their legitimacy inside the country. The theory of the dictatorship of the proletariat provided them with an ideological justification for their power, while the mass repressions helped them to eradicate all those who disagreed with them. It is true that the Soviet leaders never denied the importance of the election of governmental bodies for the confirmation of their legitimacy as the rulers of the country. For this reason, the 1918 dismantling of the Russian Constituent Assembly by Bolsheviks, who were themselves democratically elected in November 1917, was a historical fact that Soviet propaganda tried its best to avoid, because this event was one of the major arguments used by Western countries against recognizing the legitimacy of Bolshevik power.

However, even after formally recognizing that government elections could serve as a major source of legitimization, the Soviet leaders never carried out honest elections of any kind (not even for electing members of a trade union committee to an office) throughout seven decades of their rule. When they praised the legitimacy of their order, they preferred to refer to their ideology and the party. The Soviet apparatchiks used "the party" as an almost mystical force to supervise the behavior of Communists, who should tremble at the mere thought of being suspected of being disloyal to the party. Soviet leaders – Stalin and Brezhnev – introduced special articles about the leading role of the party in the Soviet system into their constitutions The 1990 deletion of the notorious sixth article from the last Soviet Constitution, created in 1977, was the most powerful signal of an imminent break in the Soviet order.

In the early 1930s, Stalin began to use the supposed continuity of his regime with the past as another pillar for legitimizing his regime. He wanted to persuade Russians that his rule had deep roots in Russia, which was, in fact, mostly true. Stalin started to introduce the attributes of the prerevolutionary monarchy into the Soviet Union, a process that he continued even after the victorious war.[7] After the revolution in 1917, the refusal of the Bolshevik regime to carry

[7] He restored the shoulder boards in the army; during the civil war, this element of the uniform was the symbol of tsarist times. He also restored the terms "officer" (instead of "commander") and "minister" (instead of "people's commissar"), as well as almost all of the military ranks of the tsarist army, from "marshal" to "corporal." He restored the tsarist ranks for several other professions, such as those who worked in the state justice system, as well as the railroad and coal industries. Again, following the example of tsarist Russia, he put uniforms on civilians in several branches of bureaucracy and introduced various types of medals. Stalin also introduced separate schools for boys and girls and restored military colleges for youths, along with several other measures that demonstrated the commonalities between his and the tsarist regimes. In his pantheon of prominent people, Stalin included several individuals who had also been highly respected by the monarchy, such as the military leaders Suvorov and Kutuzov. Of course, Stalin ordered his apparatus and media to show high respect for the cruelest tsars of the past, such as Ivan the Terrible and Nicolas I. The reconciliation with the church and its transformation into a loyal state institution were other elements of the rapprochement of the monarchist and Soviet

out free parliamentary elections was the reason that Western states refused to recognize a new Russian state (along with the official Soviet determination to foment a world revolution). These reasons account for why the USSR was not recognized by many countries for almost eight years (Italy was one of the first to do so in 1924, while the United States did not recognize the Soviet Union until 1934).[8] The refusal of leading countries to establish diplomatic relations with the USSR and recognize the legitimacy of the new regime in Moscow, which stretched on for many years, was a great irritant for the Kremlin, which saw it as an indication that the world did not believe in the durability of the Soviet system.[9] The existence of a large Russian emigrant community in Europe, with a high proportion of military people among them, was also on the minds of the Soviet leaders in the 1920s.

It was for this very reason that Soviet diplomacy expended a lot of effort in using the conflicts of various countries, and their economic interest in Soviet Russia, to gain legitimization for the Moscow regime. The world finally recognized the Soviet regime after its victory in World War II, when the Soviet Union, as one of the world's great powers, became a founder of the United Nations and a permanent member of the UN Security Council.[10]

After the war, the USSR began to struggle against the United States in a race to change regimes in various countries in each country's favor.[11] Denouncing the imperialist policy of the United States and its allies, none of the post-Stalin leaders talked about a foreign-based danger to the Soviet regime. Given the major thesis of Soviet propaganda about the "political and moral unity of the Soviet people with the party," it would have been rather humiliating and counterproductive for the masters of the Kremlin even to mention the existence of a threat of restoring the "capitalist regime." The official and highly authoritative *History of the Communist Party of the Soviet Union* talked a lot about

regimes. The imperial restorations survived Stalin's rule and continued to flourish through the Soviet period.

8 A. Prokhorov (ed.), *Bol'shaya Sovetskaia Entsiklopediia*, 3rd ed. (Moscow: Sovetskaia Entsiklopediia, 1977), p. 169.

9 Reflecting the views of the Soviet leadership in the early 1920s, Lenin wrote, "Soviet Russia is encircled by people, classes, governments which openly hate us and we have to remember that we are close to various invasions." A few years after Lenin's death, the Central Committee stated that "the danger of a counterrevolutionary war against the USSR is the most important issue of the current period." See V. Lenin, *Sobranie sochinenii*, vol. XXVII, 3rd ed. (Moscow: Politizdat, 1931) p. 117. The comparison of Soviet Russia with the revolutionary regime in France in 1789–93, which fought fiercely through the use of foreign interventions, was a fixture in Lenin's speeches and publications. See Dmitrii Shlapentokh, *The French Revolution and the Russian Anti-Democratic Tradition: A Case of False Consciousness* (New Brunswick, NJ: Transaction, 1997).

10 For the history of diplomatic recognition of the USSR see Nikolai Lebedev, *SSSR v mirovoi politike* (Moscow: Mezhdunarodnye Otnosheniia, 1982).

11 Vasily Grossman made a very shrewd note in his *Life and Destiny* (1960), writing that it was only after the Stalingrad victory that Stalin realized that the survival of his regime was guaranteed from that point forward.

international relations on the eve of Perestroika but never mentioned a threat to the Soviet system as an issue of Soviet foreign policy.[12] Indeed, this idea of a foreign threat to the Soviet order was deeply alien to Nikita Khrushchev. He scared Americans with his promise to "bury them." The same was true of Leonid Brezhnev, whose reports to the party congresses were always full of elation about the foreign successes of the Soviet Union.[13] The West was blamed for plotting against the regimes in Soviet satellites, such as Poland, Hungary, and Czechoslovakia, but never against the USSR.[14] Even in the 1970s, when the USSR was at odds with the West, Japan, and China simultaneously, Moscow did not return to the ideology of encirclement.

Since that time, the legitimacy of their own rule was never an issue for the Soviet leaders, as their legitimacy was accepted not only by the Soviet people but by Western politicians. Even Churchill, known for his hatred of the Bolsheviks, never cast doubt on the legitimacy of Stalin as the leader of Russia and found a lot of words of commendation to use in speaking about the dictator.[15] The public essentially considered any new party leader elected by the Politburo and confirmed by the Central Committee to be as legitimate as the democratically elected presidents of Western countries. Even more important for our purposes, however, is to note that the issue of legitimacy, as well as the attitudes of foreign governments toward the political order in Russia, fully disappeared from the Soviet foreign agenda. After 1945, only marginal authors of Soviet propaganda continued to insist upon the existence of various American plans to destroy the Soviet Union. In 1971, they invented the Dulles plan, which supposedly plotted the destruction of the USSR through the corruption of Soviet cultural and moral values.[16] However, Soviet leaders paid no attention to this or to other concoctions of their propagandists. In any case, this subject did not pop up at all in the numerous meetings between Soviet and American leaders after 1953. Even Reagan's famous 1983 phrase, characterizing the Soviet Union as an "evil empire," was not treated as evidence of the intention of the American president to start a crusade against the USSR. The same lack of direct threat from the United States is seen in the various American predictions about the future of

[12] B. Ponomarev (ed.), *Istoriia Kommunisticheskoi Partii Sovetskogo Soiuza* (Moscow: Politizdat, 1985), pp. 537–87.

[13] See, for instance, his report to the Twenty-Third Party Congress (*XXIII S'ezd Kommunisticheskoi Partii Sovetskogo Soiuza. Stenograficheskii otchet* [Moscow: Politizdat, 1966], pp. 20–8).

[14] W. Taubman, S. Khrushchev and A. Gleason (eds.), *Nikita Khrushchev* (New Haven, CT: Yale University Press, 2000); W. Thompson, *The Soviet Union under Brezhnev* (Harlow: Longman, 2003); R. Edmonds, *Soviet Foreign Policy – the Brezhnev Years* (Oxford and New York: Oxford University Press, 1983).

[15] See Ministry of Foreign Affairs of the USSR (compiler), *Correspondence between Stalin, Roosevelt, Truman, Churchill and Atlee during WWII* (Honolulu: University Press of the Pacific, 2001).

[16] The text was initially published in a 1971 novel, *The Eternal Call* (in Russian: *Vechnyi Zov*) by Anatoly Ivanov.

the Soviet Union. Up through 1991, there were almost none that promised the collapse of the USSR.[17]

What is more, the Soviet regimes themselves were so confident that they could afford to eschew aggressive acts in the international arena; they did not need them to provide evidence of their success as leaders. Post-Stalin Soviet leaders rarely praised their success in using force to expand or protect the Soviet influence in the world in public propaganda, preferring to play the card of the defender of the peace for their ideological purposes. Afghanistan is a typical example. The 1980 invasion of this country was hushed in the Soviet media from the very beginning. The same had been true of the military actions in Hungary in 1956 and Czechoslovakia in 1968. What a contrast with Putin! In his quest for legitimization as a successful leader, he even tried to use the war with Georgia in 2008, which was humiliating for the Russian army.

Putin's Revival of the Legitimacy Issue: Domestic Policy

Putin's rule presented a stark contrast in its perennial preoccupation with legitimacy. The question of the legitimacy of the Russian political order emerged as a crucial one starting from Putin's election in March 2000. Despite a popular victory, the fact that he was handpicked as a successor by the catastrophically unpopular Boris Yelstin suggested a dynastic transfer of power rather than a democratic one, internalized by the elites and then handed down to the voting population at large. This was further highlighted by a number of flaws in the elections themselves. First of all, it was obvious to the Russians and the world that the "election" of Putin as president was mostly fictitious – the opposition was not allowed to include its candidate in the ballot, and Putin was simply appointed by "the Tsar Boris." The first period of Putin's reign was totally devoted to justification for his staying in the Kremlin.

Unlike his Soviet predecessors, Putin was unable to create a serious official ideology with an appealing historical perspective for the justification of his regime. He had to rely on an ideology that promised to revamp the current economic and social conditions in the country. Putin made saving the country from the disarray of the 1990s a central feature of his propaganda throughout

[17] Western intelligence services and politicians, including the American ambassador in Moscow, Jack Matlock. completely failed in their predictions of the Soviet future. Among those who described themselves as being surprised were Secretary of State James Baker, Secretary of State Lawrence Eagleburger, and the high State Department official Robert McFarlane. Dozens of other journalists, intelligence officers, and politicians in the United States and Europe confessed their sense of surprise (see David Arbel and Ran Edelist, *Western Intelligence and the Collapse of the Soviet Union, 1980–1990: Ten Years That Did Not Shake the World* (London: Frank Cass, 2003), p. 200); regarding the predictions of American Sovietologists see Vladimir Shlapentokh, "Soviet society and American Sovietologists: A study in failure" in Michael Cox (ed.), *Rethinking the Soviet Collapse: Sovietology, the Death of Communism and the New Russia* (London: Cassel, 1998).

his terms (and reiterated this desire in 2012). Indeed, the chaos of the 1990s was used by Putin in much the same way the low level of the economy of prerevolutionary Russia in 1913 was used as the reference point in Soviet propaganda until 1941, to show Soviet progress in all domains of social life after the revolution. The successful fight against separatism in Chechnya and other regions, as Putin's propaganda suggested, was evidence in favor of solidifying Putin's image as the savior of the country. The stability – a key word in Putin's propaganda – of delivering pensions and salaries on time was another important argument that helped legitimize the propaganda. To enhance the legitimization of his regime, Putin positioned his rule as the natural continuity of the Soviet, and even the prerevolutionary, past.[18] Nikita Mikhalkov, a film director and Putin's friend, likes to flaunt his "monarchist convictions." In Mikhalkov's movie *Barber of Siberia*, he depicted Alexander III, who was known for his acerbic nationalism and despotism, as an ideal Russian ruler.[19] Putin's positive attitudes toward Stalin's regime have been even more clearly pronounced as a way of legitimizing his regime.[20] The restoration of such powerful symbols as the Stalinist hymn and the flag of the USSR in the army was, of course, a good indication of Putin's attitude toward the Soviet past.

Even more strongly than the Soviet leaders had, Putin, with a weak ideology and a feeble party lacking in authority, considered elections to be the major basis for the legitimacy of the regime, even if they looked bad. As the head of a feudalized society, Putin saw securing necessary outcomes in presidential and parliamentary elections, rather than enabling social or economic progress in their respective regions, as the first duty of local barons or governors. While the vassals of the Middle Ages provided the king with knights for war, Putin's vassals delivered him "the votes," using whatever technology was necessary.

Putin's concern about the legitimization of his status as the leader of the country and his determination to observe the letter of the constitution – which prohibited a person from serving more than two consecutive terms as president – were so strong that instead of simply walking into his third term in 2008, as his colleagues in Belorussia, Kazakhstan, and Uzbekistan (most Russians would have approved this action without contention) did, Putin involved himself in a complicated and risky operation that formally made Dmitry Medvedev the next president. In reality, he was just a placeholder for his boss, who returned to the presidency in 2012. In 2007, many Russian and Western analysts predicted that Putin would not risk abandoning the power of supreme leader, even if only

[18] Clifford J. Levy, "Nationalism of Putin's era veils sins of Stalin's," *New York Times*, November 26, 2008; Leonind Parfenov's interview with Ekho Moskvy radio, December 14, 2008. See, for instance, Yuri Afanasiev, "My – ne raby? Istoricheskii beg na meste: 'Osobyi put" Rossii," *Novaya Gazeta*, December 5, 2008.

[19] Vladimir Bondarenko, "Poteshnaia monarkhiia Mikhalkova," *Zavtra*, November 2, 2005.

[20] See Shlapentokh and Bondartsova, "Ideology and public opinion."

temporarily; they clearly underestimated the importance Putin attributed to the legitimacy of his presidency.[21]

Foreign Policy Enters the Fight for Legitimization

The confrontational element in Putin's foreign policy depended very much on the attitudes of foreign governments toward his regime. Xenophobic propaganda increased immediately upon Putin's arrival in power, as an argument in favor of his role as the defender of the nation. In addition to the United States (always a favorite target), the roster of enemies has, from time to time, included countries such as England and Poland and former Russian republics including the Ukraine, Belorussia, the Baltic republics, and, of course, Georgia. Decrying the "threats to Russia" on an almost everyday basis, the Kremlin returned to the propaganda of "encirclement," even if, this time, it was not a "capitalist" encirclement. The Russians had not heard statements like this for almost sixty years.[22]

In the first years of his presidency, Putin enhanced anti-American propaganda, which was already quite strong by the end of Yeltsin's rule. In the late 1990s, this propaganda described the United States as hostile to the Russian Federation and as being responsible for the failure of the country's economic reforms.[23] Official anti-Americanism was enthusiastically greeted by political and military elites, given their nostalgia for the Soviet empire and their envy of American economic and military might – which suggested that they were living in a second-rank country, spoiling their enjoyment of their status.[24]

However, the ideological hostility toward the United States was combined with a rather conciliatory practice toward that country. Indeed, Putin showed tolerance for several American actions in the international arena. In the first

[21] Some active admirers of Putin, such as the famous Russian film director Nikita Mikhalkov, asked to make Putin a tsar, saying it was the best way to make Russia stable rather than expose the country to the vagaries of an election. Vladislav Surkov, Putin's major ideologue from 2000 to 2012, advanced almost the same idea – "Putin as the national leader, is forever" – even if it was not couched in monarchic terms. See Vladislav Surkov, "Vladimir Putin byl poslan Rossii bogom," *echo.msk.ru*, July 6, 2011, http://www.echo.msk.ru/news/791683-echo.html, accessed May 15, 2012.

[22] See, for example, Putin's speech at the meeting of the Foreign Intelligence Service (SVR), in which he gave a long roster of the threats to Russia in the contemporary world. Putin called on the intelligence service to increase its activities. See "Putin call on intelligence service to increase its possibilities," *ITAR-TASS Daily*, July 25, 2007, 2012, http://dlib.eastview.com/sources/article.jsp?id=12350541, accessed May 15.

[23] See Vladimir Shlapentokh, "'Old,' 'new' and 'post' liberal attitudes toward the West: From love to hate," *Communist and Post-Communist Studies* 31.3 (1998), 119–216.

[24] Capturing the spirit of the period, the Moscow political scientist Andrei Piontkovskii (2000) published an article at the end of Putin's first year in office that described the "pathological anti-Americanism of our elite." (See Andrei Piontkovsky, "Russkii patsient," *Obshchaiia Gazeta*, December 7, 2000.)

half of 2001, some of President George Bush's actions were perceived by the Russian military establishment with horror (for instance, the exit of the United States from the ABM treaty and the declaration that they would build up their National Missile Defense program). Putin's reaction, however, was quite mild, and his meeting with President Bush in Slovenia in June 2001 was friendly. Putin's thinking was demonstrated by his policy following the events of September 11, 2001. Overnight, he became an almost cordial ally of the United States (at least publicly) and charmed the American president with his friendliness.[25]

Ignoring the fury of the military establishment, Putin practically welcomed the creation of American military bases in former Soviet Central Asia, long regarded as a zone of Moscow's influence. Citing financial considerations, Putin liquidated the former Soviet military bases in Cuba and Vietnam, generating a very positive reaction from the United States. Moscow only protested mildly against the inclusion of the former Soviet Baltic republics in NATO, a reaction that Russians would have regarded as unbelievable only a few years earlier.

The Crucial Turn in the Fight for Legitimacy: The Orange Revolutions

The Orange Revolutions in Tbilisi in 2003 and in Kiev in 2004 radically changed Putin's attitudes toward America and ended the Kremlin's feelings of nearly absolute safety for the current regime, vis-à-vis their potential domestic enemies. Putin plunged the country into a state of political nervousness that Russia had not felt since the 1920s. After these events, Putin's regime drastically changed its domestic policies and started an intensive process of dedemocratization.

Revolutions abroad, whatever their nature – nationalist, socialist, or conservative – have always generated fear in the dominant elites of various countries. Russian history is full of examples of how a revolution abroad influenced the course of events in Russia. Catherine the Great feared the impact of the French Revolution on her subjects (the writer Nikolai Radishchev was sent to Siberia because of those fears). Nicholas I was concerned about the effects of the Hungarian rebellion in 1848 (he instigated a harsh crackdown on a rather small circle of liberals that included the writer Fyodor Dostoyevsky), and Brezhnev was scared by the Czech Spring in 1968 (he initiated a period of political reaction and new repressions against dissidents in the country). In the opposite direction, the Russian revolution of 1917 had great impact

[25] Putin declared a moment of silence in the country in the aftermath of the tragic events and showed a great deal of sympathy toward America in his speech to the country on September 24, 2001. His reaction to the September events, much like his response to NMD, surprised most Moscow politicians, because one-third of the population had openly gloated over the tragedy in America. See V. Shlapentokh, J. Woods and E. Shiraev (eds.), *America: Sovereign Defender or Cowboy Nation?* (Burlington, VT: Ashgate, 2005), p. 58.

on developments in Western Europe, America, and Asia, while Gorbachev's revolutionary Perestroika sparked radical changes in East Europe, as well as violent events such as the Tiananmen Square massacre in China in 1989.

The revolutions in Georgia and the Ukraine, which pushed these countries toward democratically elected governments whose legitimacy in the aftermath of the mass protests was irreproachable, became a permanent source of irritation for Putin. In these revolutions, he saw a call to the Russian masses to follow their example. In fact, the existence of a true democratic regime in Georgia, a core Soviet republic (in the mind of the Kremlin, the Baltic republics that became part of the Soviet Union two decades after Georgia do not occupy the same status), represented a constant challenge to Putin's legitimacy.[26] In his annual call-in show on December 14, 2011, in the wake of mass demonstrations against alleged rigging in the parliamentary elections that month, Putin spoke about similar developments on Maydan Square in Kiev in November and December 2004 with the same emotion and vehemence as he had in their immediate aftermath. In December 2011, the Kremlin organized a special meeting aimed at attacking the concept of the Orange Revolution, as if the developments in Kiev had only recently occurred.[27]

Putin bears an intense animosity toward Mikhail Saakashvili, the Georgian president who emerged as the elected leader following the Georgia's Rose Revolution in 2003, verging on an almost physiological aversion, demonstrated when Putin promised "to hang [Saakashvili] by the balls" (his hatred of Viktor Yushchenko, who became the Ukrainian president as a result of the Orange Revolution in 2004, was somewhat less passionate).[28]

The war against Georgia in 2008 was a war of an authoritarian regime against a democratic one – similar to the several wars that reactionary Russia led against foreign champions of democracy, from the Hungarian revolutionaries in 1848 to the Czech liberals in 1968.

The Color Revolutions in Kiev and Tbilisi as the Western Rehearsal of Russian Regime Change

The color revolutions, in and of themselves, looked dangerous to Putin. However, his hatred of them was multiplied by his conviction that they were all staged by the West, which he believed was viewing these uprisings as rehearsals

[26] Russian liberals like Yulia Latynina constantly used the Georgian successes in democracy, and particularly in fighting corruption, in their attacks against Putin's regime. See Yulia Latynina, "Gruziia – potriasaiusche reformirovannaia strana," *Newsland.ru*, November 22, 2009, http://www.newsland.ru/news/detail/id/436485/, accessed May 15, 2012.

[27] "Na Vorob'evykh gorakh nachalsia miting protiv 'oranzhevoi prokazy'," *Lenta.ru*, December 24, 2011, http://lenta.ru/news/2011/12/24/sparrowhills/, accessed May 15, 2012.

[28] Only Senator McCain, who was very critical of Putin during the American presidential campaign of 2008 and who promised the fate of Colonel Qaddafi to the Russian leader, shares Saakashvili's intense hatred of Putin.

for doing the same thing in Russia. Indeed, the Orange Revolutions clearly intensified the West's critique of Putin's regime and its legitimacy. This deeply upset the Kremlin. Putin and the Russian elite, with their great personal material interests in the West, were made nervous by the fact that the public and officials in both America and the European Union saw the political processes in Russia as deeply antidemocratic. With the utmost displeasure, Moscow watched the West intensify its efforts to spread the view that Russia was in the process of "dedemocratization" – a term used in a prestigious report by the National Council on Foreign Affairs entitled "Russia's Wrong Direction" (2006). In 2007, Freedom House included Russia in a group of forty-five countries that it ranked as "not free,"[29] The Kremlin was even more irritated by the public criticism offered by then-high-ranking American officials, including Condoleezza Rice and Dick Cheney.[30]

Putin's regime, as mentioned earlier, was far from being as self-confident as Khrushchev's or Brezhnev's regime, and even further from being as self-assertive as Stalin's regime after the war. Therefore, Putin's Kremlin considered the Western ideological attack against it to be a danger, because it assumed that, with the slightest relaxation of pressure on the opposition, the Western critique would embolden active liberals to stage uprisings that could spread to the population at large.

In 2003–4, the Kremlin launched a counteroffensive against Western attempts to undermine the legitimization of the regime. Putin's emissaries did not mince words when they insisted that "the soft conquering of Russia" by "our foreign friends" with their "orange technology" was on "their agenda." According to Vladislav Surkov, since the orange technology "was quite successful in four countries" (he listed Ukraine, Georgia, Kyrgyzstan, and Moldova), the West was confident of its victory in Russia as well.[31] In April 2007, the pro-government *Izvestiya* daily published an article titled "The Crisis in Ukraine Was Arranged by Orangists and the USA."[32] In 2007, Putin himself showed

[29] See *Freedom House* (2007), http://www.freedomhouse.org/template.cfm?page=372&year=2007, accessed May 15, 2012.

[30] V. Kashin, "Not a Cold War yet. The US State Department explains what it thinks of Russia; Secretary of State Rice is still optimistic about relations with Russia," *Vedomosti*, May 4, 2006; M. Spetalnick, "Cheney rebukes Russia on democracy, energy 'blackmail' Vilnius," *Reuters*, May 4, 2006.

[31] Surkov, in a supposedly mild tone, talked about the "State Department that works close to us" (a reference to its subversive activity in Russia) and "much faster than we do." In order to suggest to his listeners (and readers) that these activities should be taken seriously, he reminded them of the American dictum about two types of cowboys: "the quick and the dead." (See V. Surkov, "Rossiia i demokratiia," *Ekspert*, July 3, 2006).

[32] See I. Yavlyansky, I. "Krizis na Ukraine splanirovali 'oranzhevye' i SshA," *Izvestiia*, April, 16, 2006. At the same time, *Nezavisimaia Gazeta*, an influential newspaper in Moscow, continued to insist that the United States planned "new color revolutions in Belorussia as well as in Russia" (see A. Terekhov, "Strategicheskaya piatiletka Vashingtona," *Nezavisimaia Gazeta*, April 17, 2007). In July 2007, the Kremlin-connected political analyst Sergei Markov contended, at a

that the developments in Tbilisi in 2003 and Kiev in 2004 continued to irk him when he spoke in Munich, where he gave a famously aggressive speech against the West and called on the Organization for Security and Cooperation in Europe (OSCE) to stop interfering in the internal affairs of other countries, and to stop imposing new regimes favorable to the West in those countries.[33]

Putin's belief in the West as the power behind all Orange Revolutions, past and future, suggested a worldview, one that was shared by post-Soviet Russian elites, in which the masses were unable to defend their own rights and fight for democratic principles by themselves. Moscow accepted this view almost immediately with respect to Georgia and Ukraine, as well as for Kyrgyzstan's so-called Tulip Revolution. Russian officials, including Putin, also explained the Arab Spring (2011), particularly in Egypt, in the same fashion.

The Actions against Western Material Support of Russian Democracy

As mentioned previously, together with the military intervention and ideological attacks against the Russian Federation, Western material aid to the opposition has always caused nervousness in Russian governments. In Stalin's times, the major target of the KGB was the National Alliance of Russian Solidarists (NTS), an anti-Soviet organization created by Russian emigrants, with headquarters in Germany, which had been active since 1930.[34] The Soviet authorities exaggerated the activity of this organization in helping oppositional elements inside the Soviet Union and used its existence in Stalin's time mostly for an ideological purpose – as further evidence of the danger of the "restoration" of capitalist order. More serious, however, were the activities of foreign diplomats, the CIA, various democratic organizations, and single individuals, in smuggling the books banned in the Soviet Union into Russia, as well as their help in smuggling back manuscripts like Pasternak's *Doctor Zhivago* or Svetlana Allilueva's *Twenty Letters to a Friend*.

With the collapse of the Soviet Union, the activity of prodemocratic organizations based abroad became fully legal. With his ideological counteroffensive against the West, however, Putin tried to turn back history in the leniency shown toward oppositional organizations inside Russia. Indeed, in 2006, the Kremlin declared a war against NGOs (nongovernmental organizations) by

meeting of the pro-Putin youth organization Nashi [Ours], that "the threat of lawless revolutions, such as those in Georgia and Ukraine, hangs over Russia" (see D. Nowak, "Putin gets heated in nashi talk," *Moscow Times*, July 25, 2007).

33 See Vladimir Putin, "Speech and the following discussion at the Munich Conference on Security Policy," February 10, 2007, http://kremlin.ru/eng/speeches/2007/04/26/1209_type70029type82912_125670.shtml, accessed May 15, 2012; Vladimir Putin, "Press statements and press conference with Prime Minister of Luxembourg Jean-Claude Juncker," May 24, 2007, http://www.kremlin.ru/eng/speeches/2007/05/24/1950_type82914type82915_131242.shtml, accessed May 15, 2012.

34 M. Nazarov, *The Mission of the Russian Emigration* (Moscow: Rodnik, 1994).

asserting that many of them were fronts for the West, with the goal of undermining political stability in the country under the pretext of promoting democracy. As a prominent Moscow journalist noted, "The new law against NGOs is a reaction to the series of 'color' revolutions."[35] The attack on "the stream of foreign money that is used for intervention in our internal affairs" continued in 2007 and 2008.[36] Putin devoted a special passage in his presidential address in 2007 to this issue. He also talked about it in his speech in Munich in February 2007, and again at a press conference in Luxemburg in May 2007.[37] The Duma and the federal council, along with the Kremlin, continued to lambaste the West for helping the forces that were perceived as being hostile to Russia.[38] With the mass demonstrations against the regime in 2011–12, the Kremlin again made the West's financial assistance to Russian liberals a main topic of its propaganda.[39] The pressure on NGOs grew in the wake of Putin's return to the Kremlin in May 2012. The following month, the State Duma rushed through a bill that would force NGOs receiving foreign financing to be declared "foreign agents." After the bill went into effect in November 2012, it sparked a series of debilitating searches and checks on a number of leading NGOs, involving prosecutors, tax authorities, and other law enforcement agencies.

The Second Turning Point in the Fight for Legitimacy: The Presidential Election

Putin's belief of Western intervention as a major threat to his legitimacy resurfaced again at the end of 2011. It was the result of something of a domino effect of events: (1) Putin's declaration on September 24 of his intention to swap jobs

[35] The highly publicized case of British diplomats who were supposedly arrested in Moscow for spying on January 24, 2006, represented a new example of xenophobic propaganda. (See K. Kosachev, "Britanskie diplomaty i rossiiskie pravozaschitniki deistvuyut neadekvatno," *Izvestiia*, February 3, 2006.) The spy scandal was arranged in the style of the cold war. It was used to denounce Russian NGOs for cooperating with enemies, and to scold those who were still trying to defend democratic values. (See A. Buribaev and A. Matveeva "Shpiony sredi nas," *Gazeta*, January 24, 2006; M. Rostovsky, "Skvernoi dorogoi idete, tovarishchi," *Moskovskii Komsomolets*, January 31, 2006; Y. Politov, "Bit' v nuzhnuiu tochku, po vsem pescheram. Vladimr Putin otsenil rabotu chekistov protiv terroristov i shpionov," *Izvestiia*, February 8, 2006.)

[36] The attack against the British Council was particularly heinous because its Russian employees were harassed by the FSB (E. Zubchenko and E. Shergina, "Za 'Delo Litvinenko' otvetili," *Novye Izvestiia*, January 15, 2008; V. Skosyrev, "FSB vzyalas' za britanskii sovet," *Nezavisimaia Gazeta*, January 17, 2008).

[37] See Vladimir Putin, "Speech and the following discussion at the Munich Conference on Security Policy," February 10, 2007, http://kremlin.ru/eng/speeches/2007/04/26/1209_type70029type82912_125670.shtml, accessed May 15, 2012.

[38] "Ch'ia by korova mychala...," *Slovo*, April 20, 2007.

[39] "Putin: Klinton, raskritikovav vybory v Gosdumu, dala signal 'deiateliam' vnutri RF," *Forbes.ru*, December 8, 2011, http://www.forbes.ru/news/77295-putin-klinton-raskritikovav-vybory-v-gosdumu-dala-signal-deyatelyam-vnutri-rf, accessed May 15, 2012.

with President Dmitry Medvedev without consulting voters, which upset many Russians, especially the educated urban middle class (the swap entailed that Medvedev would not even consider running against Putin); (2) the parliamentary elections on December 4, 2011, which drew an unprecedented number of election observers from the disgruntled middle class, thus revealing voting irregularities and fraud that, while present in past elections, had never before become the subject of such wide discontent; (3) the election and the fraud uncovered triggered an unprecedented outburst of antigovernment demonstrations in Moscow on a scale not seen in Russia since 1989, which continued throughout the winter in a series of authorized mass rallies and marches; and (4) the upholding of the results of the presidential election in which Putin was reelected despite widespread fraud and voting irregularities.[40] Russia's middle class, grappling with a sense of betrayal after Medvedev and Putin decided together to swap jobs (even if few actually believed that Medvedev could have emerged from Putin's shadow as an independent politician), ultimately refused to take the elections seriously or consider them legitimate in any way. This ultimate disbelief in the legitimacy of democratic procedure was illustrated by the refusal of Alexei Navalny, the most popular protest leader to emerge from the antigovernment demonstrations, even to try to run for any kind of office, on the grounds that what was happening in March 2012 was not an election but a coronation.

Facing mass dissent for the first time in twelve years, Putin resorted to playing "the foreign card," as he had with the threat posed by the Orange Revolution, insisting that the demonstrations could not have happened spontaneously, but were the work of paid agents. In two talks in December 2011 – one at a meeting of his political allies and another on his talk show – compared the protestors to chattering monkeys who were led astray, or paid to show up. Putin denigrated and derogated his disgruntled compatriots as never before[41] He declared that the United States was behind the protest actions in Russia.[42] In December 2011, Putin directly accused Secretary of State Hillary Clinton of creating anti-regime manifestations in Russia. He evidently prompted the harassment of the

[40] "Putin nazval protsent fal'sifikatsii na prezidentskikh vyborakh," *Polit.ru*, March 7, 2012, http://www.polit.ru/news/2012/03/07/putin-police/, accessed May 15, 2012.

[41] He likened the participants of the protest actions to *bandarlogs* from Rudyard Kipling's *Jungle Book*. Putin described the protesters as pawns of the opposition leaders, used in an attempt to destabilize the country. In order to humiliate protest participants even more, he labeled their white ribbons "condoms." (See "Putin sravnil belye lentochki oppozitsii s kontratseptivami," *Argumenty i Fakty*, December 15, 2011.)

[42] He insisted that that the participants "were paid for coming" by foreign agents seeking to undermine Russia. Putin said that nongovernmental organizations who accepted foreign grants were traitors akin to Judas Iscariot. He asserted that student participants "were paid and were herded like cattle by their leaders." In the same show, he accused unidentified Russians of working for foreign interests: "There are people who have Russian passports but work for the interests of a foreign state, for foreign money."

new American ambassador in Moscow, who was also declared to be a designer of protest actions; Putin lambasted him on the official Russian TV channels.[43]

Real Geopolitics

"Material" foreign politics, related to Russia's geopolitical role on the world stage and the protection of its interests abroad, plays a relatively minor role in Putin's foreign policy. Of course, Putin would have been happy to rule Russia as a superpower on a permanent quest for expansion, similarly to his Soviet predecessors. By relying on oil as his major geopolitical weapon, though, Putin (seemingly since the very beginning of his tenure) assumed that Russian military power, even with all the additional money he spent on the army, could not even remotely claim to have military parity with that of the United States, as previous Soviet leaders had claimed as a source of pride. Putin's evident indifference to the miserable state of science in his country and to the incessant flight of the best minds from Russia can only be explained by his refusal to play a significant geopolitical role in the world. It is also remarkable that Putin did not focus on using all of his opportunities to consolidate international political influence, even in interactions with the former Soviet republics. Instead, he put pure economic calculations (mostly related to oil and gas exports) ahead of political considerations. This tendency was clearly evident in his interactions with Ukraine and Belarus. When the Kyrgyz government asked Moscow to send troops to restore order in 2010 – with no objections from the international community – the Kremlin rejected this opportunity to expand its military presence in Central Asia.

"Material" Geopolitics for an Ideological Purpose: The Aggressiveness of Weak Countries

When Putin undertook "material" confrontational acts toward the United States or the West, he mostly saw them as arguments for persuading his Western partners to stay out of domestic Russian politics (Libya in 2011, Iran in 2000–12, Syria in 2011–12). However, relations between Russia and the United States during Putin's watch never reached the level of the real and dangerous confrontations that occurred in Soviet-American relations during the Cuban crisis in 1962 or the Soviet invasion of Afghanistan in 1979. What is more, Putin's Russia has been a serious and often cooperative partner to the

[43] In 1947, at the peak of the cold war, Stalin was able to order a servile newspaper to publish an article – "Harry Truman" – with personal attacks against the American president, yet the Kremlin accorded the American ambassador at this time, Walter Bedell Smith, full respect. It is evident to us now that if Smith had been treated in the same way as the current American ambassador, he would have immediately packed his belongings. (Boris Gorbatov, "Garri Truman," *Literaturnaia Gazeta*, September 1947.)

West in such areas as the fight against international terrorism and the war against the Taliban in Afghanistan.[44]

Putin's behavior in the international arena fit very well with the behavior of small countries in history that, despite a lack of resources, have positioned themselves to be great international actors. This is a vitally important move for governments seeking to enhance their legitimacy in the world's eyes as well as those of its own population. Examples of this include acts by Fidel Castro and Nicolae Ceauşescu. Not only did Castro goad Washington with regular offensive broadsides against the United States, but he also challenged America through Cuba's military intervention in Angola's civil war. This was in addition to the participation of Cuban soldiers against American troops in the defense of the leftist regime in Grenada. During the 1970s and 1980s, Castro was able to persuade his subjects to accept that he, and therefore Cuba, played a key role in international politics. Similarly, Nicolae Ceauşescu challenged the USSR in every possible way. Romania's case is even more remarkable because, unlike Cuba, which could hope for intervention from Moscow, Romania was on its own.[45] The spirit of Romania as a quasi-great country was fueled by the glorification of its past as a major heir of the Roman Empire. In both Romania and Cuba, the population considered their country almost equal to the superpowers and hailed their leaders as being highly influential and the wisest politicians in the world. In many respects, the substance of Putin's foreign policy is reminiscent of Castro's and Ceauşescu's aggressive acts against the superpowers of forty or fifty years ago. The reality, however, was that if nuclear weapons were taken out of the equation, Russia – with its reduced economic and military potential – is far removed from the might and abilities of the USSR. This means that its capacity to provoke the United States is not much greater than was Cuba's or Romania's power to do so.

The Magnitsky Affair and Private Property as a Driver of Putin's Foreign Policy

The feudalization of Russian society and the leading role of big money in a state that lacks functional rule of law influenced Russian foreign policy in another

[44] In 2012, Putin allowed NATO to use a Russian city, Ulianovsk, as a transit hub for goods shipped to and from Afghanistan. He ignored the protests of Communists and nationalists against his decision (see Andrew Kramer, "NATO plans in Russian city are protested," *New York Times*, April 22, 2012).

[45] In 1968, Romania refused to support the invasion of Czechoslovakia by the countries of the Warsaw Pact. Nor did Ceauşescu sever relations with Israel after the Six Day War in 1967, as the USSR and its allies had. Romania also participated in the 1984 Summer Olympics in America, which was boycotted by the USSR and its satellites. Even more important, however, is that Romania maintained cordial relations with China after the 1969 battle on Damansky Island, even as the rest of the world debated the chance of a large-scale Soviet-Chinese military confrontation.

important way. Never in Russian history were their leaders so absorbed with enrichment – for themselves and for their elites – as Putin and Yeltsin. In making his foreign policy moves, Putin acted the way a feudal monarch in the Middle Ages would have, taking into account how much his actions would endanger his and his friends' assets abroad and how much they would help to continue his enrichment.

The personal component played a particular role in Putin's attitude toward the foreign activity of Gazprom. The promotion of foreign trade activity for this major Russian company was obviously dictated not only by economic interests based on raw materials export, but by Putin's personal interests as well. It is highly remarkable that Putin established his best relations with those leaders in Europe who had a clear reputation as corrupt politicians, such as Silvio Berlusconi and Gerhard Schroder.[46] Perhaps the best illustration of private property as a determining factor in Putin's foreign policy is the Magnitsky Act debacle. The passage by the U.S. Congress of the Russia and Moldova Jackson-Vanik Repeal and Sergei Magnitsky Rule of Law Accountability Act in December 2012 infuriated Putin to such an extent that he signed a bill not only retaliating by similarly blacklisting certain Americans from Russian soil, but also by banning the U.S. adoption of Russian orphans, depriving hundreds of children of chances for lifesaving medical treatment, and straining U.S.-Russian relations to a level that was unprecedented during Putin's tenure.

The story of this bill – and the Magnitsky affair that sparked it – is central to understanding the role of private property and capital in Russia's foreign policy. It also helps clarify Putin's insistence on democratic procedure as the source of his legitimacy in the absence of real democratic institutions. To improve understanding of the enrichment mechanisms that were set in motion, and how they wound up determining a key decision in Russia's foreign policy, we should look at the operating conditions of the American fund manager William Browder, who began working in Russia during the late 1990s.

The accumulation of wealth – whether as personal enrichment for Putin or for members of his elite – would not have been possible without aggressive foreign investment. Attracting foreign investment, in fact, has been somewhat an obsession for Putin ever since he headed the External Affairs Committee in the administration of the St. Petersburg Mayor Anatoly Sobchak in the early 1990s. During that stint, Putin used connections he had developed while serving as a KGB officer in Dresden to facilitate a number of privatization deals in St. Petersburg through joint ventures with German firms and banks. The legality of this activity – and critics, most notably the late Marina Salie, have alleged widespread corruption and embezzlement on Putin's part – is of secondary importance; even if a lot of this activity wound up benefiting the economy of St. Petersburg (or, according to Salie, harming it), it illustrates Putin's priorities

[46] Janine R. Wedel, *Shadow Elite: How the World's New Power Brokers Undermine Democracy, Government, and the Free Market* (New York: Basic Books, 2009).

when it comes to governance, either on a municipal level in St. Petersburg or on a federal level.

This imperative toward enrichment was not Putin's invention, however. But it was also an imperative that was dependent on the goodwill of foreign investors, many of whom were comfortable doing business with a moderately authoritarian leader, just not one of the Alexander Lukashenko variety, so long as that leader provided access to the country's resources.

William Browder, who began aggressively investing in Russian companies through his fund, Hermitage Capital Management, in 1996, became a typical example of this kind of relationship. By 2005, Hermitage Capital had invested an estimated $4 billion in major state corporations such as Gazprom and Transneft. But Browder, who engaged in a form of greenmail with Russian companies, overestimated his standing with Russian authorities.

Until he was personally barred entry into Russia in 2006 – a development linked to his encroachment on the financial interests of the major companies he was investing in – Browder, like many foreign investors, was willing to tolerate infringements on democracy and even corruption as long as the government was on his side. Even as Western leaders voiced concern over the imprisonment of Mikhail Khodorkovsky in 2003, Browder had continued lavishly and unabashedly praising Putin and his regime. In an interview with one of the authors in 2011, he admitted that he had an "alignment of interests" with Putin: "My original feelings about Putin were based very narrowly on what he did for us in the first three years of his regime. Since I was fighting with a number of these oligarchs who were stealing money from the companies I was investing in I was delighted when Putin would step into the fight on our side. For a period of time, we had an alignment of interests."[47]

Browder's misinterpretation of that "alignment" led to catastrophic results. If Browder saw Putin's persecution of oligarchs as part of an ideological policy, it was, in fact, merely a tactic of solidifying power. When Browder's greenmailing encroached on the interests of those close to Putin (interests that the Putin elite equated with national strategic interests), he was barred from entering Russia on the pretext of being a security threat. At one point, Browder even approached Putin's future successor, Dmitry Medvedev, for help in reinstating his visa. But help was denied: instead, Browder's company, Hermitage Capital, became fair game in a tax scam that was common in Russia, whereby corrupt tax officials (who, in this case, were protected by high-placed officials in the FSB and the Defense Ministry) would use fake firms to embezzle tax refunds. When Sergei Magnitsky, a lawyer hired by Browder, uncovered the scam, he was jailed on similar accusations. As a form of pressure, prison officials refused to treat an underlying medical condition, and Magnitsky died in prison in 2009.

[47] A. Arutunyan, "The mystery behind Magnitsky's death," *The Moscow News*. November 14, 2011. http://www.themoscownews.com/business/20111114/189204869.html.

The scandal that ensued pushed Browder to lobby the U.S. Congress to pass the Magnitsky Act, blacklisting officials implicated in Magnitsky's death and other corruption-related offenses and freezing their assets. The passage of this act in 2012 infuriated Putin and those close to him because it curtailed the vacations and foreign assets that a number of high-placed officials in Russia enjoyed. But there was also another reason. For years, Putin had been struggling to get the Jackson-Vanik Amendment repealed, seeing it as an obstacle to trade and foreign investment in Russia. The fact that the U.S. Congress repealed the amendment only to implement another limitation stung precisely because it hit at the foreign investment and enrichment aspect that was so central to Putin's foreign policy as a whole.

The seemingly unrelated U.S. adoption ban – an apparently populist measure that had been in the works for years – baffled the protesting middle class not only because it would deprive about a thousand orphans each year of adoptive homes, but also because it was directly linked to a geopolitical statement.

During Putin's major press conference in December 2012, he fielded about eight pointed questions about the adoption ban, in which one adoptive parent even called it "cannibalistic." Nowhere in his answers did he deny that he saw it as an appropriate response to the Magnitsky Act. Moreover, he admitted just how infuriated he was by the act: "Mr. Magnitsky personally is not the issue at stake. The issue is that US lawmakers, having got rid of one anti-Russian, anti-Soviet act – the Jackson-Vanik amendment (and they were forced to do so for economic reasons) – decided they would pass another anti-Russian act immediately."[48]

The apparent contradiction of focusing so much on foreign investment despite an apparently hostile attitude toward the United States has continued to baffle observers to this day,[49] but given the priorities outlined previously, it would make perfect sense for Putin to demonstrate a tough stance politically while aggressively courting investors back home. A delicate balance of legitimacy and financial interests bolster each other: with Putin's legitimacy dependent on investment and investment dependent on legitimacy.

Conclusion

The foreign policies of the Soviet leaders and Putin differed in many key ways. On the one hand, we saw a strong, highly centralized, and totalitarian state,

[48] See official transcript of news conference of Vladimir Putin, December 20, 2012. http://eng.kremlin.ru/news/4779.

[49] Timothy Heritage of Reuters marveled in June 2012 that "no one is sure who [Putin] is trying to be." First he showed a "prickly, though and uncompromising" side during a meeting with the U.S. President Barack Obama, reviving "memories of Cold War diplomacy." But just three days later, "Putin was back in his home town of St. Petersburg and turning on the charm for investors." See: "Russia's Putin: Who does he want to be in new term?" Reuters, June 22 2012, http://www.reuters.com/article/2012/06/22/russia-putin-idUSL5E8HM43I20120622, accessed April 11, 2013.

while on the other, we saw a feudalized society with a weak centralized state and a leader whose private interests included defending the legitimacy of his power against rivals and protecting the personal fortunes of his elites. While big money was absent as a political factor during Soviet times, its role in Putin's Russia became crucial in influencing development in the country, including that regarding foreign policy. The illegal sources for the big money of most of the Russian political and economic actors made all of them enemies of democracy. This was especially true of Putin himself: his retaining power and maintaining legitimacy became an issue of not only his political and economic survival but also of his physical survival.

The Soviet regimes before 1945 were extremely concerned about legitimacy. These worries declined radically after the victory in World War II and were practically absent in the politics of the subsequent Soviet leaders until the collapse of the USSR. They reemerged as a leading problem for Putin's regime. As happened in the first three decades after the revolution, Putin's regime, which failed to build its legitimacy on democratic process, faced hostility and suspicion from the West concerning its legitimacy. With questionable legitimacy at home, Putin – unlike any post-Stalin Russian leader before him – considered his foreign policy first as an instrument to defend his legitimacy against foreign powers, which he thought could help domestic opposition. The color revolutions exacerbated Putin's fears about the safety of his regime, mostly because he assumed that the West sponsored the regime changes in some of the former Soviet republics.

At the same time, Putin's real geopolitics were very timid and mostly served the purpose of strengthening his legitimacy as leader. In some ways, his policies toward the United States followed the pattern of Castro's Cuba or Ceauşescu's Romania: teasing a superpower for the purpose of gaining prestige inside the country, while never actually getting close to a real confrontation.

Perhaps a key factor in Putin's foreign policy was that, unlike those of any Soviet leader, his decisions were influenced by his wealth and the necessity of maintaining access to the West, where many of the elites kept their assets, and ensuring the flow of foreign investment. Putin encouraged economic relations with any foreign country that could be helpful to his and his clan's material interests.

The differences between Putin's foreign policy and his Soviet predecessors' are enormous and have been largely determined by the new social order that emerged in Russia after 1991, closely dependent on private assets.

8

A Freedom That Putin Dearly Loves – The Right to Leave His Country

The list of freedoms violated in some way by Putin's regime is quite long. This regime has significantly restrained the freedom of the media; it has a track record of destroying independent TV channels. The regime has considerably curtailed freedom of speech by limiting access to electronic media to either the leaders of opposition parties or authors critical of the regime. Putin's regime has restricted freedom of election from all political bodies in the country; it has not permitted leading politicians to be included on the ballots of presidential and parliamentary elections. The regime has also systematically rigged the results of all elections in the country, including the presidential election on March 4, 2012.

Putin's regime has made it very difficult for Russians to use the freedom to assemble by either banning unendorsed gatherings outright or limiting the number of participants, reaching this end through subservient local authorities who have the formal power to allow or ban rallies; the regular and brutal use of special police forces (the notorious OMON) against protesters has scared many Russians away from taking part in political demonstrations. The Kremlin has regularly restricted the registration of political parties, fundamentally undermining the people's freedom of assembly.

In addition, Putin's regime has been far from impeccable in its implementation of religious freedoms. Various federal agencies and many local authorities continue to restrict the rights of some religious minorities. The international community does not believe Putin's Russia is either very free or very democratic for many of these reasons; in 2011, Freedom House characterized Russia as "not free." Despite all of this, there is one freedom that is respected in Russia no less than it is in any democratic country in the world: the freedom to move in and out of the country. The Soviet people were completely deprived of this freedom. In fact, the Soviet people's assignment to either the "travelable" list (this represented only a tiny minority of trusted people who passed KGB clearance) or the "not travelable" list (the majority of citizens, who were suspected of being likely to defect during a foreign trip) was a humiliating ordeal for many. The right to emigrate from the USSR was at the center of political life in that country and in the world in the 1970s and 1980s, until Perestroika changed the game.

Several people accused Andrei Sakharov of paying too much attention to the right to emigrate in his fight for democracy in Russia, which, at the time, only concerned two minorities in the country: Jews and Germans. But Sakharov, in his wisdom, saw the fight for "freedom of departure" – a term from those times – as the optimal way to start the general offensive for the democratization of Soviet society. For the same reason, my friends in Moscow saw the Jackson-Vanik Amendment in 1974 as more than simply an act in favor of the freedom of emigration for Jews; it was also an appeal to the Soviet government to join the group of nations that respect freedom of emigration.

Sakharov and all of us were confident – and considering the developments in post-Soviet Russia, here is where we made a mistake – that the materialization of the freedom to leave the country would be incompatible with an authoritarian regime and would wreck the entire Soviet order. The Soviet anecdote about the meeting between the general secretary and Brigitte Bardot, a popular French actress of that time, conveyed this belief well. The French film star begged Brezhnev, whose sympathy for beautiful women was well known, to allow everybody who wants to leave the country to be able to do so. "Oh, you little rogue," retorted the Soviet leader with amusement, "you want us to be alone," implying, of course, that if given the freedom to leave the country, all Soviet people would leave Russia, and nobody would disturb the couple.

Very few Russians – none who remember Soviet times – could have predicted that of all the freedoms eliminated or limited during Putin's rule, freedom of movement would be left intact. But this miracle happened. Despite a turn towards authoritarianism, the freedom to leave the country has survived. During all the years of Putin's rule, there has not been one case when somebody (who was not incarcerated, of course) was denied the right to leave the country. We do not know of even one case when somebody's foreign passport was withdrawn. To illustrate this lax control over transportation into and out of the country, consider that even the most ardent of Putin's foes, like Boris Nemtsov, who was not allowed to appear on state TV stations, was not obstructed in his travel to European ski resorts after his fiery speech on Bolotnaya Square on December 24, 2011. After giving his speech at the gathering, in which he demanded Putin be ousted from power, the writer Boris Akunin was allowed to go to his estate in France. Viktor Shenderovich, an avid Putin critic, was recently allowed to travel to the United States and earn money with his satirical shows poking fun at Putin. The writer Dmitry Bykov was allowed to host similar shows within the country. It was impossible to imagine such events in the Soviet past, when even a cautious critical remark about the life of the Soviet

Union, made by a Soviet citizen while abroad publicly or privately would mark him forever as "not travelable."

During his tenure as president and prime minister, Putin's absolute tolerance of the freedom of departure for Russians has passed many tests. Putin has endured the ceaseless departure of the best minds in the country. He is indifferent, for instance, to the fact that 15 percent of the graduates of Ph.D. programs leave the country each year, and the majority of them, especially the brightest, never return to Russia. Similarly, in the last decade, more than a hundred thousand scholars and engineers have left their homeland, never to return. It was exactly these people who could have advanced the locomotion of Russian science and industry and who would have been vitally important for the military-industrial complex.

This is another indication that Putin has little concern for the real geopolitical position of his country in the near future. Note that Stalin – without question a tyrant – was looking toward the future, even when the country was literally bleeding during the war, as he exempted all students in technical colleges as well as all scholars with Ph.D.s from military service. Conversely, Putin, during his numerous public statements, has almost never complained about the loss of intellectual capital. What is more, he seems to want to make the flight of Russians even easier. A key priority for Russia's EU policy is a visa-free regime for Russian citizens. It is, perhaps, the one thing that Russian leaders want most from the EU.

In his tolerance of emigration, Putin has surpassed the Soviet people's wildest dreams about living life abroad. Putin went so far as practically to endorse a change of citizenship for Russians. It is difficult to imagine a similar tolerance during Brezhnev's time, when people who expressed their desire to emigrate immediately became outcasts and often faced tribulations for many years, as "refuseniks." Putin, in speaking about his friend, the businessman Gennady Timchenko (many people link the origin of Putin's wealth with Timchenko, the co-founder of the oil processing company Gunvor), did not find anything abnormal in the fact that Timchenko acquired Finnish citizenship, commenting only that "it can help his business." It is nearly impossible to imagine an American or Chinese president hailing a powerful CEO for taking foreign citizenship.

Indeed, as a great advocate of open borders, Putin has no rivals among foreign leaders. While the heads of most of the affluent countries regularly bemoan the move of capital abroad for a variety of reasons (e.g., loss of domestic job opportunities and taxes), Putin has never uttered one word of regret about this practice; rather, he systematically justifies it.

Putin appears nonplussed by the flight of capital from Russia, which increased to $85 billion in 2011, doubling the previous year's amount. In a meeting with Russian political scientists in February 2012, Putin could not find even mild words of regret for this process and even praised Viktor Vekselberg, one of the moguls closest to him, for his investment in a Swiss company. Evidently, he did not drop Roman Abramovich from his circle of friends either, when this oligarch bought, among his many other foreign assets, the Chelsea football club in England, infuriating many Russian patriots. How can we explain Putin's remarkable love for freedom of movement? Is it due to his devotion to democracy? No. In fact, the freedom of movement serves the private interests of the Russian leaders and members of the whole ruling class, who wish to have free access to their bank accounts and villas abroad, as well as to Western schools, hospitals, and resorts. The life of the Russian elite is so deeply intertwined with the West that Moscow's biggest fears are no longer reserved for new American weapons – the main concern of the Politburo on the eve of Perestroika – but a ban prohibiting Russian officials from going to the West.

Ironically, the ruling class and the masses totally converge in their attitudes regarding freedom of movement. Indeed, as numerous surveys show, the ordinary Russian values freedom of movement to a degree that is two to three times greater than his or her value of the freedom to elect a government or even exercise free speech. In 2011, no less than 20–30 percent of Russians considered freedom of movement one of their most cherished Russian achievements.

Article 27 in the Russian Constitution states that that "everyone who is lawfully in the territory of the Russian Federation has the right to freely move and choose a place to stay or live." So far, Putin's regime, whatever its motivation, has completely honored this freedom. But it is a pity that his government has done so little to discourage Russians from leaving their country.

The developments in Russia related to the inauguration of the new president in May 2012 significantly changed the political climate in Moscow. Putin began his third term as president with a growing aggressiveness against those who took to the streets to demonstrate their refusal to recognize the legitimacy of his regime. The Kremlin responded quickly, with the arrests of hundreds of protesters and with police brutality that has not been seen in Russia in decades. Russian analysts now ponder whether these events will portend another step in the hardening of the regime in the near future. Will the regime punish oppositional activists by withdrawing their freedom to leave the country and return? Ironically, it is the material interest of the ruling elite that serves as a guarantee of existing freedoms, including the freedom to leave the country. These material interests are also what prevent Putin from cracking down harder on dissent. The probability of closing the borders haunts the minds of not only the people in the opposition but of many Russians who are far removed from political battles.

It is, of course, strongly in the West's interests for Russia to remain open, as it has been since Gorbachev's Glasnost.

Conclusion

The Uniqueness of Putin's Regime in Light of Russian History

Russia is a remarkable experimental ground for the study of various authoritarian regimes. In fact, over its thousand-year history, Russian society has been dominated either by an authoritarian state in a mostly centralized society (as happened in monarchist Russia from the sixteenth century until 1917, and then in Soviet Russia until 1991) or by a combination of authoritarianism and feudalism (as it was from the emergence of the Kievan Rus until Ivan the Terrible, and from 1993, when Yeltsin installed his dictatorship, until the present). The third segment of society – the liberal one – only held a leading role for a few months in the aftermath of the February revolution in 1917, and for a few years after the collapse of the Soviet Union (1991–3). In the quest for liberal traditions in Russian history some Russian historians such as Vasily Kluchevsky described the Russian city Novgorod, as well as the neighboring city Pskov, both located in the northwest of European Russia, in the twelfth through fifteenth centuries as democratically ruled city-republics of the Hanseatic type with the public assembly (Veche) as the key political institution.

There is an arsenal of means that an authoritarian state can use to keep subjects under control and prevent the destruction of the regime. This includes physical repressions against real or potential enemies, control over the minds of the masses, material rewards for the people in the repressive apparatus (beginning with the political police and the army), and the stimulation of the intellectual elite – material or coercive – to engage them in ideological work useful to the state. Authoritarian regimes mostly differ from each other in the intensity of their repressive actions and in the role of single instruments used for coercion of their subjects.

The choice of repressive methods always depends on the leader of the regime. In fact, the head of an authoritarian regime is like a driver who can choose one exit or another on a highway, for good or bad, for himself or for the country, choosing one level of repression or another, choosing the physical extermination of opponents to the regime or "merely" firing them from their jobs or expelling them abroad. His or her attitude toward repressions depends on various factors. First of all, he and the people who have connected their fate with him have to make up their minds as to which is more dangerous to the survival of the regime and its leader, harsh repressions or a liberal policy. The leader also has to calculate the international and economic situation, as well as the power of the opposition and its potential for seizing power, in deciding the question of repression. The policy of the predecessor will also play an important role: the probability of more liberal policies is higher if the previous leader emphasized repressions, and vice versa. Neither should the personality of the leader in an authoritarian regime be overlooked. The personalities of Stalin, Brezhnev, and Putin account for a lot of the repressive measures seen during their regimes.

Of course, the level of repressions is not the only criterion for distinguishing between authoritarian regimes. A comparison of the authoritarian regimes that existed in Russia before the October revolution of 1917 shows that the differences in the social and economic structures of the regimes were no less important, in some cases, than the character of the repressive mechanisms used. Indeed, the other two segments of society – feudal and liberal – had a great impact on the functioning of society. The regimes of Nicholas I and Alexander II were quite different, not only because the level of the repression was high in one case and relatively low in the other, but also because the role the liberal sector played was almost nil under Nicholas, while it became quite important by the end of the reign of his son.

The differences between some of the other authoritarian regimes in Russian history can be reduced almost exclusively to the level of coercion used, physical and ideological. Such is the case if we compare the regimes of Catherine the Great, on one hand, and Alexander I, on the other. There were no serious disparities in the political, economic, and social structures of the two reigns, even if Alexander did make some attempts to liberalize society in the beginning of his rule, all of which were aborted. The level of repression under his watch declined significantly, however, when compared with that of the previous regimes. A comparison of the next two regimes – Alexander I and Nicholas I – produces the same result: no disparity in the social, political, and economic structures but an enormous disparity in the level of repression. The real predecessor of the KGB – the notorious Third Section of the Chancellery, headed by the general Alexander Benkendorf – was created by Nicholas. Like the KGB, the new organization installed control over all Russians involved in any sort of public activity, at the same time it created censorship guaranteeing that no text even remotely critical of the monarchy could be printed.

The number of victims of the Third Section of the Chancellery was staggering for that time. It included about six hundred arrested as participants of the Decembrist plot, as well as forty members of the Petrashevsky revolutionary circle. Aside from the five executed Decembrists, in both cases, all those sentenced by the court were sent to Siberia. The new (liberal) regime of Alexander II freed them in 1856. (One hundred years later, Khrushchev's liberal regime did the same with Stalin's victims.)

The differences among the various Soviet regimes, like the differences between the regimes of Alexander I and Nicholas I, were only in the level of repression. In fact, the political, social, and economic institutions that were shaped in the first five years after the emergence of the Soviet order did not change until Perestroika. Physical repressions reached a peak during Stalin's reign, the harshest of all Soviet regimes. According to the official data of the KGB, roughly 3.8 million people were arrested and sentenced by nonjudicial bodies (the notorious troika) to death, internal exile, or the Gulag. Of this group 786,000 people were executed from the 1930s to the early 1950s. These figures, as the KGB data asserted, do not include the victims of dekulakization, starvation, and deportation. In this time, not only the behavior but even the minds of all Russians were controlled by the state apparatus, which kept strict control over each printed word, and over the activities of each scholar, teacher, writer, painter, musician, or movie or theater director.

First and foremost, fear of the state and political police embraced all strata of the population, mostly because the informers were insiders, even in such small units as a college class or a small provincial theater. Fear in Stalin's time was so overwhelming that it could wield enormous influence on the relations not only between colleagues and neighbors but also inside the family – between parents and children, and even between spouses.

The fear in Stalin's time was so strong that even seven decades later, when Russia was supposedly a different country, it continued to linger in the mentality of many Russians, even among the younger generations. This continuity of fear, which can hardly be detected in the post-Communist Baltic republics or in Poland, can only be ascribed to the fact that, from Stalin forward, Russians have not even had a single decade where they lived in a society that was not dominated by authoritarian institutions and repression.

The Soviet regimes that followed Stalin, up until Perestroika, only varied in the intensity of their physical repression and their ideological control over the population, particularly over the so-called creative intelligentsia. The major political institutions of an authoritarian (or, rather, totalitarian) regime remained the same in all of the Soviet regimes after the civil war. The political order was always deeply antidemocratic, with key roles played by the party and political police, as well as with its fake elections, and with the state monopoly on media, education, science, and the arts. Unlike with the political order, the building of the totalitarian economic system demanded more time, and Stalin finished the job by the middle of the 1930s after he exterminated the remnants of the liberal economy of the early 1920s and carried out mass collectivization. However, in the next fifty years the structure of the Soviet economy remained essentially intact. Khrushchev, for example, tried to stimulate economic growth with some decentralization of economic decisions. He was ousted from his position in 1964, when there were lines for bread in every city and a nationwide shortage of almost all consumer goods. Although its methods were different from those of Khrushchev, Brezhnev's regime made the same efforts to decentralize the management of the economy (the so-called Kosygin reforms), or at least to improve it by using computers and mathematical methods of planning. Brezhnev's attempts failed as badly as Khrushchev's, and none of the post-Stalin regimes could claim to have created their own economic order.

It is true that confrontations with the West diminished after Stalin's death, but not radically. Until the collapse of the USSR, the militarization of society was practically the same as it had been in Stalin's times. The Soviet state continued to participate in the weapons race without any respite. Khrushchev's and, in particular, Brezhnev's steps to soften Soviet animosity toward the West from time to time did not change the atmosphere of the cold war in any essential way. After 1953, all of the subsequent regimes continued to consider the West as the enemy; the cold war determined the foreign policies of Khrushchev and Brezhnev, not to mention Andropov, who elevated international tension to the level that existed in the last years of Stalin's reign, when the Korean War could have triggered a global conflict between the two superpowers. The USSR continued to protect its dominance in Eastern Europe by means of brute force (the suppression of the Hungarian insurrection by Khrushchev, and of the Prague Spring by Brezhnev), and the attempts to expand control over other countries continued after Stalin on a full scale; the intervention in Afghanistan under Brezhnev was the post-Stalin culmination of Soviet geopolitical efforts.

However, it was the level of repression that truly formed the face of each post-Stalin Soviet regime. Khrushchev's regime did not enter history as that which made the USSR a superpower (as suggested by Sergei Khrushchev in his book *Nikita Khrushchev and the Creation of a Superpower*) but as a thaw after Stalin's terror. This regime practically declared Stalin a criminal, releasing hundreds of thousands of prisoners from the Gulag and giving a postmortem acquittal to legions of Stalin's victims; it alleviated censorship; it allowed the emergence of new Soviet literature – all but making Solzhenitsyn, with his harsh criticism of Gulag atrocities, a hero of Soviet literature; empirical sociology and mathematical economics, which had previously been regarded as bourgeois sciences, were given new life under Khrushchev; many foreign authors were translated; and contacts with the West were increased. Fear declined somewhat throughout the country, and people became more open with each other.

Brezhnev's regime entered history with signs of being the opposite of Khrushchev's. On the whole, Brezhnev's regime was a partial return to Stalin's times, particularly after the invasion of Czechoslovakia in 1968. It was this regime that started re-Stalinization in ideology; it revived the persecution of dissidents, carrying out trials against some of them; expelled Solzhenitsyn abroad and exiled Sakharov to the provinces; it declared a war on the intelligentsia; fired and even arrested some intellectuals who participated in protest actions; and persecuted liberal scholars. It also encouraged Russian chauvinism and increased the level of anti-Semitism. At the same time, Brezhnev's regime made one very important move in its politics of repression: it allowed Jewish emigration, for the sake of a temporary improvement of relations with the United States – an unprecedented act that greatly influenced future developments in Russia.

The differences between the Soviet regimes and post-Soviet regimes (Putin's, first and foremost) are of a very different nature than the differences among the Soviet regimes. The core of the differences can be seen in the emergence of liberal and feudal segments that existed only in an embryonic stage in Soviet times. The interactions of these three segments in post-Soviet times produced a very specific, even unique society with a very particular authoritarian power.

Among the elements of the liberal segment that became embedded in Russian life were several freedoms, including free movement inside and outside the country; the total openness of the country to the external world; freedom of speech in private and, to a limited degree, in the public sphere; and the freedom, though limited, to assemble. However, the most important element of liberalization was the legalization of big business in society, which had immense consequences for a society with strong feudal tendencies, including a weak state and low observance of the rule of law. The emergence of big business as a crucial actor in Russian society led to the expansion of corruption to a level that would have been unbelievable in any of the Russian regimes in the nineteenth and twentieth centuries, and that also, consequently, led to the concentration of big money in the Kremlin. With the elimination of the financing of various pro-Soviet regimes abroad, and with the drastic reduction in military expenditures, a gigantic amount of money accumulated at the personal disposal of the Kremlin's master. The curtailment of expenditures on public goods – science, education, culture, and health services – only increased the resources at Putin's disposal. Legislators' decisive voice in how to use taxpayers' money has always been the main instrument for controlling executive power in a truly democratic society. It is well known that the fight against absolutist monarchy has often begun with a demand from the elected parliament to control the budget. However, the Duma – the Russian parliament – had, in fact, no real impact on the use of the budget or the enormous extra budgetary resources controlled by Putin's regime. Of no less importance was the free access the Kremlin had to the resources of big corporations – state, private, and mixed. The corporations whose very existence was at the mercy of the Kremlin (as was the case for many Russian fortunes) were ready to satisfy any of the Kremlin's demands for money – whether to fulfill the personal needs of the rulers or for their pet projects, like the Olympic Games.

It is obvious that without universal corruption and lawlessness – both of which are products of feudal tendencies – such a concentration of money in the Kremlin would have been impossible in the past. All Russian regimes, at least in the nineteenth and twentieth centuries, fought corruption as well as feudal tendencies, even if they had different results. The two post-Soviet regimes, Yeltsin's and Putin's, were the first in Russian history in which the government not only was *not* fighting corruption at the highest echelons of power but, in fact, encouraged it as the best way to ensure the loyalty of bureaucracy and big business to the regime. None of the previous leaders promoted feudal elements in the country to such an extent that allowed officials at all levels of bureaucracy – such as those who were included in the Magnitsky Act – to use their offices as feudal fiefs for personal enrichment, with a guarantee of immunity against prosecution by law enforcement agencies.

None of the regimes before 1991 – and again, the parallels with the early Middle Ages are obvious here – intentionally made governors into feudal barons, like Alexander Tkachev, the governor of Krasnodar region, who could do anything in their power in their provinces; they enriched themselves and the members of their families and maintained ties with criminal structures. The only demands Putin's regime made of the governors were to ensure that their population voted in favor of the Kremlin and to guarantee the absence of mass protests. None of the previous authoritarian leaders could make feudal servants of their business bosses, as Putin did with Oleg Deripaska, who put his resources at the total disposal of the Kremlin, or as Mikhail Prokhorov, who demonstrated his readiness to play a role in political shows at the Kremlin's behest, in exchange for various privileges.

Putin's regime was so immersed in corruption that it did not even dare to fight it inside law enforcement agencies. All the Russian regimes in the past considered the integrity of their political police to be a necessary condition for fulfilling its duty as their watchdog. This was not the case for Putin's Kremlin, which saw the corruption inside the FSB, the heir of the KGB, as well as in the Ministry of Internal Affairs or the Investigative Committee, or inside other governmental structures, with clear equanimity. During the first two decades of post-Soviet history, not one high official or big business executive was sued in court, and none went to trial. For instance, Yury Luzhkov, former Moscow mayor, was not prosecuted, even though his corruption activity was divulged in several documentary movies in 2012.[1]

In fact, unlike every other regime in Russian history, Putin's administration used corruption in order to tie not only the holders of various state offices to the regime, but also millions of ordinary people, like doctors and teachers, traffic officers and the inspectors of fire departments and sanitation units, who were bribed by citizens both to implement their legal rights and to skirt them.

It was the possibility of personally operating with immense resources, and mostly for their own benefit, that greatly changed the behavior of post-Soviet leaders in comparison with their predecessors. It looks as if the gigantic military

[1] A new anti-corruption campaign that the Kremlin launched in the first half of 2013 was in fact only for show since again none of the leading politicians or businessmen in the country were brought to court.

machine controlled by Soviet leaders and the ability – at least in post-Stalin times – to push the button to start a nuclear war did not make them as self-interested and self-important as big money, with its control of resources (gas and oil), made Putin. Soviet leaders led an ascetic life by the standards in Putin's times, and could not transfer any assets to their offspring. Almost none of the heads of the Russian state in the nineteenth and twentieth centuries, nor their ruling elites, was as absorbed with personal enrichment as Yeltsin and Putin. None of the previous leaders, even taking into account Nikita Khrushchev, who was known for his emotional outbursts, and definitely not the highly educated Russian monarchs, ever used language as vulgar as did Putin. Stalin – who sent a lot of people to their deaths with the wink of an eye – never allowed himself to behave like a lout in public, as Putin does. None of the Russian leaders would have dared to perform circus stunts, as Putin does, to show the public how macho he is. It is simply not possible to imagine that one of the Russian (or foreign) leaders in history would have done the same (only Mao Zedong swimming in the Yangtze River at Wuhanin in 1966 comes to mind). Putin's public stunts include piloting a fighter jet, swimming in a Siberian river, scuba diving in the Strait of Kerch, shooting a polar bear to tranquilize him, shooting a whale with a crossbow, swimming with dolphins, participating in a car race, riding barechested on a horse through the Siberian wilderness, and copiloting forest fire planes. Putin's demonstration of machismo in September 2012 involved his piloting a hang glider to lead cranes on a migratory route. Only an extraordinary level of self-confidence allowed him to disregard the reaction of the public – domestic and international – that openly mocked the extravaganzas put on by the Russian leader.

In fact, big money in the Kremlin deeply influenced not only Putin's personality but his mechanisms of repression. The leaders in Putin's regime protected themselves against enemies through the use of big money. Of course, Putin's regime did not neglect the traditional means of repression either, taking advantage of fear, as did the Soviet regimes, as the major instrument in dealing with intellectuals, not ignoring the material benefit of making them in effect their servants. A few murders of journalists and politicians ascribed to the regime by the public, as well as jail terms for a few recalcitrant opposition figures were sufficient to spread enough fear among the critics of the Kremlin and local governors to prevent the most brazen among them from taking action. What is more, with the prominent feudal elements in society, the persecution of opponents to the regime ceased to be highly centralized, as it had been in Soviet times, and could be performed by various bodies, at the national and local levels, on their own initiative, even up to the thugs of the Chechen leader Ramzan Kadyrov, one of Putin's feudal barons, who were able to kill their enemies in the capital and abroad, appearing in Moscow.

Still, big money allowed Putin's regime to diminish the overall number of repressions considerably, in comparison with the past. With big money, Putin reduced the size of the opposition to his regime, particularly among state employees and retired people, forcing them to refrain from protest actions and to vote for him and his party. Instead of arresting or expelling intellectuals to Siberia or abroad, Putin enrolled many of them in the defense of his rule in the media, by awarding fabulous honoraria and by financially supporting their theaters and orchestras. He was able to suggest that intellectuals become his special emissaries during the presidential election. Putin neutralized many real or potential activists of the opposition by luring them into his business with a considerable income and favor; those who were not completely subdued were at least restrained from taking action that was too aggressive against the government. With the same money, Putin guaranteed the loyalty of the special riot police and the highest officers in the army, making them relatively wealthy people.

None of the previous leaders was so apathetic toward the long-term future of Russia. None of them was so unconcerned about the state of science and education in the country. What is more, none of them was so lukewarm about the military preparedness of the army, focusing attention solely on the repressive apparatus.

None of the authoritarian leaders of prerevolutionary Russia, nor those in the Soviet past, would have subjugated the foreign policy of the country to the financial interests of corporations, because they were the source of wealth for leaders and their circles. None of them was ready to sacrifice relations with natural allies such as former Soviet republics, as Putin was, if these relations did not satisfy the financial expectations of the ruling elite. Unlike Putin, none of them indulged his whims or personal feelings toward the leaders of foreign countries when making important decisions on foreign affairs. None of them – prerevolutionary or Soviet leaders – insulted the heads of foreign countries unless they were at war with them. At the same time, none of the past leaders was as low in esteem or as weak on the international scene. None of the leaders was so degraded and mocked by domestic and international public opinion. None of them was as concerned about the legitimacy of his position as the head of state as Putin, even though he was able formally to use the state apparatus to be elected in a rigged election because he never permitted honest competition with his political rivals. At the same time, none of the Soviet leaders so cynically or openly articulated their determination to stay in power for an indefinite period, as Putin did, even if they hoped to do so.

Putin differed radically from the Soviet leaders in ideological matters. He did not, in fact, pay much attention to ideology, unlike all of the previous general secretaries. The Soviet leaders operated with a relatively cohesive ideology. Lenin's socialism and Russian nationalism combined well in the common glorification of the state and the dictatorship of the party. The big state apparatus was involved in the ideological indoctrination of the masses. At the same time, though, Putin was satisfied with his very eclectic ideology, which simultaneously had to justify the state, democratic procedures, and the dominant feudal, or oligarchic, elements in society and has minimal impact on the mind of the Russians.

It is remarkable that none of the Soviet leaders were so indifferent to social equality in society or so tolerant of the conspicuous consumption of the ruling elite. None of them (including, to some degree, the Russian tsars) tolerated the deep – in fact, treacherous and antinational in nature – ties of this elite group with the West, which they considered to be the best place to keep their assets, educate and provide a permanent residence for their children, and, ultimately, provide a refuge for them, in case of turmoil. Putin's regime was also a unique regime in Russian history in the role that it awarded to the Orthodox Church in political and ideological life in the country. Certainly, in Soviet times this church was the object of permanent persecution (the period of the war with Germany was an exception) and under the full control of the KGB could not even publicly voice any political statement. However, even in monarchist Russia the church was an instrument of the state and never played an independent role. Meanwhile, in Putin's Russia the church was a leading political actor and the patriarch was considered by many Russians as the second leader after Putin. Never, of course, in prerevolutionary Russia was the church so materially supported by the state, and never were church dignitaries so involved in conspicuous consumption as in Putin's times.

The comparison of Putin's regime with the Soviet, as well as the prerevolutionary, authoritarian regimes helps us better understand the nature of Russia in the first decades of the twenty-first century. However, in no way does the author claim to predict when Putin's regime will collapse – not in the foreseeable future, or in one decade, or in three decades, or at any moment – as many pundits in Russia and outside tried to do in 2010–13.

On the eve of the anniversary of the second (February) Russian revolution, a Moscow journalist from the popular newspaper *Argumenty i Fakty* talked to a ninety-six-year-old Russian noble, Baron Eduard Falzfei, who clearly remembered how the three-hundred-year-old Romanov Empire dissipated before his eyes in a few days. As he recounted, even one week before the February revolution, none of the Russian nobles in his family or around him had predicted such a catastrophic change in their lives. Of course, many mutually exclusive ideas about how to transform politics in Russia were circulating in Petrograd in 1916 (the most radical among them was the replacement of the tsar). Less than three weeks before the resignation of the emperor, during a meeting with Nicholas II, Mikhail Rodzianko, a liberal monarchist, demanded radical changes in the government and tried to scare the emperor with the prospect of revolution. The tsar, however, did not take this threat seriously. He treated it as merely one of the many gloomy prophesies that could be found in any society and in any time. Vasily Shulgin, another monarchist (he was among those who attended the ceremony of Nicholas's abdication), in his famous memoir *Years,* recounted that two days before the start of the revolution, the tsar still hated the State Duma and signed an edict that stopped its activity for an uncertain period. The committed enemies of the monarchy were no shrewder on this issue than the imperial court. In exile in Zurich, Vladimir Lenin bitterly lamented in 1916 that his generation would never see a revolution in Russia, the dream of the liberal intelligentsia.

However, on February 23, a demonstration by women in Petrograd who demanded bread was strong enough to trigger the events that brought about the abdication of Nicholas II within ten days. It meant the collapse of the Russian monarchy, along with its repressive apparatus, its loyal Orthodox Church, and the cult of the tsar. The velocity with which the Russian Empire vanished amazed the Russians themselves as well as the rest of the world.

In the 1970s and early 1980s, many analysts supported Alexander Zinoviev's vision of the Soviet Union, as described in his famous book *The Yawning Heights* (1973), as being a perfect society for ordinary people who were concerned only about stability and the satisfaction of their basic needs, and not freedom. A legion of postmortem prophets has advanced, with admirable conviction, dozens of causes of the empire's instant death. None of them, however, was able to predict the demise of the USSR when it was alive. The memoirs of the many Soviet politicians, including people close to Gorbachev, then the leader of the USSR, showed that the collapse of the Soviet system in August 1991 was totally unexpected. Even Gorbachev himself ultimately recognized that he did not expect the collapse, either in August or later. This was evident when Gorbachev made his first statement while at the airport, after returning from seclusion in Foros, in August 1991. It was clear that the Soviet president did not understand that he was returning to a new country. He later acknowledged this fact himself. Alexander Bessmertny, the last Soviet foreign minister, insisted that "Gorbachev did not feel that the USSR was about to collapse." He said, "I don't think there was any Soviet intelligence documents which mentioned this future collapse," and "I, like most of the Politburo, understood that the USSR was changing, but it never occurred to us that it could cease to exist."

Western observers who were living in Moscow at the time were as surprised as the Soviet people. Jack Matlock, who served as the American ambassador in Moscow for four years before the August events and who had perfect knowledge of Russian language and history, wrote in 1995:

> Other empires may have shattered under the pressure of war or revolution, but the Soviet Union expired quietly.... Within minutes, while most Americans were opening presents or preparing Christmas dinner, Russia replaced the Soviet Union as a nuclear power.... The enormity of what had happened soon sank in. I had expected the outcome, but I also realized that, with all my acquaintance with the society and its politicians and my own participation in some of these events, I could not explain with confidence just how it had happened.... How could such a state simply have destroyed itself?

Western intelligence services and politicians were no more successful than Ambassador Matlock in their predictions of the Soviet future. David Arbel and

Ran Edelist named several dozen politicians, intelligence officers, and journalists in Washington who used the word "surprise" to characterize their reactions to the fall of the Soviet Union. Among those who described themselves as surprised were Secretary of State James Baker, Secretary of State Lawrence Eagleburger, and State Department official Robert McFarlane. Dozens of other journalists, intelligence officers, and politicians in the United States and Europe also did.

The author of this text was in Moscow in May 1991 and witnessed the drastic deterioration of the standard of living and the universal discontent. However, among the people with whom he talked (from outstanding social scientists to taxi drivers), many predicted (the author included) a strong counter-offensive by the Communists, not the fall of the USSR. Eduard Shevardnadze, then a member of the Politburo and the minister of foreign affairs, predicted this event in December 1990 at a meeting of the Fourth Congress of People's Deputies. Indeed, in August 1991, the Soviet ruling elite undertook a putsch, which, to everybody's surprise (and to the relief of liberals), was dismantled in three days. The self-proclaimed junta did not dare order the army to shoot into the crowd and quickly capitulated. Neither the Communists nor the KGB resisted Yeltsin's decision to bury the Soviet Union. There was not even one member of a party committee at any level (from the regional to the factory level) who publicly defended the regime, which served, supposedly, as the basis of their status and well-being. For the Russian people, the fall of the regime was a total surprise – and a moment of déjà vu for those who remembered February 1917.

The comparison of Putin's regime with the Soviet regimes, if not a very effective instrument, is still helpful for evaluating its stability and its vulnerability with respect to domestic and international challenges. Putin's regime had neither an effective party and state apparatus nor a powerful KGB and strong ideology. But never in Russian history had such a large number of Russians lived as well as they did under Putin. Never in history had the opposition lacked charismatic leaders as much as in Putin's Russia. And yet, never in Russian history, except, maybe, for the Yeltsin years, had its leader been so virulently and openly criticized as in Putin's Russia. Despite the clampdown on the televised media, despite the growing repressions, despite the lack of political freedom, we are seeing an autocrat being shown unprecedented levels, at least in Russia's historical context, of public derision inside his own country. And if that dissent is not very visible on national television, it exists everywhere else: in national newspapers, on independent television channels like Dozhd, and on social networking sites like Facebook and Twitter. As we have shown, private commerce and private capital are the chief driving forces behind these paradoxes. Still, the coexistence of unprecedented freedoms with haphazard repression, of autocracy with private commerce, signifies that Putin's Russia has emerged as a strikingly unique authoritarian society, one that may be increasingly hard to predict.

The most vulnerable spot in the stability of Putin's regime were the prices of oil and gas. Their dramatic decline would have had a tremendous impact on political life in Russia. However, in this case, the well-paid FSB, police, and army might have had a good chance of coping with the mass protests of a pauperized population. Other unpredictable shocks, like big technological disasters, might also have great effects on people's lives.

Although the protests of 2011–12 have made a considerable dent in Putin's popularity and the stability of his hold on power, his regime – whether with Putin himself at the helm or someone like him – has a good chance of persisting for the next decade or two. There is too much at stake for the elites as a whole – in terms of the capital that they control – to risk considerably reforming the mixed, soft authoritarianism that Russia has seen emerge under Putin. This may, indeed, be one of the key factors behind the failure of the middle-class protest movement – the contingent is too affluent to risk a loss in the standard of living for drastic political reforms. And even while the educated classes continue to bemoan a "moral crisis" of the political regime,[2] it is still a power system that benefits far too many people, in terms of capital, for drastic change to be likely any time in the near future. Even in the unlikely case that Putin is replaced before the end of his presidential term, we expect a very similar leader to take his place, and for the kind of rule we characterize as the "Putin regime" to continue.

[2] See opinions like those voiced by the Kommersant columnist Konstantin von Eggert after Vladimir Putin's press conference in December 2012. Eggert, as did many other journalists, emerged from the press conference depressed and talking of a moral collapse not just of Putin, but of the political class as a whole. "My v pryamom efire nablyudali moralny krakh presidenta Putina I vsego rossiiskogo pravyaschego klassa," *Kommersant FM*, December 21, 2012, http://www.kommersant.ru/doc/2094769, accessed December 31, 2012.

Bibliography

Acemoglu, Daron, James Robinson and Pierre Yared, "Reevaluating the modernization hypothesis" (CEPR Discussion Papers 6430, August 2007).

Albats, Yevgenia, *KGB: State Within a State* (London: IB Taurus, 1995).

Alexeeva, Ludmila and Valerii Chalidze, *Mass Rioting in the USSR* (Silver Springs, MD: Foundation for Soviet Studies, 1985).

Andrei Soldatov and Irina Borogan, *Novoe dvorianstvo: Ocherki istorii FSB* (Moscow: United Press, 2011).

Andrew, Christopher and Vasily Mitrokhin, *The Sword and the Shield: The Mitrokhin Archive and the Secret History of KGB* (New York: Basic Books, 1999).

Arbel, David and Ran Edelist, *Western Intelligence and the Collapse of the Soviet Union, 1980–1990: Ten Years That Did Not Shake the World* (London: Frank Cass, 2003).

Arendt, Hannah, *The Origins of Totalitarianism* (s.l.: Harcourt Brace, 1951).

Aron, Leon, *Russia's Revolution: Essays 1989–2006* (Washington, DC: AEI Press, 2007).

Yeltsin: A Revolutionary Life (New York: St. Martin's Press, 2000).

Bacon, Edwin, *Contemporary Russia* (New York: Palgrave Macmillan, 2010)

Bakatin, Vadim, *Izbavlenie ot KGB* (Moscow: Novosti, 1992).

Banfield, Edward, "Corruption as a feature of governmental organization," *Journal of Law and Economics* 18 (1975), 587–605.

Barro, Robert, "The Determinants of Democracy," *Journal of Political Economy* 107 (1999), 158–83.

Bauer, Raymond A., Alex Inkeles and Clyde Kluckhohn, *How the Soviet System Works: Cultural, Psychological, and Social Themes* (New York: Vintage, 1956).

Belikova, Galina and Alexander Shokhin, "Chernyi rynko: Liudi, veshchi, fakty," *Ogoniok* 36 (1987), 6–8.

Bloch, Sidney and Peter Reddaway, *Psychiatric Terror* (New York: Basic Books 1977).

Blum, Douglas W., *Russia and Globalization: Identity, Security, and Society in an Era of Change* (Washington DC: John Hopkins University Press, 2008).

Bollen, K. and R. Jackman, "Democracy, stability, and dichotomies," *American Sociological Review* 54 (1989), 612, 618.

Boulding, Kenneth, *the Image: Knowledge in Life and Society* (Ann Arbor: University of Michigan Press, 1956).

Bredikhin, V. (ed.), *Lubianka – Staraia ploschad, Sekretnye dokumenty TsK KPSS i KGB o repressiakh 1937 – 1990 gg. v SSSR* (Munchen: Posev Publishing House, 2005).

Brovkin, Vladimir, *Russia after Lenin: Politics, Culture and Society, 1921–1929* (New York: 1998).

Buchanan, James, Robert Tollison and Gordin Tullock (eds.), *Toward a Theory of the Rent Seeking Society* (College Station: Texas A&M University Press, 1980).

Bukovsky, Vladimir, *I vozvraschaetsia veter* (Moscow: Novoe Izdatelstvo, 2007).

Judgment a Moscou (Paris: Robert Lafont, 1995).

Case, William, "Can the 'halfway house' stand? Semidemocracy and elite theory in three Southeast Asian countries," *Comparative Politics* **28** (1996), 437–64.

Chernyaev, Anatoly, *Dnevnik pomochnika presidenta SSSR* (Moscow: s.n., 1997).

Sovmestnyi iskhod.Dnevnik dvukh epoch (Moscow: s.n., 2008).

Chernyaev, Anatoly S., *Sovmestnyi iskhod: Dnevnik dvukh epoch* (Moscow: Rosspen, 2008).

Coicaud, Jean-Marc and David Ames Curtis, *Legitimacy and Politics: A Contribution to the Study of Political Right and Political Responsibility* (Cambridge: Cambridge University Press, 2002).

Colton, Timothy J. and Stephen Holmes, *The State after Communism: Governance in the New Russia* (Lanham, MD: Rowman & Littlefield, 2006).

Colton, Timothy J., *Yeltsin: A life* (New York: Basic Books, 2008).

Conquest, R., *Russia after Khruschev* (London: Pall Mall Press, 1965).

Coppedge, Michael and Wolfgang Reinicke, "Measuring polyarchy," *Studies in Comparative International Development* **25** (1990), 51–72.

Cottam, Martha L., Beth Dietz-Uhler and Elena Mastors, *Introduction to political psychology*, 2nd ed. (New York: Psychology Press, 2010).

Dahl, Robert, *A Preface to Democratic Theory* (Chicago: University of Chicago Press, 2006).

Democracy and Its Critics (New Haven, CT: Yale University Press, 1989), pp. 241, 316–7.

Polyarchy: Participation and Opposition (New Haven, CT: Yale University Press, 1971), pp. 2, 8, 231–5.

Daniels, Robert, "Russian political culture and the post-revolutionary impasse," *The Russian Review* **46.2** (April, 1987), 165–75.

Danilov, V., "Rossiiskaia vlast' v 20 veke" in T. Zaslavskaia (ed.), *Kuda idet Rossia. Vlast'. Obshchestvo. Lichnost'* (Moscow: Vysshaia Shkola sotsial'nykh i ekonomicheskikh nauk, 2000), p. 6.

Davies, Sarah, *Popular Opinion in Stalin's Russia: Terror, Propaganda and Dissent, 1934–1941* (Cambridge: Cambridge University Press, 1997).

Davydchenkov, Vasily, "Organizatsiia sotsiologicheskogo obsledovaniia i vnedrenie poluchennykh rezul'tatov v tsentral'noi gazete," in Vladimir Shlapentokh (ed.), *Sotsiologiia pechati* (Novosibirsk: Nauka, 1970), pp. 147–77.

Delyagin, Mikhail, *Rossiia posle Putina. Neizbezhna li v Rossii "oranzhevo-zelenaia revoliutsiia"?* [Russia after Putin. Is the orange-green revolution unavoidable?] (Moscow: Veche, 2005).

Diamond, Larry, "Thinking about hybrid regimes," *Journal of Democracy* 13.2 (2002) 21–35.

Doroshenko, V., I. Pavlova and P. Paak, "Ne mif: Rech' Stalina 19 avgusta 1939 goda," *Vorposy Istrorii* 8 (2005), 3–5.

Duby, Pierre, *Feudalism* (Paris: Presses Universitaires de France, 1998).

Edmonds, R., *Soviet Foreign Policy – the Brezhnev Years* (Oxford and New York: Oxford University Press, 1983).

Fadeyev, Alexander, *Razgrom* (Moscow: s.n., 1927).

Fainsod, Merle, *How Russia Is Ruled* (Cambridge, MA: Harvard University Press, 1963).

Felshtinsky, Yury and Vladimir Pribylovsky, *Korporatsiia: Rossiia I KGB vo vremena prezidenta Putina* (Moscow: TERRA, 2010).

Feofanov, Yuri and Barry, Donald D., *Politics and Justice in Russia: Major Trials of the Post-Stalin Era* (New York: M. E. Sharpe, 1996).

Filippov, A. and Poliakov, L. *Noveishaia istoriia Russii 1945 – 2006* (Moscow: Prosveshchenie, 2007).

Friedrich, Carl and Zbigniew Brzezinski, *Totalitarian Dictatorship and Autocracy* (Cambridge, MA: Harvard University Press, 1956).

Furmanov, Dmitry, *Chapaev* (Moscow, 1923).

Gaidar, Yegor, *Anomalii eknomicheskogo rosta* [Anomalies of economic growth] (Moscow: Evraziia, 1997).

Collapse of an Empire: Lessons for Modern Russia (Wahington, DC: Brookings Institution Press, 2007).

Dolgoie vremia. Rossia v mire. Ocherki ekonomicheskoi istorii [Long time. Russia in the world. Essays in economic history] (Moscow: Delo, 2005).

Galeotti, Mark (ed.), *Russian and Post-Soviet Organized Crime* (London: Ashgate, 2002).

Gaman-Golutvina, O. V., "Burokratiya ili oligarkhiya," in T. I. Zaslavskaya (ed.), *Kuda idet Rossiya? Vlast, obschestvo, lichnost* (Moscow: Moskovskaya Vysshaya Shkola Sotsialnykh i Ekonomicheskikh nauk, 2000), p. 162.

Gessen, Masha, *The Man without a Face: The Unlikely Rise of Vladimir Putin* (Riverhead, NY: Riverhead Books, 2012).

Girling, John, *Corruption, Capitalism and Democracy* (New York: Routledge, 1997).

Gogol, Nikolay, *Revizor* (s.l.: s.n., 1836).

Goldman, Marshall I., *Petrostate: Putin, Power, and the New Russia* (New York: Oxford University Press, 2008).

Goldman, Marshall, "Russian energy: A blessing or a curse," *Journal of International Affairs* 53 (1999), 74.

Goldstein, Jeffrey, "Emergence as a Construct: History and Issues," *Emergence: Complexity and Organization* 1.1 (1999), 49–72.

Gorbatov, Aleksandr, *Years of My Life: The Memoirs of General of the Soviet Army, A.V. Gorbatov* (London: Constable, 1964).

Gorzka, Gabriele and Reinhard Krumm (eds.), *Rossiia: itogi poslednego destialetiia (1998–2008) i perspektivy razvitiia* (Moscow: ROSSPEN, 2010).

Grigorenko, Pyotr, *Memoirs* (New York: Norton, 1982).

Grishin, Viktor, *Ot Khruscheva do Gorbacheva* (Moscow: Aspol, 1996).

Grossman, Vasily, *Life and Fate* (London: Collins Harvill, 1985[1960]).

Grushin, B. A., *Chetyre zhizni Rossii v zerkale oprosov obshchestvennogo mneniia. Epokha Brezhneva* (Moscow: Progress-Traditsia, 2001).

Hale, Henry E., *Why Not Parties in Russia? Democracy, Federalism, and the State* (Cambridge and New York: Cambridge University Press, 2007).
Harrison, Lawrence E. and Samuel P. Huntington, *Culture Matters: How Values Shape Human Progress* (New York: Basic Books, 2000).
Herspring, Dale Roy (ed.), *Putin's Russia: Past Imperfect, Future Uncertain* (Lanham, MD: Rowman & Littlefield, 2007).
Holsti, Olc, "Cognitive Dynamics and Images of the Enemy," in J. C. Farrell and A. P. Smith (eds.), *Image and Reality in World Politics* (New York: Columbia University Press, 1967), pp. 14–34.
Ilf, Ilia and Evgeny Petrov *Zolotoi Telenok* (s.l.: s.n., 1931).
Inglehart, Ronald, Basanez, Miguel and Moreno, Alejandro, *Human Values and Beliefs* (Ann Arbor: University of Michigan Press, 1998).
Inglehart, Ronald, *Modernization and Postmodernization: Cultural, Economic, and Political Change in 43 Societies* (Princeton, NJ: Princeton University Press, 1997).
Inkeles, Alex, *Social Change in Soviet Russia, Vol. 57* (Cambridge, MA: Harvard University Press, 1968).
Inkeles, Alex and Bauer, RA, *The Soviet Citizen: Daily Life in a Totalitarian Society* (Cambridge, MA: Harvard University Press, 1959).
Inozemtsev, Vladislav, "Chto sluchilos's Rossiei," *Neprikosnovennyi Zapas* **6**.74 (2010), 74.
Ivanov, Anatoly, *Vechnyi Zov* [*The Eternal Call*] (Moscow: Sovetskii Pisatel', 1971).
Jain, A. (ed.), *Economics of Corruption* (Dordrecht: Kluwer Academic, 1998).
Johnson, Simon and James Kwak, *13 Bankers: The Wall Street Takeover and the Next Financial Meltdown* (New York: Pantheon Books, 2010).
Johnston, Michael, *Syndromes of Corruption: Wealth, Power, and Democracy* (Hamilton, NY: Colgate University, 2005).
Karl, Terry Lynn, "The hybrid regimes of Central America," *Journal of Democracy* **6** (1995), 72–87.
Karpovich, Oleg, *Corruption in Present Day Russia* (Bloomington, IN: AuthorHouse, 2008).
Katsenelinboigen, Aron, "Color markets in the Soviet Union," *Soviet Studies* **29**.1 (1976), 976.
Khlebnikov, Paul, *Godfather of the Kremlin* (New York: Harcourt, 2000), pp. 152–3.
Khrushchev, Nikita, *Vremia, Liudi, Vlast' (N. S. Khruschev Vospominania)* [Time, People, Power], edited by Sergei Khrushchev (Moscow: Moskovskiye Novosti, 1999).
Khrushchev, Sergei, *Khrushchev on Khrushchev: An Inside Account of the Man and His Era* (Boston: Little, Brown, 1990).
Nikita Khrushchev and the Creation of a Superpower (New Haven, CT: Yale University, 2000).
Kirpichnikov, A., *Vziatka i korruptsiia v Rossii* (St. Petersburg: Alfa, 1997).
Kliamkin, Igor' and Lev Timofeev, *Tenevaia Rossiia: Ekonomiko-sotsiologicheskoie issledovanie* (Moscow: RGGU, 2000).
Kopelev, L, *Khranit' Vechno* (Ann Arbor, MI: Ardis, 1975).
Sotvorim Sebe Kumira (Ann Arbor, MI: Ardis, 1978).
Ease My Sorrows: A Memoir (Moscow: Slovo, 1991).
Korzhakov, Alexander, *Boris Yeltsin: Ot rasveta do zakata* (Moscow: Interbuk, 1997).
Kostin, Aleksandr, *Petlya Putina: razbor poletov za 10 let* (Moscow: Algoritm, 2010).

Kostyrchenko, Gennady, *Gossudarstvennyi antisemitizm v SSSR* (Moscow: Mezhdunardnyi. fond "Demokratiia", 2005).

Kryuchkov, Vladimir, *Bez sroka davnosti* (Moscow: Prosveschenie, 2006).

Kuzio, Taras, "Regime type and politics in Ukraine under Kuchma," *Communist and Post-Communist Studies* 38.2 (2005), 167–90.

Latynina, Yulia, "Patent na blagorodstvo: vydast li ego literatura kapitalu?" *Novyi Mir* 11 (1993), 191–5.

Lebedev, Nikolay, *SSSR v mirovoi politike* (Moscow: Mezhdunarodnye Otnosheniia, 1982).

Lee-Chai, Annette Y. and Bargh, John A., *The Use and Abuse of Power: Multiple Perspectives on the Causes of Corruption* (Philadelphia: Psychology Press, 2001).

Lefebvre, Vladimir, *Algebra of Conscience* (Dordrecht: Kluwer Academic, 2001).

Lenin, Vladimir, *Sobranie sochinenii*, 3rd ed. (Moscow: Politizdat, 1931), vol. XXVII.

Collected Works, vol. 43 (Moscow: Politizdat, 1955), p. 206.

Levada, Yury (ed.), *Prostoi sovetstkii chelovek* (Moscow: Interxentr, 1993), pp. 46, 69, 176, 187.

Levada, Yury, "Chelovek sovietkii: Chetvertaia volna," *Vestnik Obshchestvennogo Mnenia* 4 (2004).

LeVine, Steve, *Putin's Labyrinth: Spies, Murder, and the Dark Heart of the New Russia* (New York: Random House, 2009).

Levitsky, Steven and Lucan A. Way, "Elections without democracy: The rise of competitive authoritarianism," *Journal of Democracy* 13.2 (2002), 51–65.

Levitsky, Steven, "Mapping the great zone: Clientelism and the boundary between democratic and democratizing," paper prepared for the Annual Meeting of the American Political Science Association, Boston, MA (August 28–31, 2002).

Lipset, Seymour Martin, "Some social requisites of democracy: Economic development and political legitimacy," *American Political Science Review* 53 (1959), 69–105.

Maiminas, E. Z., "Sootnoshenie vlasti, obschestva i lichnosti," in T. I. Zaslavskaya (ed.), '*Kuda idet Rossiya?: Vlast, obschestvo, lichnost* (Moscow: Moskovskaya vysshaya shkola sotsialnykh i ekonomicheskikh nauk, 2000), p. 207.

Malia, Martin, *Russia under Western Eyes* (Cambridge, MA: Harvard University Press, 1999).

The Soviet Tragedy: A History of Socialism in Russia, 1917–1991 (New York: Free Press, 1994).

Mauro, Paolo, "Corruption and the composition of government expenditure," *Journal of Public Economics* 69 (1998), 263–79.

McFaul, Michael, *Russia's Unfinished Revolution: Political Change from Gorbachev to Putin (*Ithaca, NY: Cornell University Press, 2001), p. 265.

Medvedev, Roi, *Vladimir Putin: Tret'ego sroka ne budet* (Moscow: Vremia, 2007).

Medvedev, Zhores, *Andropov* (Oxford: Basil Blackwell, 1983).

Mezhuev, V., "Traditsiia samovlastiia v sovremennoi Rossii" in T. Zaslavskaia (ed.), *Kuda idet Rossia.Vlast'. Obshchestvo. Lichnost*' (Moscow: Vysshaia Shkola sotsial'nykh i ekonomicheskikh nauk, 2000), pp. 81, 86.

Ministry of Foreign Affairs of the USSR (comp.), *Correspondence between Stalin, Roosevelt, Truman, Churchill and Atlee during WWII* (Honolulu: University Press of the Pacific, 2001).

Naishul, Vital, *Vysshaia i posledniaia stadiia sotsializma: Pogruzhenie v triasinu* (Moscow: Progress, 1991).

Nazarov, M., *The Mission of the Russian Emigration* (Moscow: Rodnik, 1994).

Nemtsov, Boris and Milov, Vladimir, *Luzhkov: Itogi* (Moscow: Eksmo, 2010).

Okonta, Ike and Douglas, Oronto, *Where Vultures Feast: Shell, Human Rights, and Oil* (New York: Verso, 2003).

Orlova, Raisa, *Memoirs* (New York: Random House, 1983).

Ostrovsky, V. (ed.), *Lichnoie Podsobnoie Khosiastvo* (Moscow: Nauka, 1988).

Piontkovsky, Andrei, *Tretii put' k rabstvu* [*The third way is to slavery*] (Moscow: Moskva, 2011).

Neliubimaia strana (Moscow: RDP "Yabloko", 2006).

Pipes, Richard, *Russia under the Bolshevik Regime* (New York: Vintage Books, 1995), p. 511.

Russia under the Old Regime (s.l.: Collier Books, 1992).

"Private Property, Freedom, and the Rule of Law," *Hoover Digest* 2 (April 30, 2001).

Property and Freedom (New York: Alfred A. Knopf, 1999).

Pirani, Simon, *Change in Putin's Russia: Power, Money and People* (London and New York: Pluto Press, 2010).

Pivovarov, Yury, *Russkaia politika v ee istoricheskom i kul'turnom otnosheniiakh* (Moscow: ROSSPEN, 2006).

Platonov, Andrei, *Gorod Gradov* (s.l.: s.n., 1927).

Politkovskaya, Anna, *Putin's Russia: Life in a Failing Democracy* (New York: Holt Paperbacks, 2007).

Ponomarev, B. (ed.), *Istoriia Kommunisticheskoi Partii Sovetskogo Soiuza* (Moscow: Politizdat, 1985), pp. 6–8.

Pridemore, William A. (ed.), *Ruling Russia: Law, Crime, and Justice in a Changing Society* (New York: Rowman & Littlefield, 2005).

Pridemore, William A. (ed.), *Ruling Russia: Law, Crime, and Justice in a Changing Society* (Lanham, MD: Rowman & Littlefield, 2005).

Prokhorov, A. (ed.), *Bol'shaya Sovetskaia Entsiklopediia*, 3rd ed. (Moscow: Sovetskaia Entsiklopediia, 1977).

Radzinsky, Edvard, *Stalin: Zhizn' i smert'* (Moscow: AST, 2007).

Ringen, Stein, *The Possibility of Politics* (New Brunswick, NJ: Transactions, 2006).

Robertson, Graeme B., *The Politics of Protest in Hybrid Regimes: Managing Dissent in Post Post-Communist Russia* (Cambridge: Cambridge University Press, 2011).

Rose, Richard, William Mishler and Neil Munro, *Popular Support for An Undemocratic Regime: The Changing Views of Russians* (Cambridge: Cambridge University Press, 2011).

Rose-Ackerman, Susan, *Corruption: A Study in Political Economy* (New York: Academic Press, 1978).

Rosefielde, Steven and Stefan Hedlund, *Russia since 1980: Wrestling with Westernization* (Cambridge: Cambridge University Press, 2009).

Rutland, Peter, *The Politics of Economic Stagnation in the Soviet Union: the Role of Local Party Organs in Economic Management* (Cambridge: Cambridge University Press, 2010).

Sakharov, Andrei, *Progress, Coexistence, and Intellectual Freedom.* (New York: Norton, 1968).

Sakwa, Richard, *Russian Politics and Society*, 4th ed. (New York: Routledge, 2008).
Putin: Russia's Choice, 2nd ed. (London and New York: Routldge, 2008).
The Quality of Freedom: Khodorkovsky, Putin, and the Yukos Affair (Oxford: Oxford University Press, 2009).
Satarov, Georgy (ed.), *Diagnostika: Rossiiskaia korruptsia* (Moscow: Indem, 2002).
Schechter, Darrow, *Beyond Hegemony: Towards a New Philosophy of Political Legitimacy* (Manchester: Manchester University Press, 2005).
Scott, John, *Behind the Urals: An American Worker in Russia's City of Steel* (Bloomington: Indiana University Press, 1989).
Sears, David O., Leonie Huddy and Robert Jervis (eds.), *Oxford Handbook of Political Psychology* (Oxford: Oxford University Press, 2003).
Seigelbaum, Lewis, *Making Workers Soviet: Power, Class, and Identity* (Ithaca, NY: Cornell University Press, 1994).
Shalit, Ben, *The Psychology of Conflict and Combat* (New York: Praeger, 1988).
Shchekochikhin, Yuri, *Raby KGB. Religia predatelstva.* (Samara: Izdatel'skii dom "Fedorov", 1999).
Shevtsova, Lilia and Antonina W. Bouis, *Lonely Power: Why Russia Has Failed to Become the West and the West is Weary of Russia* (2010).
Shevtsova, Lilia, *Russia – Lost in Transition: The Yeltsin and Putin Legacies* (Washington, DC: Carnegie Endowment Press, 2007).
Shevtsova, Lilia, *Putin's Russia* (Washington, DC: Carnegie Endowment for International Peace, 2005).
Shlapentokh, Dmitry, *The French Revolution and the Russian Anti-Democratic Tradition: A Case of False Consciousness* (New Brunswick, NJ: Transaction, 1997).
Shlapentokh, Dmitry and Vladimir Shlapentokh, "Letters to the editor on the ideologies in the USSR during the 1980s," in Anthony Jones (ed.), *Research on the Soviet Union and Eastern Europe* (Greenwich, CT: JAI Press, 1990), pp. 145–72.
Soviet Cinema in 1918–1991: Ideological Conflict and Social Reality (New York: Aldine De Gruyter, 1993).
Shlapentokh, Vladimir (ed.), *Chitatel i Gazeta : Itogi Izucheniia Chitatelskoi Auditorii Tsentralnykh Gazet. Vyp.2, Chitateli "Literaturnoi Gazety"* (Moscow: Institut Konkretnykh Sotsial'nykh Issledovanii, 1969).
Shlapentokh, Vladimir "Standard of living and public discontent," in Ellman, Mikhael and Kontorovich, Vladimir (eds.), *The Destruction of the Soviet Economic System* (Armonk, NY: Sharp, 1998), pp. 30–40.
Shlapentokh, Vladimir, "'Old', 'new' and 'post' liberal attitudes toward the West: From love to hate," *Communist and Post-Communist Studies* 31 (1998), 30–40.
"Bounjour stagnation: Russia's next years," *Europe-Asia Studies* 49.5 (1997), 865–81.
"Catastrophism on the eve of 2000: Apocalyptic ideology between Russia's past and future," *Demokratizatsia* 5 (Winter 1997), 10–18.
"How Russians will see the status of their country by the end of the century," *The Journal of Communist Studies and Transition Politics* 3 (September 1997), 1–23.
"China in the Russian mind today: Ambivalence and defeatism," *Europe-Asia Studies* 59 (2007), 1–21.
"Contemporary Russia: The best parallel to it – Feudal Europe," *Europe-Asia Studies* (Spring 1996), 393–411.
"Four Russias," *The Tocqueville Review* 19.1 (1998) 9–34.

"George Orwell: Russia's Tocqueville," in Thomas Cushman and John Rodden (eds.), *George Orwell into the Twentieth Century* (Boulder, CO: Paradigm, 2004), pp. 267–85.
"Moscow identity crisis," *Foreign Service* 4 (April 1997), 10–13.
"Russia after the election," *Transition* 4 (1996), 16–20.
"Russia: Privatization and illegalization of social and political life in Russia," *The Washington Quarterly* 19 (1996), 65–85.
"Soviet society and American Sovietologists: A study in failure" in Michael Cox (ed.), *Rethinking the Soviet Collapse: Sovietology, the Death of Communism and the New Russia* (London: Cassel, 1998), 30–40.
"Sovietskie liudi v nachale 60kh godov: Razmyshlenia po povodu knigi Borisa Grushina," *Monitoring obshchestvennogo menia* 4.54 (2001), 42–8.
"The Changeable Soviet Image of America," *The Annals of the American Academy of Political and Social Science* 497 (1988), 157–71.
"The four faces of Mother Russia," Transition 4.5 (October 1997), 331–6.
"'Normal' Russia," *Current History* 212 (October 1997), 331–6.
"The study of values as a social phenomenon: The Soviet case" *Social Forces* 61.2 (December 1982), 403–17.
"Wealth versus political power: The Russian case," *Communist and Post-Communist Studies* 37 (2004), 135–60.
A Normal Totalitarian Society (Armonk, NY: M. E. Sharpe, 2001).
Public and Private life of the Soviet People:Changing Values in Post-Stalin Russia (New York: Oxford University Press, 1989).
Contemporary Russia As a Feudal Society: A New Perspective on the Post-Soviet Era (New York: Palgrave Macmillan, 2007).
Shlapentokh, Vladimir, Eric Shiraev, and Eero Carroll, *The Soviet Union: Internal and External Perspectives on Soviet Society* (New York: Palgrave Macmillan, 2008).
Shlapentokh, Vladimir, *Fear in Contemporary Society: Its Negative and Positive Effects* (New York: Palgrave Macmillan, 2006).
Russia: Privatization and Illegalization of Social and Political Life (Cambridge, UK: Conflict Studies Research Center, Royal Military Academy, Sundhurst, 1995).
Sociology and Politics: The Soviet Case (Falls Church, VA: Delphi Associates, 1985).
Soviet Intellectuals and Political Power (Princeton, NJ: Princeton University Press, 1990).
Soviet Public Opinion and Ideology (New York: Praeger, 1986).
The Last Years of the Soviet Empire: Snapshots from 1985–1991 (New York: Praeger, 1993).
The Politics of Sociology in the Soviet Union (Boulder, CO: Westview Press, 1987).
Shlapentokh, Vladimir and Vera Bondartsova, "Stalin in Russian ideology and public opinion: Caught in a conflict between imperial and liberal elements," *Russian History* 36.2 (May 2009), 302–25.
Shlapentokh, Vladimir and Eric Shiraev, *Fears in Post-Communist Society* (New York and Basingstoke: Palgrave, 2002).
Shlapentokh, Vladimir and Joshua Woods, *Feudal America: Elements of the Middle Ages in Contemporary Society* (University Park: Pennsylvania State University Press, 2011).

Shlapentokh, Vladimir, Joshua Woods and Eric Shiraev (eds.), *America: Sovereign Defender or Cowboy Nation?* (Burlington, VT: Ashgate, 2005).

Shleifer, Andrei and Daniel Treisman, "A normal country," *Foreign Affairs* (March–April 2004), 20–38.

Shubkin, Vladimir, *Sotsiologicheskie opyty* (Moscow: Mysl, 1970).

Shubkin, Vladimir , *Trudiaschaiasia molodezh': Obrazovanie, professiia, mobil'nost'* (Moscow: Nauka, 1984).

Simes, Dimitri K., *After the Collapse: Russia Seeks Its Place as a Great Power* (New York: Simon & Schuster, 1999).

Simis, Konstantin, *The Corrupt Society* (New York: Shuster, 1982).

Sixsmith, Martin, *Putin's Oil: The Yukos Affair and the Struggle for Russia* (New York: Continuum International Publishing Group, 2010).

Sluch, S., "Rech' Stalina, kotoroi ne bylo," *Otechestvennaya Istoriia* 1 (2004), 113.

Smith, Anthony, *The Concept of Social Change: A Critique of the Functionalist Theory of Social Change* (New York: Routledge, 2010).

Soldatov, Andrei and Borogan, Irina, *The New Nobility: The Restoration of Russia's Security State and the Enduring Legacy of the KGB* (2010)

Soldatov, Andrei and Irina Borogan, *Novoe dvorianstvo: Ocherki istorii FSB* (Moscow: United Press, 2011).

Stuermer, Michael, *Putin and the Rise of Russia* (London: Weidenfeld & Nicolson, 2008).

Sukhovo-Kobylin, Aleksandr, *Delo* (s.l.: s.n., 1861).

Surinov, A. (ed.), *Rossiiskii statisticheskii ezhegodnik 2010 (*Moscow: Rosstat, 2010).

Taubman, W., S. Khrushchev and A. Gleason (eds.), *Nikita Khrushchev* (New Haven, CT: Yale University Press, 2000).

Taylor, Brian D., *State Building in Putin's Russia: Policing and Coercion after Communism* (Cambridge: Cambridge University Press, 2011), pp. 102, 107.

Terekhov, Alexander, *Germans* (Moscow: AST. 2012).

Timofeev, Lev, *Institutsional'naia korruptsiia: Ocherki teorii* (Moscow: Rossiiskii Gosudarstvennyi Gumaniratnyi Universitet, 2000).

Tompson, W., *The Soviet Union under Brezhnev* (Harlow: Longman, 2003).

Travin, Dmitrii, *Putinskaya Rossiia: Ot rassveta do otkata* (St. Petersburg: DELO, 2008).

Tregubova, Yelena, *Tales of a Kremlin Digger* (Moscow: AdMarginem, 2004).

Treisman, Donald, "The causes of corruption: A cross-national study," *Journal of Public Economics* **76** (2000), 399.

Truscott, Peter. *Russia First: Breaking with the West* (New York: I. B. Tauris, 1997).

TsK KPSS, *Istoriia Vsesoiuznoi Kommunisticheskoi Partii (bol'shevikov): Kratkii kurs* (Moscow: Politizdat, 1938).

Tucker, Robert, *Philosophy and Myth in Karl Marx* (New York: Cambridge University Press, 1961).

Swolen State, Spent Society: Stalin's Legacy to Brezhnev's Russia (s.l.: s.n., 1980).

Stalin in Power: The Revolution from Above (New York: W. W. Norton, 1990).

Ulam, Adam, *The Communists: The Story of Power and Lost Illusions, 1948–1991* (New York: Scribner, 1992).

The Kirov Affair (New York: Harcourt, 1988, p. VII).

Ulanovskaya, M. and N. Ulanovskaya, *Istoria Odnoi Sem'i.* (New York: Chalidze, 1982).

Verkhovskaya, Alla, *Pis'ma v redaktsiiu i chitateli* (Moscow: Izdatel'stvo Moskovskogo Universiteta, 1972).

Wallace-Hadrill, Andrew, *Patronage in Ancient Society* (New York: Routledge, 1989).

Wanke, Paul, *Russian/Soviet Military Psychiatry, 1904–1945* (New York: Rutledge, 2005).

Weber, Max, *Economy and Society* (Berkeley: University of California Press, 1978).

Wedel, Janine R., *Shadow Elite: How the World's New Power Brokers Undermine Democracy, Government, and the Free Market* (New York: Basic Books, 2009).

White, Stephen (ed.), *Politics and the Ruling Group in Putin's Russia* (New York: Palgrave Macmillan, 2008).

Wilson, Andrew, *Virtual Politics: Faking Democracy in the Post-Soviet World* (New Haven, CT: Yale University Press, 2005).

Wilson, Ronald, *Ancient Republicanism: Its Struggle for Liberty against Corruption* (New York: Peter Lang, 1989).

Witkin, Zara, *An American Engineer in Stalin's Russia: the Memoirs of Zara Witkin, 1932–1934* (Berkeley: University of California Press, 1991).

XXIII S'ezd Kommunisticheskoi Partii Sovetskogo Soiuza. Stenograficheskii otchet (Moscow: Politizdat, 1966).

Yevtushenko, Evgenii, *Volchii Passport* (Moscow: Vagrius, 1998).

Zyuganov, Gennady, *My Russia*, edited by Vadim Medish (Armonk, NY: M. E. Sharpe, 1997), 9–10.

Postizhenie Rossii (Moscow: Mysl', 2000).

Zorin, Valentin, *Sober Man* (s.l.: s.n., 2001).

Zoschenko, Mikhail, *Slabaia Tara* (s.l.: s.n., 1932).

Zvyagintsev, A. *Pod sen'iu russkogo orla. General-prokurory Rossii* (Moscow: "Dovgan", 1997).

Zvyagintsev, Alexander and Orlov, Yury, *V epokhu potriasenii i reform. Rossiiskie prokurory 1906–1917* (Moscow: ROSSPEN, 1996).

Index

For EU product safety concerns, contact us at Calle de José Abascal, 56–1°, 28003 Madrid, Spain or eugpsr@cambridge.org.

www.ingramcontent.com/pod-product-compliance
Lightning Source LLC
LaVergne TN
LVHW011521200926
848484LV00001B/98

* 9 7 8 1 1 0 7 0 4 2 1 4 8 *